THE DOLLAR DRAIN AND AMERICAN
FORCES IN GERMANY

i

Gregory F. Treverton

The Dollar Drain
And
American Forces In Germany

Managing The Political Economics
of Alliance

Ohio University Press: Athens, Ohio.

iv

For Nancy

TABLE OF CONTENTS

Preface ix
   Note on Sources xii
   Acknowledgements xiii
   Notes to Preface xiv
Chapter
I: THE BALANCE OF PAYMENTS AND AMERICAN FORCE LEVELS
    IN GERMANY 1
    I. American Forces in Europe: Costs 3
    II. American Forces in Europe: Rationales 18
    III. The Clash of Two Orthodoxies 26
    Notes to Chapter I 28
II: FOREIGN EXCHANGE AND FORCE LEVEL AT ISSUE BETWEEN
    ALLIES 31
    I. The Origins of Offset 32
    II. The 1966 "Crisis" 34
    III. The Trilateral Negotiations 37
    IV. Offset and Force Level after 1967 39
    Notes to Chapter II 51
III: BONN 56
    I. Prelude to the Erhard Visit 60
    II. The Fall of the Erhard Government 74
    III. Offset and the Grand Coalition 80
    Notes to Chapter III 92
IV: WASHINGTON 97
    I. Organizational Perspectives 99
    II. The 1966 "Crisis" 110
    III. Trilateral Negotiations 122
    Notes to Chapter IV 133
V: BETWEEN WASHINGTON AND BONN 136
    I. Allied Interactions over Offset and Force
      Level: Washington between Bonn and London 138
    II. American Policy-Making 154
    Notes to Chapter V 164
VI: MANAGING THE POLITICS OF ALLIANCE 166
    I. Misperception and Misunderstanding between Allies 166
    II. The Overlap of Politics and Economics 172
    III. Managing Decentralized Operations 179
    IV. Limits on Reorganization 185
    V. The Politics of Alliance 193
    Notes to Chapter VI 206
LIST OF PERSONS INTERVIEWED 208
BIBLIOGRAPHY 212
INDEX 221

PREFACE

This study derives from my abiding interest in how the great governmental machines of the United States and its major postwar allies interact. In particular, I sought to examine dealings with respect to a set of issues which involved, at once, considerations of politics, economics and military security; considerations which conflicted with each other, for leaders in Washington and in allied capitals. Issues and dealings of that sort were rare in the two decades after the Marshall Plan, as issues of different sorts most often were delegated to different arenas to be resolved separately after study by distinct groups of experts. I began with the presumption that the separation will not characterize the years ahead, of however much benefit it may have been in the past to countries on both sides of the Atlantic. Events which have transpired in the several years since I began work on this project, the 1973 oil embargo and its economic aftermath notable among them, have confirmed that judgment. The challenges posed for the making of United States policy are considerable.

The several episodes described in this study offer a retrospective look at the nature of those challenges. From 1961 onward, the United States engaged the Federal Republic of Germany in periodic negotiations over economic mechanisms whereby Germany could "offset" the balance-of-payments drain experienced by the U.S. due to stationing American forces on West German soil (after 1960 that force was never less than 200,000 strong). In the process, an economic issue—the kind and amount of German "offset"—became linked to a central matter of politics and security—the number of American forces in the

German Federal Republic. That made the "offset" negotiations serious business for both governments. The link, in part, reflected Washington's tactical purposes in "offset" negotiations. But it also stemmed from deeper features of policy-making in Washington, from the politics of relations among the major foreign policy departments of government and, especially, of the dialogue between the Executive Branch and the American Congress.[1] Those sets of relationships are a theme of this study.

My primary case is a "crisis" and its aftermath. In 1966, Bonn and Washington, misperceiving one another's intentions, acted in pursuit of different purposes. Their differences with regard to the issues of "offset"* and force level culminated in an unhappy German-American summit conference in Washington, in September 1966. The result of that conference played a part in bringing down the government of German Chancellor Ludwig Erhard. After Erhard's downfall, the issues were taken up in tripartite negotiations involving the United Kingdom. Those discussions, the so-called Trilateral Negotiations, were brought to a successful conclusion in May 1967.

I can make no claim that those two instances are representative of alliance relations in general, of relations involving the intersection of politics and economics, or even of dealings between Washington and Bonn. They serve, in the first instance, only as examples. They illustrate some of the dangers when allies, particularly the United States, engage their partners in joint enterprises whose fulfillment depends upon a conjunction of actions, some of which may come to be matters of contention in the domestic economics and politics of the allies. Since the events of 1966 and 1967 were a crisis, they are to that extent atypical even of dealings with respect to offset and force level in more normal times. Yet the events of 1966–67, more dramatic than subsequent events in the history of offset and force level, are not mere curiosities in that history. In them are displayed many features which continued to characterize the handling of offset and force level, by both Bonn and Washington. Each of the chapters that follow contains glances at events after 1967. In a final chapter, I compare the instance of offset with other recent cases in the making of American policy which it resembles in certain respects.

*"Offset" is a wooden term and one which, as will be seen later, is not entirely accurate as a description of the arrangements it labels. Nevertheless, I use it to refer to the financial arrangements and, in shorthand, to the conjunction of those arrangements and the issue of troop level. Quotation marks will hereafter be dropped as needless clutter.

This book is an attempt to explain why recent events in alliance relations turned out as they did, and to speculate on the significance of that explanation for the future making of American foreign policy. It is not primarily a test of explanatory methods; for that reason I have freely borrowed concepts or techniques from wherever suited my purposes and have not, in general, made that borrowing explicit. But the roots of the study's style of analysis should be clear enough. The issues at play were ones on which the major institutions of government, both American and German, had strong views; the details of those issues were technical, and they customarily were played out between the two governments in official secrecy. Those reasons suggest that insights from the writings now labeled "bureaucratic politics" would be helpful. They have, as has the literature on the transnational extension of those politics, "alliance politics" from the title of Richard E. Neustadt's pioneering study.[2]

Yet the handling of the issues within and between the two executives in Washington and Bonn hardly took place in a vacuum. In the United States, Congress was frequently exercised over the issues, and the debates within government were paralleled without, in the press and among influential former officials and other members of the limited public attentive to foreign affairs, the "Establishment" in popular reference. Hence I have been helped by writings on Congress and on interest group politics.[3]

Finally, deliberations between the two governments took place within the context of perceptions of "national interest"—differences that separated Americans and Germans but views that were shared widely among people of different official positions and party politics in each of Washington and Bonn. For instance, Defense Secretary McNamara's use of the words "deterrence" and "defense," controversial enough in Washington in the 1960s, was bound to evoke quite different connotations in the ears of Germans, for whom "defense" could not but suggest the possibility of a war that would be fought on German soil. If I devote less attention to these conceptions of state interest than to what went on in the two capitals, that reflects no general judgment about the importance of particular sets of factors in producing given outcomes. Rather this is an inquiry into how much difference was made by political and governmental deliberations within the vague limits of state interest, and into how much space there was for the governmental processes in each country to make their broader interests compatible in specific instances.

No author, I imagine, is ever completely comfortable releasing a study which by its form advertises itself as a final product. There are always further details to be captured, refinements in both presentation of fact and interpretation to be made. In my case the sense of unease is sharp. My facts are case materials, recent episodes in relations between the United States and major allies in western Europe. Much more is knowable than I now know. My focus on the making of American policy compounds my discomfort, for my judgments several times turn on nuances in the calculations of officials, American or German, or on shadings in the actions of governments or the effects of those actions.

My account of the German side, in particular, is less precise than I would like it to be. German documents pertaining to the events of 1966–67 were inaccessible to me; by 1973, when I made my initial foray into German deliberations, several key participants were dead, while others remained reticent about discussing the events of that period. At several junctures, my judgments, particularly those touching the motivations of senior German officials and relations among those men, become reasoned conjectures, based on interviews and supported by fragments of evidence from published sources.

Note on Sources

This study is based on several score of interviews of participants and observers at close range of the events recounted, conducted both in the United States and in Europe. Those interviews were conducted on a background basis, and no specific reference to them is made in the text or notes. The persons interviewed all consented to be listed; their names appear at the conclusion of the study. I have also drawn on newspaper articles, on parliamentary documents from the United States, Germany and Britain, and on other published accounts. I cite these sources occasionally as places to find additional information. More often, especially in the case of newspaper articles, they serve as partial corroboration for statements I believe true from sources I cannot cite. If the account cited is approximately right but lacks in or errs on particulars, I try to point that out.

In preparing a version of the offset cases for the federal Commission on the Organization of Government for the Conduct of Foreign Policy, I was given access to classified government documents under rules which precluded quotation or direct citation. That material no doubt colors the discussion in the pages which follow. It has sharpened the description of events and added precision to the discussion of deliberations within the United States government, but the classified record does not, I believe, differ in fundamental respects from what I obtained through interviews and from sources in the public domain. The general shape of deliberations in both capitals is discernible from public sources. Most details can be found between the lines in those sources. The press was active in both countries, most notably during 1966 but later as well, especially in Germany where the import of even the routine episodes was great. My inability to offer full, academic documentation for the study is a cost of doing research on certain kinds of current issues of public policy. I believe the research important and that cost of doing it is one I am willing to pay. Yet, alas, reader and author alike must bear it. The study and conclusions derived from it must stand, finally, on the reader's judgment of its internal consistency and plausibility. Only the reader can determine whether or not I have lived up to my implicit compact with him.

Acknowledgments

In the course of this study I have incurred the customary number of debts, intellectual and other. I am happy to acknowledge them all. First and foremost, it is a pleasure to record my gratitude to my teachers, now colleagues, at Harvard in and around the Kennedy School of Government, especially Richard E. Neustadt, Graham T. Allison, Francis M. Bator, Ernest R. May and Joseph S. Nye. My intellectual debt to them will be clear enough, I think, in the pages which follow. It is a large one. The study also bears the mark of thoughtful comments from many other people, especially I. M. Destler, Abraham F. Lowenthal, C. Fred Bergsten and Morton Halperin. There could have been no study without the cooperation of the many officials and ex-officials—American, German and British—who found the time and patience to answer my questions, in many cases on more than one occasion. To each I offer my sincere appreciation.

I owe a debt of another sort to the Twentieth Century Fund, which aided in financing research for this project. For the assistance and consideration of members of the Fund I am grateful. The research program of the federal Commission on the Organization of Government for the Conduct of Foreign Policy commissioned me to prepare a case study based on this project. That provided me the chance to test some of the arguments in this study against a wider audience and afforded me the opportunity to check my version of the case materials against the classified government record. The Kennedy School was kind enough to provide me a quiet, happy place to work and generous amounts of time free from other duties. I also express my thanks to the Deutsche Gesellschaft für Auswärtige Politik in Bonn and to various of its staff members for twice having provided me a base and guidance for initial—and fascinating—looks at German politics. I completed final revisions on the manuscript during a pleasant and productive year as a research associate at the International Institute for Strategic Studies in London.

The customary reminder that I alone remain responsible for any errors in fact or judgment is necessary because I would like the foregoing list of people and institutions, and others too numerous to name, to be implicated in whatever is worthwhile in what follows but spared identification with the study's shortcomings.

London
July 1976

NOTES TO THE PREFACE

[1]There is an extensive literature on linkage as a foreign policy strategy; similarly, there has been considerable writing on links between national systems and international politics. Both sets of writings, however, touch my purposes in this study only obliquely. What concerns me are the implications of linkage not as a strategic choice in foreign policy but as an imperative arising out of the interplay of alliance relations and domestic politics. In 1961 Secretary of Defense McNamara may have been making a strategic linkage across issue areas by erecting offset arrangements tied implicitly to force levels, but I doubt that he thought so; for him, both issues lay squarely within his bailiwick. The preoccupation of this study is the difficulty posed for the American government as that linkage, whatever its initial motivation, hardened into a political imperative. Those problems, particularly severe, may find parallels in other sets of linked issues, and the offset case may be suggestive of the dangers even of linkages which better fit the traditional conception of strategic choice. For a recent discussion of linkage, one akin to my own thinking but one which also discusses the dangers of linkage strategies, *see* William Wallace, "Issue Linkage Among Atlantic Governments," *International Affairs,* LII, 2 (April 1976), 163–79.

[2]Richard E. Neustadt, *Alliance Politics* (New York: Columbia University Press, 1970). The basic sources on the "bureaucratic politics" approach are Graham T. Allison, *Essence of Decision: Explaining the Cuban Missile Crisis* (Boston: Little, Brown, 1971), and Morton H. Halperin, *Bureaucratic Politics and Foreign Policy* (Washington: The Brookings Institution, 1974); for a briefer summary, *see* Allison and Halperin, "Bureaucratic Politics: A

Paradigm and Some Policy Implications," in Raymond Tanter and Richard H. Ullman, eds., *Theory and Policy in International Relations* (Princeton: Princeton University Press, 1972). Working from the perspective of behavioral psychology, John Steinbruner has developed a "cybernetic" model or paradigm that is, in a sense, a generalization of Allison's Model II, labeled by him "organizational process" and rooted in the work on organizations by Simon, and Cyert and March.

An additional reason why I have not made these or other perspectives explicit in this book is that doing so encourages a misunderstanding of them. It suggests that each is a complete and alternative mode of explanation in and of itself; they are not, a fact recognized by the authors I have cited but not always clearly understood by critics of the so-called "bureaucratic politics" school.

Thus far there have been too few attempts at putting the models together, at seeing what foreign policy contexts or parts of the policy process are best explained (and predicted) by which models. One interesting attempt at such a synthesis is Ernest R. May, "The 'Bureaucratic Politics' Approach: U.S.-Argentine Relations, 1942–47," in Julio Cotler and Richard R. Fagen, eds., *Latin America and the United States: The Changing Political Realities* (Stanford: Stanford University Press, 1974). My implicit synthesis in this study parallels his; it derives from the common-sense notion that organizational models, like Allison's Model II, will be most useful in explaining those parts of the policy process dominated by the day-to-day routines of large governmental organizations. Hence I discuss in some detail the perspectives of those organizations, American and German, as shapers of the offset/force level issues. Their handling of the issues in normal times was imbedded in organizational routines, procedural "channels" whose assumptions influenced the way the issues were perceived even after they were elevated to high-level attention. At higher levels, Model II yields in explanatory power to Neustadt's style of analysis, Allison's Model III, "governmental politics," which focuses on the interactions of senior officials and the political considerations represented by them. If there were an extended implementation phase, as there was not in offset, organizational perspectives and processes would again have become central in explaining outcomes at that stage.

[3] Good analyses of interest groups and their influence on foreign policy, either directly or through Congress, are few. Several useful sources are Lester Milbrath, "Interest Groups and Foreign Policy," in James Rosenau, ed., *Domestic Sources of Foreign Policy* (New York: The Free Press, 1967); and William Zimmerman, "Issue Area and Foreign Policy Process: A Research Note in Search of a General Theory," *American Political Science Review*, LXVII, 4 (December 1973), 1204–12. The now classic study of interest groups and Congress is Raymond A. Bauer, Ithiel de Sola Pool and Lewis Anthony Dexter, *American Business and Public Policy: The Politics of Foreign Trade* (New York: Atherton Press, 1963). See also Theodore Lowi's review of that book, "American Business, Public Policy, Case Studies and Political Theory," *World Politics*, XVI, 4 (July 1964), 677–715.

Equally rare are examinations of the flows of real influence in and through Congress, not to mention studies of how Congressional actions short of passing laws influence foreign policy-making in the Executive Branch. For a recent discussion of Congress' role in the realms of arms control and defense, *see* Alton Frye, *A Responsible Congress: The Politics of National Security* (New York: McGraw-Hill, 1975).

CHAPTER I: THE BALANCE OF PAYMENTS AND AMERICAN FORCE LEVELS IN GERMANY

WHEN Lyndon Johnson met his German counterpart, Chancellor Ludwig Erhard, at a summit conference in Washington at the end of September 1966, offset and the level of American forces in Germany figured prominently on the agenda. In making decisions with respect to those issues before and during the meeting, the President confronted a snarly tangle of choices. He and his successor faced similar clusters of decisions on other occasions, albeit times less imbued with high drama than were the weeks surrounding the summit conference with a German Chancellor in desperate political straits at home.

To take decision with respect to offset and force level was to attempt to square a circle. The objectives weighed by the President conflicted with one another. On the one hand, Washington wanted to increase NATO capacity to defend Europe by conventional means, hence to deter Soviet adventures. The United States also wanted to strengthen the cohesion of the NATO alliance and the European commitment to it. For those purposes, the more American troops in Europe the better. On the other hand, the troops in Europe cost money and consumed manpower desperately needed for Vietnam. The President was well aware of the political risk he courted on those

1

scores, from both those in Congress who opposed stationing troops abroad at all and those who gave priority to the war in Vietnam.

The American garrison in Europe also cost foreign exchange. To run persistent balance-of-payments deficits was both bad policy and bad politics. That concern was pressed upon the President by the "gold bugs" and "dollar drainers" in Congress, among the New York banking community and within his own Administration. There were but two ready means of reducing the foreign exchange drain occasioned by the stationing in Europe: bring troops back to the United States or press the Germans to "offset" the drain, perhaps by spending dollars on military weapons purchased in the United States. In either case, Washington's purposes were served by bargaining hard with Bonn over offset and by insisting that the U.S. might be forced to reduce its garrison in Germany if the Federal Republic did not offer an attractive offset. If Bonn were niggardly, that would serve to justify an American troop cut.

A final set of objectives entered the balance. In 1966, the Federal German economy fell into recession, and Chancellor Erhard sought relief from the offset commitments his government had given previously. Bonn could not scrape up the budget money, he argued, to purchase as many weapons as it had agreed to buy. President Johnson knew that Erhard would come to Washington hat in hand, asking to be forgiven part of his offset obligations. In fact, several of the President's senior advisors believed the Chancellor's government would fall if Washington held firm. That nastiness to the loyal leader of a major ally, bad enough in itself, might risk impairments in Bonn's long-term relations with Washington or with NATO serious enough to give Washingtonians cause for concern.

Sorting out the welter of objectives at play in the issues of offset and force level is my task in this chapter. Since the two issues have been interconnected, it is important to look at both: at costs and rationales for the stationing, and at the economic effects of the various offset agreements entered into by the United States and the Federal Republic of Germany. In 1966, the two issues came before an official Washington—Executive and Congress—which was divided. The difference between the halves was one not merely of substance but of perspective. The division, grown hard with time, neither began nor ended with the Trilaterals, nor did its effect touch only the issues of offset and troop levels in Europe. That division is the subject of a final section of this chapter. It was of crucial importance to the course of

2

deliberations within the American government during 1966 and 1967, and its influence persisted beyond that episode.

The next chapter turns from objectives to cases. It contains a brief overview of my primary instance: events before and during the Trilateral Negotiations of 1966 and 1967. To set them in context, the chapter glances at what transpired before and after the trilaterals, at how the issues of offset and force level have been played out between Bonn and Washington and among them and their allies in western Europe.

Chapters III, IV and V present the case of 1966 and 1967, with occasional glimpses of subsequent episodes. Chapter III is an examination of the politics and procedures surrounding offset and force level in Bonn; chapter IV is a similar, and more detailed, treatment of Washington. Chapter V places events in the two capitals side by side, looking at how the actions of one government related to the deliberations of the other. My central interest is policy-making in Washington, and the overlay of deliberations in Bonn and Washington permits evaluation of Washington's actions: to what extent did Washington misperceive and misunderstand what was occurring in its ally's capital? Or to what extent were its politics incompatible with Bonn's at various junctures in the offset history during 1966–67?

Chapter VI frames an answer to those questions. It asks what special obstacles to the management of alliances arise from the problem of competing objectives which confronted President Johnson in the late summer of 1966. That intellectual problem was given substance in deep differences among departments of government and their secretaries, mirrored in Congress and among the limited public attentive to foreign affairs. Is the offset affair a rarity in relations between the United States and nations conceived of, by tradition and common purpose, as allies and friends? Or will the kinds of dangers apparent in the instance of offset plague dealings among the allies in the years ahead? If so, and I believe so, what lessons are there for the conduct of American policy?

I. AMERICAN FORCES IN EUROPE: COSTS

In 1950 there were somewhat more than 100,000 American soldiers in western Europe. By 1953 there were more than 400,000. Since 1953 there have never been fewer than 300,000, nor fewer than

200,000 in the Federal Republic of Germany, where virtually all the land-based U.S. forces are located. The decision to send four Ameri-

Table I

APPROXIMATE U.S. MILITARY STRENGTH IN GERMANY AND IN ALL OF WESTERN EUROPE, 1950–1974

Year	Strength in Germany (thousands)	Strength in Western Europe, Including Germany (thousands)
1950	98	122
1953	254	407
1955	261	430
1956	262	418
1957	250	401
1958	235	386
1959	240	379
1960	237	365
1961	242	371
1962	280	419
1963	265	383
1964	263	368
1965	262	353
1966	237	320
1967		
1968	210	
1969		
1970	213	300
1971		
1972	221	307
1973	228	313
1974	228	319

Sources: 1950–66, 1970–73. *U.S. Forces in Europe,* Hearings before the Subcommittee on Arms Control, International Law and Organization of the Senate Committee on Foreign Relations, 93 Cong., 1 sess. (1973), pp.18,149–196.

1968. Horst Mendershausen, *Troop Stationing in Germany: Value and Cost,* RM-5881-PR (Santa Monica: The Rand Corporation, 1968), p.52.

1974. Richard D. Lawrence and Jeffrey Record, *U.S. Force Structure in NATO: An Alternative* (Washington: The Brookings Institution, 1974), p.93.

can divisions to Europe was made in 1951, when U.S. forces were engaged in war with Chinese forces in Korea, when the Soviet Union lately had become a nuclear power and when the possibility that the cold war in Europe might become hot preoccupied serious people on both sides of the Atlantic.

At the time the forces were sent, Secretary of State Marshall asserted to Congress that there was nothing "magic" about the figure of four-plus divisions.[1] In fact, there has been considerable magic about that figure, for reasons which will be suggested in the pages to follow. The level of American forces in Germany reached a peak of about 280,000 at the time of the Berlin crisis in 1961–62 and dipped to about 210,000 at the height of the war in Vietnam, in 1967–68. (Table I lists approximate American troop strengths in the Federal Republic, and in all of western Europe, 1950–1974.)

Budgetary Costs

The budgetary costs of troops stationed in western Europe by the various NATO members are, in general, borne by the country contributing the troops.[2] Conceivably, NATO forces in Europe might be paid for jointly—since the security they provide is an essentially public good—but the allies have never come close to an agreement on a budget-sharing arrangement of that kind.

Neither the United States nor most of its NATO allies allocates defense costs by geographic area, and comparisons of area figures seldom enter negotiations among the allies (while comparisons of total military expenditure, perhaps as a percentage of GNP, often do). Cost estimates for U.S. forces in Europe are sensitive to assumptions made in their calculation, hence slightly artificial. It is also important to note that of the American forces maintained primarily for European contingencies, only a portion is stationed *in Europe*.

It is relatively simple to calculate *operating* costs (pay and allowances, supplies, maintenance and transportation), but these understate real resource costs to the United States. Estimates must be made as well of the annual costs of military equipment and construction, and the European garrison must be allocated a share of direct support costs (administration, training and central logistics).[3] Rough estimates of budgetary costs, in 1974, for forces stationed in the German Federal Republic and in the rest of NATO Europe are presented in Table II.

How much could be saved through reductions in the American

Table II

ROUGH ESTIMATES: BUDGETARY COSTS OF U.S. FORCES
IN GERMANY AND IN THE REST OF NATO EUROPE, AND OF ALL
GENERAL PURPOSE FORCES COMMITTED TO NATO, FY 1974

	Forces Abroad		
	Operating Costs (billions of $)	Support Costs (billions of $)	Total Costs (billions of $)
Forces in Germany	3.1	2.9	6.0[a]
Forces in Rest of NATO Europe	.9	.8	1.7
All Forces in Europe	4.0	3.7	7.7[b]

PLUS Forces in U.S. Committed to NATO	
	Total Cost (billions of $)
Low Estimate (includes direct costs, support costs, and a share of equipment)	17.0[c]
High Estimate (low estimate adjusted for a slightly larger force and adding shares for retirement pay, intelligence, administration and fixed support)	28.4[d]

a. All the totals are from *U.S. Forces in NATO,* Hearings before the House Committee on Foreign Affairs and its Subcommittee on Europe, 93 Cong., 1 sess.(1973), pp.260–1. The division between operating and support costs is based on that given in *United States Relations with Europe in the Decade of the 1970's.* Hearings before the Subcommittee on Europe of the House Committee on Foreign Affairs, 91 Cong., 2 sess.(1970), p.411.

b. This figure is probably on the low side. It all depends on which items are included in support costs and which are excluded.

c. This is the figure used by the Defense Department. It appears in *U.S. Forces in NATO,* cited above.

d. This estimate is based on that given by John Newhouse, and others in *U.S. Troops in Europe: Issues, Costs, and Choices* (Washington: The Brookings Institution, 1971), p. 119. It has been adjusted upward to account for inflation and pay hikes.

garrison in Europe? The artificiality of the original cost estimates becomes clear in attempting an answer. To save the entire six billion dollars per year, *all* American forces in the Federal Republic would have to be returned home *and deactivated,* and procurement, training and other support functions would have to be reduced by the amount attributed to the forces in Germany. Calculating incremental savings attainable through specified levels of reductions is tricky; it all depends on assumptions made about what will be done with the troops once they are removed from Germany (or Europe).

The central point is that merely transferring troops from Germany to the U.S. *does not* save budget dollars, quite the less so if the transfers are made under so-called dual-basing arrangements, which permit the troops withdrawn to be quickly mobilized in Europe if needed. It is not much cheaper to station troops in the U.S. than in Germany. Indeed, it may be more expensive and almost certainly was in 1966–67 due to the lower cost of local services in Germany. In 1973, Deputy Secretary of State Kenneth Rush told the United States Senate that the additional cost of keeping the troops in Europe rather than in the U.S. was $400 million per year. But at the same time, he argued that bringing the men home would cost more. He apparently had in mind the costs of duplicate equipment and supplies necessary to permit the withdrawn forces to be returned to Europe rapidly.[4] Still, the distinction is a fine one. When Washington presented Bonn with a bill for the $400 million in "additional" costs, the Federal Republic countered that the value of goods and services provided to American forces by Germany free of charge (land for bases, buildings and some services) would more than offset the $400 million.

Table III presents rough estimates of the costs and savings attached to removing one division force (about 48,000 men) from Germany under alternative subsequent uses and possibilities for return to Europe. In *budgetary* terms the significant choice is between deactivating a division and maintaining it, *no matter where.* As the table illustrates, returning one division to the U.S. and integrating it with other general purpose forces designated for European contingencies (which implies that it could not be redeployed to Europe quickly) would produce trivial annual budget savings (about $40 million); returning the division with an extra set of equipment pre-positioned in Europe would cost about the same each year as stationing in Europe (after substantial one-time costs); and any other redeployment scheme with provision for rapid return to Europe would cost *more* than stationing in Europe. Moreover, the table estimates probably understate the per division cost of dual-basing more than one division, due to the need for measures to cope with potential transportation bottlenecks in provisions for rapid return to Germany.[5]

Table III

ESTIMATED COSTS OF AND SAVINGS FROM REDEPLOYING ONE DIVISION FROM THE FEDERAL REPUBLIC TO THE U.S. UNDER VARIOUS ALTERNATIVES FOR SUBSEQUENT USE[a]

	Fixed, One-Time Cost (−) or Saving (+)	Recurring, Yearly Cost (−) or Saving (+)
1. Return to U.S. and deactivate	−50	+500[b]
2. Return and integrate with no special provisions for return to Europe (implies possible return within 90 days— D+90—with existing airlift and sealift)	−50	+40
3. Return, but purchase and pre-position in Europe an extra set of equipment, no additional airlift required (implies return by D+15)	−380	+10[c]
4. D+30 (24 C−5A's)	−750	−50
5. D+15 (56 C−5A's)	−1800	−200

Sources: The estimates are rough; they are based on figures given in *U.S. Security Agreements and Commitments Abroad, Pt. 10: United States Forces in Europe,* Hearings before the Subcommittee on U.S. Security Agreements and Commitments Abroad of the Senate Committee on Foreign Relations, 91 Cong., 2 sess.(1970), p.2168; and John Newhouse, and others, *U.S. Troops in Europe: Issues, Costs, and Choices* (Washington: The Brookings Institution, 1971), p.115.

a. Secretary McNamara originally estimated that the 1968 redeployments (35,000 men) would produce annual budget savings of $10–15 million after initial costs of $50–150 million. *United States Troops in Europe,* Hearings before the Combined Subcommittee of the Senate Committees on Foreign Relations and Armed Services, 90 Cong., 1 sess. (1967), p.17. Actual data on the 1968 REFORGER exercise (28,000 men) suggest that redeploying a full division force (48,000 men) might save $65 million annually after initial costs of about $135 million. *Military Construction Appropriations for 1970, Pt. 2: Department of the Air Force, and Department of the Army,* Hearings before a Subcommittee of the House Committee on Appropriations, 91 Cong., 1 sess. (1969), pp. 279-80. (The Hearings estimates have been adjusted upward to account for the larger redeployment and increased 20% to account for 1973 prices.) But those estimates, as the Brookings study notes, understate costs and overstate savings. In 1968 there was substantial unused base capacity in the U.S. due to the Vietnam war, and REFORGER was relatively small. Now, however, sizable redeployments might necessitate hiring additional civilians and reopening or constructing additional base capacity. Newhouse, *U.S. Troops in Europe,* cited above, p.114.

b. Operating costs only.

c. Excludes the cost of any annual exercises in Europe. The cost of the 1972 exercises carried out as part of REFORGER was $13.4 million. *The American Commitment to NATO,* Hearings before the Special Subcommittee on NATO Commitments of the House Committee on Armed Services, 91 Cong., 1 and 2 sess.(1971–72), p.14963.

Balance-of-Payments (Foreign Exchange) Costs

Why the balance-of-payments effect of the troop stationing should have been such an urgent concern to the United States is, on the face of it, puzzling. Foreign exchange costs do not represent drains on American resources additional to the budgetary costs. Some budgetary costs are immediate and direct balance-of-payments costs as well—for example, payments to West German nationals for services rendered to American bases. But in other cases exchange costs can be reduced without diminishing budgetary outlays—for instance, by reducing the local market purchases of dependents of American soldiers, perhaps by sending dependents home. By contrast, other attempts to reduce balance-of-payments costs may *increase* budgetary costs—for example, so-called "Buy American" procurement policies that gave precedence to American over foreign suppliers of military goods even if foreign goods were cheaper.

The term balance-of-payments (or foreign exchange) "drain," which I employ along with the participants in offset episodes, is itself ambiguous. Connecting a deficit in any payments subaccount with an over-all payments deficit is loose economics, as Germans consistently have pointed out. American military expenditures in the Federal Republic increase German supplies of foreign exchange, in turn stimulating increases in German purchases of American exports. But even the *net* American "drain" after accounting for increased exports may not equal the *net* German "gain," due to increases in German purchases of third-country exports. American experts have differed over the size of the feedback of U.S. military expenditures on American exports; that is, how much smaller is the *net* foreign exchange "drain" attributable to the troops than the *gross* foreign exchange expenditure related to them.[6] Given the differences of professional opinion on one side of the Atlantic, it is hardly surprising that the parties to the 1966–67 Trilateral Negotiations could not come to agreement on net "gains" and "drains" in a technical exercise undertaken in a distinctly political context. I will return to that exercise in chapter IV.

The foreign exchange issues are complicated, often technical. That technicality has varying implications for decision-making in Washington: at times decision processes in the Executive Branch may be insulated from public (or Congressional) pressure, at times be driven to respond to oversimplified public perceptions.

The American President presumably cares about balance-of-payments deficits because they may constrain the conduct of his foreign policy and, ultimately, of his domestic economic policy. Different elements of the private sector may fret over (or relish) deficits for different reasons. But why was one item in the balance of payments—military expenditures abroad—the subject of so much concern, from 1960 onward? One line of response is suggestive, though in itself not a complete answer. From the time of initial balance-of-payments concern in the United States through 1971, the nation had a substantial *surplus* in private sector foreign trade on current account. (Table IV presents a summary of the U.S. balance of payments, 1960–73, listing major accounts and net balances.) The substantial deficit *on government account* seemed to be the main foreign exchange culprit, and military expenditures abroad, including those in Europe, bulked large in that deficit. (Table V presents U.S. military expenditures in Germany and in all of Western Europe, 1961–1972; and the composition of German offset, 1968–1975.) From early in the Kennedy Administration, each department was required to calculate the foreign exchange implications of *its* activities (its "gold budget"). The McNamara Defense Department took that mission seriously and set about saving foreign exchange.

The general form of offset arrangements was from the start strange, at best a matter of political convenience. In the first place, the Germans were correct in insisting that there was no economic justification for separating a "military" subaccount from the over-all American balance of payments. Yet from Washington's perspective of the 1960s, with devaluation unthinkable, operating on subaccounts was the only remedy for American deficits. Still, to equate German procurement in the United States with American expenditure in Germany and call the former an "offset" to the latter was at best a sideshow to Washington's serious purpose: inducing the Germans and other Europeans to hold dollars and not cash them in for gold. Searching, in years after 1966, for means of filling the "gap" between German procurement and American expenditures per-

Table IV

U.S. BALANCE OF PAYMENTS: SELECTED MAJOR ACCOUNTS AND NET BALANCES

1960–1973

(billions of dollars)

Year	Merchandise			Military Transactions			Long-term Capital Flows, Net	
							U.S. Gov-ern-ment	Pri-vate
	Ex-ports	Im-ports	Bal-ance	Direct Expend-itures	Sales	Bal-ance		
1960	19.7	14.8	4.9	3.1	.3	−2.8	− .9	−2.1
1961	20.1	14.5	5.6	3.0	.4	−2.6	− .9	−2.2
1962	20.8	16.3	4.5	3.1	.7	−2.4	− .9	−2.6
1963	22.3	17.0	5.2	3.0	.7	−2.3	−1.2	−3.4
1964	25.5	18.7	6.8	2.9	.7	−2.1	−1.3	−4.5
1965	26.5	21.5	5.0	3.0	.8	−2.1	−1.5	−4.6
1966	29.3	25.5	3.8	3.8	.8	−2.9	−1.5	−2.6
1967	30.7	26.9	3.8	4.4	1.2	−3.1	−2.4	−2.9
1968	33.6	33.0	.6	4.5	1.4	−3.1	−2.2	1.2
1969	36.4	35.8	.6	4.9	1.5	−3.3	−1.9	− .1
1970	42.0	39.8	2.2	1.9	1.5	−3.4	−2.0	−1.4
1971	42.8	45.5	−2.7	4.8	1.9	−2.9	−2.4	−4.4
1972	48.8	55.7	−6.9	4.7	1.2	−3.6	−1.3	− .2
1973*	67.0	67.7	− .7	4.6	1.8	−2.8	− .8	1.8

Year	Net Liquidity Balance	Official Reserve Transactions Balance
1960	− 3.7	− 3.4
1961	− 2.3	− 1.3
1962	− 2.9	− 2.7
1963	− 2.7	− 1.9
1964	− 2.7	− 1.5
1965	− 2.5	− 1.3
1966	− 2.2	.2
1967	− 4.7	− 3.4
1968	− 1.6	1.6
1969	− 6.1	2.7
1970	− 3.9	− 9.8
1971	−22.0	−29.8
1972	−13.9	10.3
1973*	− 9.1	−10.7

*preliminary

Source: *Economic Report of the President, 1974* (Washington, 1974), pp. 350–51.

Table V

U.S. MILITARY EXPENDITURES IN GERMANY, AND IN ALL OF WESTERN EUROPE, ENTERING THE BALANCE OF PAYMENTS, 1961–1972; AND COMPOSITION OF GERMAN OFFSET, 1968–1975

	Military Expenditures Entering the Balance of Payments (millions of $)		Covered by Offset Agreements (millions of $)			
Fiscal Year	Western Europe	Germany	Total	Financial Measures	Procurement	Direct Payments
1961	1,600	641				
1962	1,600	699				
1963	1,600	734				
1964	1,600	702				
1965	1,500	703				
1966	1,600	759				
1967	1,600	801				
1968	1,600	889	725	625	100	
1969	1,600	910	725	625	100	
1970	1,700	1,030	1,520	925	525	
1971	1,900	1,176				
1972	2,300	1,388	2,034	650	1,200	184
1973						
1974						
1975		*3,300	#2,218	#843	#1,142	#231

Sources: *U.S. Forces in NATO,* Hearings before the House Committee on Foreign Affairs and its Subcommittee on Europe, 93 Cong., 1 sess. (1973), pp. 98, 332–33.

U.S. Security Issues in Europe: Burden Sharing and Offset, MBFR and Nuclear Weapons, Staff report for the Subcommittee on U.S. Security Agreements and Commitments of the Senate Committee on Foreign Relations, 93 Cong., 1 sess. (1973), p. 7.

#Department of State Press Release, April 25, 1974. The agreement, like its predecessors, was denominated in *Deutsche Marks.* Dollar figures have been coverted at 2.669 *DM* to the dollar.

petuated the artifice. However, as subsequent pages will show, once the bilateral offset form had been established, reflecting an initial convergence of political purposes in the two countries, domestic American politics made it hard to abandon. The Trilateral Negotiations resulted in the German pledge not to cash in its dollar holdings for American gold. That provided direct assistance to Washington's purposes. It did not, however, cause a fundamental alteration in the form of the issue. Bilateral offset negotiations persisted even after a fixed dollar-exchange rate ceased to be sacrosanct, in 1971.

Economic Effects of Offset

German-American offset agreements have included four kinds of offset, four forms of balance-of-payments assistance from Bonn to Washington: German purchases of American military hardware, German purchases of American civilian goods, financial measures of several kinds, and German payments in direct support of American forces. The forms have had different economic effects, and hence have been of varied attractiveness to the two governments and to their subunits engaged in the issues of offset and force level.

1. Military Purchases. It has become a convention in Washington to credit purchases of American military equipment by NATO countries against American military expenditures in those countries. The convention apparently predated the first offset agreements; it no doubt affected the form of those agreements and was in turn strengthened by their existence. There has been no doubt in subsequent negotiations about the legitimacy of military purchases as offset.

There has been, however, some uncertainty about their actual balance-of-payments effect. The worry is that they may not represent purchases *additional* to those which would have occurred in the absence of any agreement. It seems clear that there can have been little additionality in purchases made under the early agreements: the Federal German army (the Bundeswehr) was rearming and German industry was fully employed producing civilian goods. Purchases after 1967 may have been somewhat more additional, with Bonn forced to purchase equipment of marginal utility to it (though perhaps of great interest to its army) or, more likely, pressed to choose American over domestic or European producers.[7] The issue has been debated in Washington, in Bonn and between the two. It is impossible to settle conclusively. It may, however, be taken as a working presumption that the crediting of military purchases as offset produces tidy accounts more than it records truly additional foreign exchange inflows.

Under the first three offset agreements, the Federal Republic undertook to place weapons orders in the United States totaling an agreed amount during the two-year period of each agreement. Further, Bonn pledged to transfer payments to the United States Treasury for the full amount by the end of each period, no matter how many orders it had been able to place. During 1966 and 1967, German orders lagged far behind its payments. As a result, by the beginning of 1968 the Federal Republic had about $800 million on deposit with the Treasury in two special offset accounts. How to erase the overhanging balance became a constant theme of subsequent negotiations, with Washington insisting in each instance that Bonn make available "fresh" money. In the 1971 agreement, the Federal Republic was permitted to liberate about $500 million of money previously deposited and apply it toward the 1971 procurement commitment. Doing so involved some double-counting of course, since the money had been credited as offset when initially deposited.

2. *Civilian Purchases*. Purchases of nonmilitary items—by the German Federal government, by a state or local government, or by a public corporation—occasionally were counted under offset agreements, although Washington consistently objected to their inclusion. Again, the grounds for objection was additionality. And as with military purchases, the additionality agreement is inconclusive. In any case, civilian purchases were no more than footnotes to any given agreement, for reasons that will become clear in subsequent chapters.

It is worth noting that the American practice with respect to civilian purchases was at variance with the British: even the earliest Anglo-German offset arrangements included nonmilitary purchases. However, neither side really liked the arrangement. London of course worried about additionality, while Bonn disliked the enormous bookkeeping exercise. Under the first agreements, Bonn subsidized German imports from Britain, but that practice soon ran afoul of GATT regulations governing international trade and was terminated. London's qualms about additionality turned out to be well-founded: German studies done after civilian purchases ceased to be formal parts of Anglo-German agreements, in 1971, suggested that the total of such purchases remained roughly constant.

3. *Financial Measures*. The offset agreements, customarily negotiated every other year, included two types of financial provisions: the first, German purchases of U.S. Treasury notes (or other types of government securities) was a central element of every agreement

after 1967 and continually debated, both among Americans and between Americans and Germans; the second, the German pledge not to redeem dollar reserves for U.S. gold—though irrelevant after the link between dollars and gold was severed in 1968, and little publicized or understood before that—was a key feature of the Trilateral agreement in 1967.

(a) Securities Purchases. In the offset agreements reached in 1967 and 1968 the Germans agreed to make large purchases of special, medium-term United States Treasury securities at commercial interest rates (interest rates on the issues purchased under the 1967 agreement ranged between four and six percent). In effect, the Federal Republic lent foreign exchange to the United States. The securities were purchased by the German Bundesbank (central bank), not the federal government; hence they did not cost budget money. Instead, the purchases signified the willingness of the Bundesbank to hold part of its reserves in a special and relatively illiquid form.

Securities purchased under the 1969, 1971 and 1973 agreements earned *below* market interest rates. In form, that required the federal government to make a budgetary appropriation which was then transferred to the Bundesbank. In fact, the subsidy was indirect, except in 1971. By law the Bank cannot retain any profits and instead must transfer them to the federal government. Thus, by agreeing to submarket interest rates, the federal government expressed a willingness to forego revenue.

Obviously, the sales of Treasury securities to the Federal Republic affected the timing and financing of American deficits more than their magnitude. Balance-of-payments deficits had to be financed in any case; the balance had to balance. They could be financed by selling American gold to nations abroad or by incurring dollar liabilities in some form to foreigners, or by some combination of measures. Dollar liabilities, most often liquid in form and short-term, could move rapidly back across the Atlantic. Large amounts could be converted readily in the United States for other foreign currencies, perhaps signaling that another run on the dollar was in the making, or worse, the liabilities could be presented as claims against Fort Knox gold. What the special securities sold to the Federal Republic under offset offered Washington was certainty: a given portion of the American deficit could be financed by incurring dollar liabilities which were not convertible, at least in the short run. Moreover, the effective interest rates associated with the special, medium-term offset issues were somewhat lower than those attached to short-term liabilities. The interest subsidies provided by Bonn under later agreements lowered the cost to Washington still further.

In 1966, Washington officials hoped that the sales of securities to the Bundesbank would be counted as a capital inflow under the liquidity basis definition of the balance of payments, since the securities were of more than a year in duration. In fact, the sales were counted as a means of *financing* the deficit: that was because the transaction was a special one, government to government. As a practical matter, however, the difference counted for little, since the Bundesbank privately promised not to redeem the securities for a minimum period of more than a year.

Selling securities was a kind of "beggar-thy-future" measure, carrying with it the presumption that the payments deficit was a temporary phenomenon, part of whose burden could be shifted to the future. When the securities came to term, after four years in most cases, the Federal Republic had to be repaid, occasioning a balance-of-payments outflow. Yet the sales of securities did assist Washington in financing American deficits. They were reasonable enough in the several years following 1967, assuming that the United States purpose was buying time, at least staving off devaluation of the dollar until reforms in the international monetary system could be negotiated. Labeling the German purchases of securities an "offset" was, however, purely a German-American convention.

Not surprisingly, the arrangement looked less and less attractive as the years passed. Sales of securities under later agreements only enabled Washington to "roll over" the debts incurred from sales under previous agreements as those earlier liabilities came due. At various times it was argued within official Washington that only the amount of the German interest subsidy should be counted under offset agreements, or that the principal of the securities sales could be counted as inflow when the sales were made but that principal had to count as outflow for offset purposes when the securities were redeemed by the Federal Republic. Neither argument gained sway in Washington, but for reasons which had more to do with politics than with economics.

(b) The Gold Pledge. During the Trilateral Negotiations, the Bundesbank agreed—in a letter from its president, Karl Blessing, to William Martin, Chairman of the Federal Reserve—not to exchange its dollar reserves for gold. It thus agreed to help finance any subsequent American deficits to the full extent of the German surplus, by piling up dollar reserves. In that sense, the gold pledge was analogous to the purchase of securities, and more important at a time of pressing concern in Washington over losses of gold reserves.

The pledge raised, however, the question of "additionality" in a different guise: would German behavior have been much different had the pledge not been made? The Bundesbank had not made direct claims on the U.S. gold stock in the several years prior to 1967, although it had acquired some American gold through IMF gold sales and through the operations of the international Central Bank Gold Pool. No doubt it would not have made wholesale conversions after 1967 even without its formal commitment. The pledge added certainty to the management of U.S. reserves, by serving as a signal to international money managers. It also was useful as an example to other nations which had been behaving less well than the Federal Republic, notably France.

4. *Direct Support.* Not surprisingly, the Federal Republic resisted making budgetary contributions in direct support of American forces: making direct payments competes frontally with spending more money on the German Army. Just as obviously, the U.S. consistently pressed for direct support: it reduces both the budgetary and the balance-of-payments costs of the garrison. It is clear evidence that the Germans are willing to "do their share."

The 1971 agreement included, for the first time, a modest amount of direct support, but of a special kind. Bonn agreed to spend $186 million over two years modernizing the barracks used by American forces in Germany. U.S. troops, as the first postwar army in Germany, inherited the old Wehrmacht barracks, generally located in or at the fringes of cities and by 1970 quite dilapidated. The German expenditure was a budgetary and balance-of-payments gain for the U.S. *to the extent* that the American government would have picked up the tab in its absence. In fact, for years the U.S. Seventh Army had desired, and the American Congress resisted, accomplishment of the project with American money. There was disagreement within official Washington over whether or not the German outlays would replace American expenditures already budgeted, but it is fair to say that the money would have been spent eventually. Given the serious morale problem of the force in Germany, the rehabilitation program probably would have been undertaken prior to 1970 had not army maintenance budgets, worldwide, been pilfered to finance the war in Vietnam. The 1971 agreement—repeated in 1974—reflected a neat convergence of interests: by providing what the U.S. Army wanted,

17

the Federal Republic made possible an offset "break-through" (for the benefit of the American Congress) and, at the same time, improved an asset it ultimately will re-obtain.

II. AMERICAN FORCES IN EUROPE: RATIONALES

The Debate over Force Level

For a decade the size of the American garrison in Europe has been a contentious issue in Washington. The dispute has become a customary feature of Executive Branch politics and, especially, of relations between the Executive and Congress. Yet the debate has seldom been instructive. Much of the argument is rhetorical; many positions are stated only in the most general of terms. Reductions from any given level are presumed to touch off processes from which felicitous or, more often, unhappy consequences will result. But seldom are the processes or their results specified with any precision. Since offset deliberations have been so intimately related to the question of force level, it is important to examine that debate. Two features stand out; they appear and reappear in the chapters to follow.

(1) It is impossible to prove conclusively—or even argue convincingly—that *any* specific level is necessary to secure adequacy with respect to *any* objective, political or military. There is no magic number. In fact, the level of American troops in Europe diminished by a hundred thousand between 1962 and 1972 (that in Germany, by sixty thousand), for reasons that had only partly to do with analysis of the military balance between East and West.

(2) As a direct consequence of (1), the debate has addressed only the desirability of changes from whatever the existing level has happened to be. While there has been no rationally magic number, there has been much magic about any existing number. Those favoring the maintenance of at least the level in effect have feared "unraveling" of two sorts. Domestically, once it is admitted that the existing level may be slightly excessive, who knows where the process of reduction will stop, since any number is hard to defend compellingly. And, it has been argued, American reductions would weaken the resolve of the European allies to preserve the existing strengths of their own forces or, worse, induce alterations in their general foreign policies. The "troop-cutters" have responded either by denying the plausibility of those effects or by asserting that, in any case, how the Euro-

peans react is no business of ours, that it is silly for the United States to protect Europe more than it is willing to defend itself.

A look at possible rationales for the stationing and at counter arguments to them will go far in suggesting why the debate has been so murky.

Military Rationales

(1) Defending Europe from a massive conventional attack by the Warsaw Pact. This aim has long been the primary justification of the American presence; it has become a litany to the defenders of that presence. During the period through the Trilaterals, the customary assumption was that NATO conventional forces were grossly inferior to those of the presumed foe, the Warsaw Pact. That meant that the central issue was the relation between conventional and nuclear weapons under the doctrine of flexible response: the so-called nuclear threshold, how soon after the outbreak of major conventional hostilities NATO would be forced to resort to nuclear weapons.

The difficulty, of course, was determining how many American troops were necessary to set the threshold at an acceptable level. During the Trilaterals, those opposed to reductions tended to imply that there was a sharp break: the existing level was just enough to provide for a credible flexible response, while any substantial cut (say, more than 50,000) signified a return to a "trip-wire" or "plate glass" doctrine. In testimony before Congress at the conclusion of the Trilateral Negotiations in 1967, for example, Secretary of State Rusk opposed those who talked of a "plate-glass" doctrine, arguing that NATO chiefs of government would not want to be forced to nuclear weapons within forty-eight hours of the start of a conventional war.[8] The implication of his statement was plain: to propose a force reduction larger than that the Administration was prepared to make at the end of the Trilaterals (35,000 men) was to recommend adoption of a "plate glass" doctrine.

A related issue dominated debate during the Trilaterals: to what extent could American troops be withdrawn from Europe but with equipment left behind ("pre-positioned"), in the expectation that the forces would be rapidly airlifted back to Europe in time of crisis. The military judgment turned on a host of factors, some of them technical, which will be mentioned in later chapters. McNamara and civilian officials at Defense—who would have preferred redeployments even larger than the so-called "rotation" of one division agreed to in the

19

Trilaterals—were pitted against the Joint Chiefs of Staff and the Europeanists at State—who believed rotation was tantamount to reduction and opposed it.

During the 1960s a second view of the military balance in Europe developed in Washington. In this view, NATO forces were not overwhelmed by forces of the Warsaw Pact but instead roughly matched them. A series of studies led by McNamara's Defense Department Office of Systems Analysis attacked the assumptions on which the previous dark view of the balance had been based: for example, that small Soviet divisions could be equated with larger and better equipped (if fewer) NATO divisions.[9] NATO conventional forces came to be regarded as an option in themselves, not merely as the link to American nuclear weapons.[10] Suggestively, that development coincided with the emergence of something like strategic parity between the United States and the Soviet Union.

Gradually the new view of the military balance gained currency even within the American military.[11] That process was speeded by military participation in the thorough review of the military balance which was undertaken during the Trilaterals; the exercise also provided an opportunity for Washington to introduce the new logic to civilian officials and military officers of two major American allies. Once U.S. officers saw the implications of the new view, they had compelling reasons to make it their own. For if the forces of East and West were approximately equal, that made it more, rather than less, important to hold the line on American forces. By contrast, the dismal view to which the military had subscribed previously led in just the opposite direction: if NATO's situation was hopeless, the level of U.S. forces was of no military consequence. That line of reasoning offered scant argument against even large troop withdrawals.

Again, however, it is difficult to argue that any particular number of American troops is necessary to assure that NATO will be able to carry out whatever conventional role is assigned to it. In fact, the view that NATO and Warsaw Pact forces were roughly in balance gained acceptance in Washington during a period in which American forces in Europe decreased and those of the Soviet Union increased. Opponents of reduction often have attempted to have it both ways, at once applauding the fact that a strong majority of NATO forces is provided by the Europeans yet asserting that reductions in the American level would have debilitating military effect.[12] The contradiction inherent in that combination of views is diminished, but not eliminated, by the fact that American forces are, by and large, better trained and equipped and at a higher state of readiness than troops of NATO allies.

Other disputes center not on the number of American troops in Europe but on whether or not they are in the right place and prepared to fight the right war. During the 1960s, if reductions had to be made, American officials preferred to thin combat forces rather than supply units, on the argument that it was imperative to maintain NATO's capacity for reinforcement and resupply. American forces, and to a lesser extent those of its allies, were prepared to refight World War II: an initial engagement ending in a stalemate providing time to mobilize and reinforce, followed by a long war of attrition. But the forces of NATO's opponents are structured for a quick thrust, presumably to present NATO with the capture of key objectives in western Europe as *faits accomplis,* for a war measured in tens of days, not in months.

Various proposals for reshaping American forces were put forward and had begun to find acceptance in the Pentagon during the tenure of Defense Secretary James Schlesinger.[13] Under the requirements of the Nunn Amendment of 1974, 18,000 support troops were withdrawn from the European garrison, replaced by two brigades of combat forces. The supply "tail" was shortened, but combat "teeth" were increased; by 1976 the four and one-third American combat divisions of a few years before had become the equivalent of five and one-third. That might be accompanied by a general reorganization of U.S. forces in the United States which would enable combat troops to be deployed to Europe at a constant rate over several months. At present, there is a sharp break in the American capability to mobilize: the troops stationed in Europe are maintained at a high state of readiness, but once they are engaged, few additional combat troops can be brought to bear in Europe for several months. A restructuring of forces would not necessarily save men, money or foreign exchange, but at least it would provide the United States more fighting capacity at the same cost.

The location of American forces within Germany is more a product of arrangements for ending the last war than of plans for fighting the next. Most U.S. forces, by general agreement NATO's best, are located in the former American occupation zone in southern Germany, while the most likely path of a major Warsaw Pact attack is across the North German plain. Moving American troops north would seem obvious. But not only does it cost money and raise problems of command and supply, it is politically difficult as well. Germans are concerned about the problems of land use, pollution and noise that result from packing bases and troops, whatever their nationality, into a small country. The prospect of moving American troops from the sparsely populated South toward the dense and industrialized North is distressing. The additional American brigade that arrived in 1976 was deployed north, in the British sector, only after much negotiation with both British and Germans.

(2) Defending Europe against lower level probes or pressures. The essence of the doctrine of flexible response, formulated by the United States in the early 1960s and adopted by NATO in 1967, was escaping the choice of nuclear war or capitulation in response to limited, conventional aggression. Statements of American officials are littered with references to the utility of conventional forces in forestalling "piecemeal aggression," "adventurism," or "a process of political coercion."[14]

There are, however, two flaws in this rationale. The first is that the nature of the threat is never clearly specified, nor is its likelihood. The range of possibilities runs from limited, localized conventional aggression through various sorts of political pressures supported by different kinds of military threats or actions. Some postulated threats seem quite unreal from the vantage point of the mid-1970s.

Second, it is difficult to imagine how NATO capabilities in almost any scenario would be diminished by even a halving of American forces. In the unlikely event that an attack did remain limited and localized, NATO would not lack for sufficient conventional force, even with *no* GIs in Europe. More probable politico-military probes—for instance, pressure at sensitive points *à la* the 1961 Berlin crisis or demands accompanied by military buildups along borders—would be relatively slow to develop. There should be, as in the Berlin crisis, time to reinforce. Any uncertainties about the American response, in those situations, would not derive from qualms about the military adequacy of the American garrison in Europe. Rather they would be doubts about U.S. will or willingness to employ nuclear weapons, matters to be discussed below.

Political Rationales

(1) Maintaining political influence in Western Europe. This rationale virtually always has been argued in the negative, as a description of the untoward consequences that would (or might) re-

sult from American troop reductions. A variety of unfortunate European reactions have been postulated, but Washington officials seldom have been specific—at least in public statements—about the probabilities of any given reaction or the chain of causation between American reduction and European response.[15] During the Trilateral Negotiations in 1967, American officials did try to specify the sizes of troop reductions by America's European allies which might follow U.S. withdrawals. That exercise, however, took the character more of postulating "worst cases" than of framing predictions rooted in analysis.

The consequence most often suggested is that the European allies would match American cuts with reductions of their own. ". . . the process of unraveling the peacetime defense of the West would be underway and would have been begun by the United States itself." There is force to that argument, despite the exaggerated form in which it often has been made by spokesmen of the last few administrations. American steadfastness with regard to force level gives leaders of the major NATO nations of Europe a justification for not acceding to parliamentary pressures for reductions in their own armies. Those pressures have been strengthened by the combination of inflation, recession and uncertainty over the future of the world economic order which has confronted the industrialized nations in recent years. Yet again arguments offered by opponents of reduction sometimes have been contradictory. For instance, while the likely response to an American cut on the part of major European capitals would be reductions in their own forces and defense spending, even if increases in European armies occurred, that might not be desirable. It might lead to "an emergence of rivalry and mistrust among the Allies."[16]

More serious consequences have been postulated. The Europeans, losing faith in the American commitment to their defense, might "tilt" their foreign policies eastward, making bilateral arrangements with the Soviet Union or other Warsaw Pact nations.[17] That, too, is a consequence to be taken seriously. But it is not clear what "tilt" means or what actions on the part of European governments it would comprise. Making bilateral arrangements with eastern block nations was precisely the substance of Bonn's *Ostpolitik,* a policy the United States played a part in inducing and later warmly supported. Presumably, the bilateral arrangements feared by opponents of troop reduction would be those involving an explicit security component.

Again, however, arguments against reduction have lacked precision. The different effects of alternative levels of reduction have not been specified: "reduction" has been implied to be massive, tantamount to "pull-out."[18] No attention has been paid, in public, to the processes which produce European responses, no probabilities attached to various reactions which are hypothesized. There can be no gainsaying the difficulty of the analytic task, but instead of attempting it those who oppose reduction often have taken refuge in the argument that the *uncertainty per se* of what the Europeans would do in response is bad.[19] To be sure, these vague arguments against reduction are often matched by equally imprecise assertions of the value of withdrawing forces. One extreme form is the argument that an American withdrawal would provide a goad to unity and resurgence in Europe.[20] There has been little discussion of the *form* an American decision to reduce might take. Opponents have tended to assume any cuts would result from abrupt, unilateral American decisions, rather than actions taken, if not with the eager consent of the Europeans, at least after consultation and ample warning. For troop levels, as for many other issues in relations among the Atlantic allies, the form of allied decision-making may be as important as the substance of decisions taken.

In recent years, American officials have been tempted to view the U.S. troop presence not merely as a goad to offset generosity on the part of Bonn but, more generally, as a symbol of the security "chip" held by the United States in a broad range of economic dealings with western Europe. In his ill-fated "New Atlantic Charter" speech of April 1973, Presidential advisor Henry Kissinger asserted that "political, military and economic issues in Atlantic relations are linked by reality, not by choice."[21] President Nixon made the link, and with it the threat to withdraw troops, more explicit in several speeches in the spring of 1974 after the Arab oil embargo. To speak directly of diminishing the nuclear protection afforded western Europe would be to provoke immediate crisis, but threats to reduce troops amount to much the same thing in European eyes. And, as in offset negotiations, Executive Branch officials never need utter a threat; they have only to point, with sadness, to what the "zealots" in Congress might do if Europe does not "do more" for the U.S. in dealings with regard to trade or international money.

(2) Maintaining the credibility of the American deterrent, both conventional and nuclear. Officials have argued that, even were the "actual" commitment of the U.S. to Europe's defense to be undi-

minished by troop reductions, cuts still would have symbolic importance. Potential foes would be tempted and old friends disheartened. At best, the European drive for an independent nuclear capability (or desires for national capabilities) might be fueled.[22]

European NATO allies, especially the Federal Republic, have been sensitive to the relation between conventional forces and the nuclear deterrent. For them, an outbreak of major conventional war would be disaster, for the war would be fought on their soil. Deterrence is an absolute necessity. And deterrence means, to Europeans, nuclear deterrence, in which Washington has virtual monopoly. To the extent that McNamara's doctrine of flexible response smacked of *defense* by conventional means, they wanted no part of it. The doctrine was attractive only if it made *deterrence* more credible, by denying the Soviets the prospect of easy conventional victories in western Europe which would reduce an American nuclear response to futile suicide.

Still, American arguments from this rationale can be faulted on the same grounds as was the preceding justification. The task of converting lists of possibilities into assessments of probabilities, admittedly very hard, has not been undertaken publicly. Any existing situation has been presumed to be far less dangerous than that issuing from reductions (with reductions again implied to be abrupt and massive). The inertia of any existing troop level has been particularly strong with respect to this rationale: if there were only 100,000 American troops in Europe today, they would suffice, *provided* there had not been 150,000 yesterday nor were likely to be 50,000 tomorrow.

(3) Maintaining political influence in the Federal Republic. For obvious reasons, American spokesmen never assert that U.S. troops remain in Germany partly to "protect Europe from the Germans." That justification, however, is alive just beneath the surface of debate. Much of NATO military structure has been designed to contain the growth of the Bundeswehr and deny it the capacity for independent action. And Washington officials *have* worried in public that American reductions might make the German army dominant in NATO—at present it is twice the size of the U.S. force in Germany—especially if the Federal Republic compensated for U.S. cuts with force *increases*. In fact, German increases are unlikely, in the absence of some imminent international calamity. Leaders in Bonn feel the same domestic pressures as do their counterparts elsewhere in NATO. As NATO entered mutual force reduction negotiations with

the Warsaw Pact in Vienna early in the 1970s, Bonn's proposals aimed to assure that the Federal Republic would be included early in the process of reduction.

In the view of those who oppose American reductions, if Germany came to occupy a more prominent position in NATO military structures, two adverse consequences would ensue. The first has been articulated clearly, the second only hinted. Gains registered by Bonn's *Ostpolitik* might be threatened, as the fears of Germany's neighbors to the East were reawakened. And, it has been suggested gingerly, the situation "would give pause even to some of Germany's allies."[23]

(4) Obtaining reciprocal reductions from Warsaw Pact nations. With mutual force reduction negotiations underway in Vienna, why, this argument has run, throw away for free what could be bartered for reciprocal cuts. The rationale carries force; early American proposals in those negotiations were designed to make its premise come true by giving Soviet and American reductions first priority. Members of Congress and others who favor withdrawals have responded, of course, that for years the Executive has used the prospect of reciprocal reductions to beat back Congressional efforts to compel unilateral reductions, but that cuts never have materialized. Nor are they likely to result soon from any negotiations as complicated as the mutual force reduction (MFR) discussions.[24] By 1977 those negotiations had dragged on for several years with no result.

III. THE CLASH OF TWO ORTHODOXIES

When Lyndon Johnson pondered the issues of offset and force level in preparation for his meeting with Erhard in 1966, the issues did not come to him in isolation. They came in the context of other discussions and other issues. Other decisions, made or about to be, affected both the arguments about offset and force level and the character of the processes through which they were handled in official Washington. And the two issues came to the President embedded in lines of argument which had developed, and hardened, over time. Those arguments had histories, and the histories affected how the President and his senior advisors perceived and handled offset and force level. Their impact will be evident at various points in the chapters which follow.

The governmental establishment in Washington was divided along two perspectives. The division neither began nor ended with offset and force level. It was more than a bureaucratic dispute over responsibility; it went to assumptions and habits of thought, to how issues were perceived, what considerations were applied and with what force. Put crudely, the division was "politics" versus "economics."

For those opposed to troop reduction, the troop presence in Europe was a necessity, for reasons which began with military considerations but ended with the politics of alliance. The continuance of the troop stationing was, in this view, vital to sustaining the alliance with the United States' friends in Europe, America's staunchest, an alliance regarded as the cornerstone of American foreign policy. The State Department and the Joint Chiefs of Staff agreed that maintaining the existing level of troops in Europe was imperative, never mind that the paths of reasoning which led the two to that conclusion were at some variance from one another. By 1966 their view long had been fixed. And, efforts to the contrary notwithstanding, the handling of offset had not been allowed to disrupt the assumption that no American soldiers should be withdrawn from Europe.

Those on the other side of the division viewed the issues differently and attached different weights to the considerations involved. Their view was dominated by economy and efficiency, hardly a new perspective in American society or government. Concern with the balance of payments was a late addition to this orthodoxy, but by 1966 its place was secure. The representatives of this perspective in 1966 and 1967—civilians at Defense and the Treasury Department—hardly regarded the political considerations associated with the troops as imperative. That was, for them, just one set of considerations among many. For the half decade before 1966, offset had been firmly controlled by the concerns of this perspective.

Partisans on both sides within the Executive Branch were reinforced by segments of Congress and elements of the restricted public attentive to foreign affairs. The claim of the "economics" perspective on those in Congress who thought the American garrison in Europe was too large and too expensive, or that the Europeans shouldered too little of the burden, was most obvious. But those who held to the "politics and troops" perspective could count on support from those who took for granted the primacy of America's relations with western Europe.

Given the distance between perspectives, it is little surprise that the arguments about offset and the level of forces in Europe seemed to intersect so seldom. The opposing arguments were rooted in dif-

27

ferent premises, assumptions grown hard with the passage of time. Fresh analysis was difficult to perform and to bring to bear on the process of decision, for it might have challenged not only views on substance but threatened long-standing assumptions about how issues should be viewed, what lines of reasoning should be applied and what courses of actions were legitimate. To frame reasonable policies with respect to offset and force level amid those competing orthodoxies was no mean feat. President Johnson and his government were hard pressed to do so in 1966 and 1967. Succesive administrations did not find it easy in later years.

NOTES TO CHAPTER I

[1]The Secretary's dialogue with Senator Gillette appears in *Assignment of Ground Forces of the United States to Duty in the European Area,* Hearings before the Senate Committees on Foreign Relations and Armed Services, 82 Cong., 1 sess. (1951).

[2]Exceptions are relatively minor. The Federal Republic pays for most of the local goods and services required by the U.S. Berlin Brigade. In 1970 these costs amounted to about $38 million, 65 per cent of the cost of maintaining the brigade. *U.S. Security Agreements and Commitments Abroad, Pt. 10: United States Forces in Europe,* Hearings before the Subcommittee on U.S. Security Agreements and Commitments Abroad of the Senate Committee on Foreign Relations, 91 Cong., 2 sess. (1970), p. 2100. NATO infrastructure projects are jointly financed, with each country paying a negotiated percentage of the total cost. Expenditures on infrastructure totalled $151 million in 1968, with the U.S. share at 33 per cent. *Ibid.,* p.2295. The U.S. share subsequently was reduced.

[3]The debate over how large support costs are for the military as a whole and how they should be apportioned among services or theaters is a persistent one. For an excellent contribution to it, *see* a 1972 Brookings staff paper by Martin Binkin, *Support Costs in the Defense Budget* (Washington: The Brookings Institution, 1972).

[4]For the Rush comments, see *U.S. Forces in NATO,* Hearings before the House Committee on Foreign Affairs and its Subcommittee on Europe, 93 Cong., 1 sess.(1973), pp.162–3. [Hereafter cited as *U.S. Forces in NATO (House* 1973).]

[5]John Newhouse, and others, *U.S. Troops in Europe: Issues, Costs, and Choices* (Washington: The Brookings Institution, 1971), p.115.

[6]A 1968 Brookings study called the effect small, while the Institute for Defense Analyses earlier had estimated it to be substantial. *See The United States Balance of Payments in 1968,* Report by the Brookings Institution to the Joint Economic Committee of the U.S. Congress, (1968), p.197; and Lois Ernstoff, Rolf Piekarz and Elliot Wetzler, *United States Exports Induced by*

Department of Defense Expenditures in Europe, (Washington: Institute for Defense Analyses, 1965).

[7]A German scholar, Gernot Volger, argues that there has been little or no additionality. *See* his "Devisenausgleich als militär und zahlungs-bilanzpolitisches Instrument" (unpublished monograph, 1972). Joseph Aschleim of George Washington University agrees with the Volger assessment, suggesting that "offset through buying" was abandoned just at the point it would have become "real" (i.e. involve a misallocation of German resources). *See* "The Dollar Deficit and German Offsetting," Pt. 4 of *1968 Economic Report of the President,* Hearings before the Joint Economic Committee, 90 Cong., 2 sess.(1968), p.934. *See* also Horst Mendershausen, *Troop Stationing in Germany: Value and Cost,* RM-5881-PR (Santa Monica: The Rand Corporation, 1968), pp.87–93.

[8]*See United States Troops in Europe,* Hearing before the combined Subcommittee of the Senate Committees on Foreign Relations and Armed Services, 90 Cong., 1 sess.(1967), p.59. [Hereafter cited as *United States Troops in Europe (Senate, 1967).*]

[9]For public discussions of the new view, written by men who had been involved in developing it within the government, *see* the works by Alain C. Enthoven and K. Wayne Smith, *How Much is Enough? Shaping the Defense Program, 1961–1969* (New York: Harper and Row, 1971); and "What Forces for NATO? And From Whom?" *Foreign Affairs,* XLVII, 1 (October 1969), 80–96; that by Enthoven, "Arms and Men: The Military Balance in Europe," *Interplay* (May 1969); and the article by Frederick S. Wyle, "European Security: Beating the Numbers Game," *Foreign Policy,* 10 (Spring 1973), pp. 41–54.

[10]*See,* for example, the remarks by Defense Secretary Schlesinger, *U.S. Forces in Europe,* Hearings before the Subcommittee on Arms Control, International Law and Organization of the Senate Committee on Foreign Relations, 93 Cong., 1 sess.(1973), pp.60–61. [Hereafter cited as *U.S. Forces in Europe (Senate, 1973).*]

[11]*See,* for example, the comments of Adm. Thomas Moorer, Chairman of the Joint Chiefs of Staff, in *U.S. Forces in NATO (House,* 1973), pp.218–19; or the article by Michael Getler, "Study Insists NATO Can Defend Itself," *Washington Post,* June 7, 1973.

[12]*See,* for example, the testimony of Gen. Andrew Goodpaster, Supreme Allied Commander in Europe, in *U.S. Forces in NATO (House,* 1973), p. 233

[13]For a statement of the position that the support force/combat force ratio of U.S. troops in Europe is too high, *see* Edward R. Fried and others, *Setting National Priorities: The 1974 Budget,* (Washington: The Brookings Institution, 1973), pp. 356–59. Many in Congress have picked up that argument; Senator Sam Nunn, for example, called in 1974 for a reduction of 29,000–60,000 support troops. Steven Canby was among the first to call for a reorganization of American forces to fight a short war. For a detailed proposal along similar lines, see Richard D. Lawrence and Jeffrey Record, *U.S. Force Structure in NATO: An Alternative* (Washington: The Brookings Institution, 1974). Their proposals would result in the transfer of 11,000 U.S. soldiers from Europe to the United States, at an annual foreign exchange saving calculated at $121 million, (p.74). Late in 1974, Defense Secretary

Schlesinger announced a reorganization of the Army in an effort to obtain sixteen divisions instead of thirteen from existing manpower.

[14]The quoted phrases are, in order, former Under Secretary of State, Elliot L. Richardson, "U.S. and Western European Security," *Atlantic Community Quarterly,* VIII, 1 (Spring 1970), p.7; Goodpaster, cited above, p. 229; and former Under Secretary of State, Nicholas Katzenbach, in *United States Troops in Europe (Senate, 1967),* p.44.

[15]For example, former Assistant Secretary of State Hillenbrand argued that an American reduction of 150,000 "would lead to a chain of causality which would lead to the ending of NATO as we know it." *U.S. Security Agreements and Commitments Abroad, Part 10: United States Forces in Europe,* Hearings before the Subcommittee on U.S. Security Agreements and Commitments Abroad of the Senate Committee on Foreign Relations, 91 Cong., 2 sess.(1970), p.2238.

[16]The phrases quoted in this paragraph are, respectively, Deputy Secretary of State, Kenneth Rush, *U.S. Forces in NATO (House,* 1973), p. 162; and U.S. Representative to NATO, Donald Rumsfeld, *ibid.,* p.335. *See* also Richardson, "U.S. and Western European Security," p.7.

[17]*See,* for example, the comments of Rumsfeld, cited above, p.335.

[18]The equation is made by Rush, cited above, p.162.

[19]*See* Rumsfeld, cited above, p.335.

[20]For instance, an argument of that kind runs through David Calleo, *The Atlantic Fantasy: The U.S., NATO and Europe* (Baltimore: Johns Hopkins Press, 1970).

[21]Quoted in the *New York Times,* April 24, 1973.

[22]*See* Rumsfeld, cited above, p.335.

[23]*See* Richardson, "U.S. and Western European Security," p.11, and the colloquy between Katzenbach and Fulbright in *United States Troops in Europe (Senate, 1967),* p.46.

[24]*See,* for example, the statement of Senator Mansfield in *U.S. Forces in Europe (Senate, 1973),* pp.13–14.

CHAPTER II: FOREIGN EXCHANGE AND FORCE LEVEL AT ISSUE BETWEEN ALLIES

JUST as the lines of argument into which offset and troop level fell in 1966 had developed over time and continued to develop, so too was there a history of the way in which the issues had been handled within official Washington. That history affected the "face" the issues took when crisis arose in the late summer of 1966 and showed how they would be perceived during later episodes. It indicated which governmental agencies would be involved and how deeply, what analyses they would perform and what alternative courses of action they would suggest. It meant that the government's senior officials would come to the issues with different levels of expertise—hence of claim to authority—and with varying levels of interest and intensity of preference. The interplay of that history with the preexisting perspectives that had divided the American government deepened the conflict of the two orthodoxies when Washington confronted the decisions of 1966 and 1967.

This chapter begins with the origins of offset arrangements and their history to 1966. It then provides a brief overview of my primary case: the months preceding Chancellor Ludwig Erhard's visit to Washington in September 1966, and subsequent events leading to the successful conclusion of the Trilateral Negotiations in May 1967. How did it come to pass that Erhard arrived in Washington with his immediate political survival dependent upon getting the United States to forgive part of the Federal Republic's offset commitment? Why did the United States refuse to accede to his request? In retrospect, was there some way President Johnson might have met the Chancellor's needs? Or were the politics surrounding offset in Washington and Bonn incompatible in the fall of 1966?

The instance of 1966–67 was a "crisis" in alliance relations and its aftermath. That did not recur; subsequent dealings between Washington and Bonn with respect to offset and force level have not come to political crisis. Yet in other respects the 1966–67 episode is not unique. How the issues were handled by Washington and Bonn, between them, and among them and their allies in NATO: none of these changed dramatically after 1966 and 1967. What changes there have been are illuminating, particularly with regard to policy-making within the American government. This chapter outlines the history of offset and force level through 1976. I shall make occasional reference to episodes after 1967 in the chapters to follow.

I. THE ORIGINS OF OFFSET

The foreign exchange costs of American troops in Europe became a matter for serious concern in the last years of the Eisenhower Administration. For fiscal year 1961 defense expenditures abroad contributed about three billion dollars to the American balance-of-payments deficit; outlays for foreign troop stationing made up $2.4 billion of this, with the portion attributable to troops in the German Federal Republic (where two-thirds of the U.S. troops in Europe were located) calculated at over $600 million. (See Table V, page 12.)

In November 1960 Treasury Secretary Robert Anderson secured permission from President Eisenhower for a mission to Bonn. Accompanied by Under Secretary of State Douglas Dillon, Anderson proposed that the Federal Republic pay about $650 million per year in direct support of the American garrison. The German government of Konrad Adenauer, caught unaware, refused. To it, direct budgetary support was tainted with the aura of occupation costs, a constraint which recurred. During occupation the Germans had been compelled to finance the presence of the victors' armies. To 1954, when the Federal Republic became sovereign, these payments totalled $13 billion for forces in the three western zones which then became the Federal Republic. Moreover, direct support implied a German tax increase.[1]

The Anderson mission, a poorly prepared and internally ill-coordinated effort by a lame-duck administration, produced scant tangible result. The Federal Republic agreed to increase its share in the joint funding of NATO infrastructure projects. While it resisted a commitment to bilateral cost sharing, it did promise to consider a large military procurement program in the United States. That pledge conduced to the offset arrangement successfully negotiated early in the Kennedy Administration. Moreover, the Anderson mission reinforced the linkage between expenditures on American troops in Germany and more general balance-of-payments considerations. That no doubt played a part in inducing the Germans to revalue the *Deutschemark* upward, which Bonn reluctantly did at the end of 1961, thereby making German exports to the United States more expensive and American exports to the Federal Republic cheaper.

American and German interests soon converged, if not necessarily on the desirability of an offset agreement per se, at least on terms which might frame such an accord. Washington was concerned about its balance-of-payments position, West German development plans for the American-equipped Bundeswehr called for large new procurements, and the two countries shared the desire to see the American presence (about 240,000 in mid-1961) maintained, even increased, at a time of extreme tension in Berlin.

Deputy Secretary of Defense Roswell L. Gilpatrick and Defense Minister Franz-Josef Strauss concluded an agreement in the fall of 1961. Bonn was to make major new arms purchases from American sources and receive training, and supply and maintenance support from the United States. German payments for arms and services were expected to offset the foreign exchange drain occasioned by the U.S. troops for the foreseeable future. In fact, from mid-1961 through 1966 German offset payments did approximate American military expenditures in the Federal Republic.[2] The agreements were renewed in 1963 and 1965, amounting to nearly $700 million per year under the latter accord.

On the American precedent, the British separately negotiated their own agreement to offset the foreign exchange expenditure on British troops in Germany, the British Army of the Rhine (BAOR). Anglo-German offset pacts never provided the British with a full offset—the first, of March 1962, amounted to about 75%—even

33

though London was from the start willing to include civilian purchases as well as military procurement under the agreements. And the Germans found it difficult to meet their obligations, contending that it was hard to find what they needed in the United Kingdom. By early 1965, newly elected Prime Minister Harold Wilson found the existing agreement insufficient. His government succeeded in renegotiating it, in June 1965, to some British advantage; at that time the arrangement was extended to March 1967.[3]

II. THE 1966 "CRISIS"

Events on both side of the Atlantic came together in 1966 to produce a crisis in the offset arrangements. The United States continued to run persistent, though moderate, balance-of-payments deficits. Gold conversions continued, despite Administration attempts to stem them. The war in Vietnam increasingly fed the balance-of-payments deficit, although the precise amount of its contribution is difficult to measure.[4] The British economy continued to quake, and the pound sterling remained under intense pressure, culminating in a severe run on the pound in July 1966.

The gross national product of the Federal Republic failed to rise in 1966, for the first time in the nation's brief history. Tax revenues lagged and the Erhard government was faced with a large budget deficit which it could remedy only at political peril. At the same time, the rearming of the Bundeswehr begun under earlier offset agreements was regarded by many Germans as basically complete, and joint weapons projects which might have generated more procurement failed to materialize.

NATO was in disarray after the French withdrew from the integrated military command, in July 1966. Both Washington and London felt it was in their interest to enlarge their commitments in order to maintain the credibility of the alliance, but both found it increasingly difficult to do so. They needed larger offsets, not smaller. But Bonn was finding it hard to meet existing commitments. The German government was caught in a nasty bind: domestically there was little money for offsets and little desire for the arms that could be purchased with offset funds; internationally, the Federal Republic was caught between its two most important allies, the United States and France, at ever greater distance from each other over NATO structure, European defense and international money.[5]

In this context, Secretary of Defense Robert McNamara warned his

German counterpart, Kai-Uwe von Hassel, in May 1966, that American troop levels in Germany might be tied to the size of future German offsets.[6] The implicit threat created a furor in the Federal Republic and Bonn requested a formal explanation from Washington. The influential Hamburg daily, *Die Welt,* called the McNamara threat a "pretext" for the transfer of more American troops from Germany to Vietnam.[7] Von Hassel, however, continued to state in public that Bonn would meet its existing offset obligation ($1.35 billion for the two-year period ending June 30, 1967).[8]

The Anglo-German offset accord was called into question at the same time. Under the agreement then in effect, Bonn was committed to no fixed amount and had been offsetting about 55 million pounds of a total British foreign exchange expenditure of 94 million pounds. As part of the package of austerity measures taken in the wake of the July sterling crisis, Her Majesty's government sought a better offset. Chancellor of the Exchequer James Callaghan threatened to draw down the British Army of the Rhine, then 55,000 strong, to the level at which British foreign exchange expenditures equaled whatever offset Bonn was willing to provide. German Chancellor Erhard, however, had told his Bundestag earlier in the summer that there could be no full offset for London.[9] An Anglo-German study commission was set up, under the clear shadow of British withdrawals.

Over the spring and summer of 1966 officials in Washington focused on what sort of *successor* offset agreement to seek (the accord then in effect expired June 30, 1967). They recognized German economic woes, but Bonn did not clearly communicate, perhaps did not itself understand, that those problems threatened the *existing* agreement as well as the renewal. Erhard mentioned difficulties with offset in a letter to President Johnson dated July 5, 1966,[10] but the Chancellor suggested only that the two chiefs of state discuss the matter in September when Erhard came to Washington for a periodic visit. Only in early September did Washingtonians clearly understand that German compliance with the existing agreement was in doubt.

The debate in Washington over the terms of a *successor* (or "new") agreement had raged since early spring, gradually rising to the attention of the government's senior officials. The President's advisors offered divided counsel. Defense Secretary McNamara and Treasury Secretary Fowler wanted to bargain hard with Bonn for a new agreement again composed only of military procurement, while State Department and White House staff officials felt it would be

35

necessary to broaden the renewal agreement to include additional forms of offset.

Two factors forced that debate to a head. The first was the British threat to draw down the BAOR. A second stimulus to action was more direct. The American Embassy in Bonn cabled, in mid-August, that Bonn was about to begin its budget season and that if Washington did not want offset endangered by economy measures in the (calendar year) 1967 budget, it must act quickly.

Senior American officials convened around the question of what to reply to Erhard's July letter. The President's eventual decision represented a setback for the McNamara/Fowler position. The United States government would tell Erhard that it would join the Anglo-German Mixed Commission and that it would offer Bonn more offset options in the *renewal* agreement, that agreement to be hammered out in the trilateral context. However, while the reply to Erhard mentioned opening up the terms of the new agreement, it stressed Washington's expectation that the Federal Republic would comply with the *existing* offset agreement. That language, insisted on by McNamara, was not regarded as menacing by those officials who fretted about Erhard's political difficulties: if the German problem were more serious, let Bonn say so.

But Bonn did not begin a dialogue with Washington. The Germans did not understand Washington's change of policy with respect to the new agreement or did not think it important. In any event, Erhard, in deep political trouble at home, felt he needed a big "victory" sooner than seemed possible through the trilateral format. He needed to be forgiven as much as a billion dollars of Bonn's offset commitment under the existing agreement—that would have meant a billion dollars less of budget money spent on offset, sparing the Chancellor the necessity of trying to maneuver spending cuts or tax increases through a divided Cabinet. Erhard's early September reply to the American letter parried the suggestion of the trilaterals and instead asked for one more German-American meeting on the issue. The Chancellor fended off all American efforts to start a lower-level interchange on offset, and he was uninterested in proposals from his own staff. He preferred to stake everything on a face-to-face appeal to the President.

He made that appeal in Washington the last week of September 1966. By then the American government had relented part way on the existing agreement, but President Johnson was unwilling merely to "forgive" the Germans a substantial portion of their commitment.

Nor was the Chancellor adept at seizing what opportunities the President offered him. Erhard assented reluctantly to the idea of trilateral negotiations, and a German-American working group hastily constructed an arrangement for German fulfillment of the existing agreement. But that package required both additional budgetary appropriations from the Bundestag *and* action by the German Bundesbank, which was autonomous from the federal government, formally and in practice. Erhard endeavored to put the best possible face on the visit, but it was well understood in Germany to have been less successful than the Chancellor had hoped.[11]

Erhard's downfall was rapid. He had been blocked in an attempt to cut government spending in order to balance the budget, so he turned instead to tax increases. The proposal for tax increases was linked to the failure of Erhard's visit to Washington partly in fact and powerfully in symbol. The "shortfall" in German arms purchases under the existing offset agreement was suggestively close to the projected German budget deficit. It appeared that Erhard had to tax his own people because he had been rebuffed by his American "friends."

In November the Free Democratic Party (FPD), the junior partner in coalition with Erhard's Christian Democratic Union (CDU), broke with the Chancellor, leaving him at the head of a powerless minority government. After another month of negotiations, the Grand Coalition government of Christian Democrats and Social Democrats (SPD), the former opposition party, was formed. Kurt-Georg Kiesinger of the CDU was Chancellor, and Willy Brandt of the SPD, Foreign Minister. The Erhard government had barely functioned in its last months, so the change in Bonn was not a major disaster for Washington. But it was clear that the Grand Coalition would take a more independent posture vis-à-vis the United States than its predecessor, in rhetoric if not in substance. Washington escaped direct blame for Erhard's demise, but nevertheless a residue of suspicion directed at the U.S. was carried from the old government to the new.

III. THE TRILATERAL NEGOTIATIONS

British Prime Minister Wilson also agreed to join the tripartite talks, though also with misgivings, and the Trilateral Negotiations began in October 1966. John J. McCloy, former American High Commissioner in occupied Germany, represented the United States. His counterparts were Karl Carstens, Foreign Office State Secretary (under secretary), for the Germans; and George Thomson, Minister of

State for Foreign Affairs, for the British. However, serious negotiations could not begin until after the first of the year: first there was only a distracted Bonn government to deal with, then none at all, then a new one which had first to set its own house in order.

The American conception of the Trilateral Negotiations explicitly linked offset and force level; that linkage only acknowledged what had been the case anyway. Washington was thus confronted with a set of interrelated decisions: whether or not to reduce the level of its forces in Germany, and if so, by how much; what sort of offset bargain to seek with Bonn, and how tightly to link offset with the force level decision. Throughout deliberations, London's problems impinged on American decision-making. In the fall of 1966 the American government acted to forestall immediate cuts in the BAOR, while over the longer term it had to balance the desire for maximum German offset for itself with its interest in seeing Her Majesty's government obtain an offset that would minimize the need to draw down the BAOR and the consequent pressure put on Washington to do likewise.

Senior American officials remained divided on the central issues, and those divisions were played out in all of the several arenas in which policies with respect to offset and force level were debated. McCloy, who had been charged with making an independent report to the President, counseled against any troop reduction, making both military and political arguments.[12] He and his State Department allies wanted to de-couple offset and force level. They believed that a modest offset would suffice to placate Congress. On the other hand, McNamara pressed for either a large German financial offer or a substantial troop cut, probably preferring the latter. In the spring of 1967 he recommended a cut of two divisions (70,000 men).[13]

The eventual Presidential decision, made in late February 1967, was a compromise. The United States would make withdrawals, but only two-thirds of a division, and that cut was to be packaged as a "rotation," with special provisions for the rapid remobilization of the entire division in the Federal Republic. Washington also decided to abandon the notion of a dollar-for-dollar offset composed only of military procurement (a move which had been accepted implicitly the previous August). Bonn would be permitted to substitute "financial measures"—purchases of the special medium-term Treasury securities and the pledge not to convert dollar holdings for American gold—for some portion of the offset formerly provided through military procurement.

38

Washington's decision paved the way for the successful conclusion of the Trilaterals, although there was considerable further wrangling about terms for London, and Bonn was concerned at the end about the size of the U.S. Air Force withdrawal which was to accompany the troop reduction. The context of the discussions was darkened by German annoyance at what Germans called "defects" in German-American consultation with respect to Soviet-American non-proliferation treaty (NPT) negotiations. Johnson took note of Bonn's unhappiness in several letters to Kiesinger during the spring. Both that and the plane redeployment were discussed when the two men met at Adenauer's funeral, in Bonn at the end of April.

Agreement was formally announced on April 28th, with details released on May 2nd.[15] Major provisions were: (1) The United States would "rotate" one division and one air wing, involving a total reduction of up to 35,000 men, while the British would withdraw one of nine brigades of the BAOR (6500 men). (2) Bonn would make significant new arms purchases in the United States, but without specifying a commitment. Bonn did agree to a given level in Britain, and Washington committed itself to step up its procurement in the U.K. (3) Finally, the Bundesbank would buy $500 million in special Treasury securities; it also made public its pledge not to convert its dollar reserves for gold.

The agreement drew mixed reviews from Senatorial critics of the troop stationing. Senator Mansfield had introduced, in September 1966, a sense-of-the-Senate resolution calling for a "substantial reduction" in the American force in Europe. He withdrew that resolution in October, pending the conclusion of the Trilaterals, but reintroduced it in January as the talks dragged on. He let it die again when the agreement was announced, calling the American reductions "an encouraging start."[16] But he doubted that they were enough.

IV. OFFSET AND FORCE LEVEL AFTER 1967

The Trilateral agreement seemed to become unstuck almost as soon as it had been pieced together. Strains in the international monetary system continued; the creation of Special Drawing Rights (SDR's) at the September 1967 meeting of the Governors of the International Monetary Fund was an encouraging sign, but it offered neither dollar nor pound immediate help. When the British finally devalued, in November 1967, that only increased pressure on the dollar. In September, the German Cabinet approved a $350 million cut in the 1968 defense budget, and earlier there had been rumors of a secret Cabinet agreement to end offsets.[17] By early 1968 President Johnson requested "prompt negotiations with our NATO allies to minimize the foreign exchange costs of keeping our troops in Europe."[18]

In the end, however, the monetary crisis was weathered and did not envelop the Trilateral agreements. In March 1968 the governors of most major central banks agreed to limit transfers of gold to dealings among themselves (in effect establishing a "two-tier" gold market). Soon after, France lost much foreign exchange in the wake of its student rebellion and general strike; the monetary renegade could no longer play that role. The Bundesbank made its promised quarterly purchases of the special Treasury securities. German arms purchases for the one-year period of the agreement totaled about $100 million,[19] and the United States made its agreed purchases in the U.K., although there were thorny problems with more general Anglo-American cooperation in procurement. The redeployments of American military personnel agreed upon during the Trilaterals were delayed but did take place in early 1968. However, the notion of rotating the affected division's three brigades through Germany in turn was dropped, no doubt for financial reasons. Instead, the two brigades withdrawn would join the third left in place for yearly exercises.[20]

In this context the 1968 offset negotiations, once again bilateral, were successfully concluded without great difficulty, along the lines of the 1967 agreement. There was, of course, the by-then-familiar conflict: Washington preferred fewer loans and more "hard" purchases; Bonn, the opposite. The eventual agreement, signed in June, covered a total of $785 million for the next fiscal year, up from Bonn's initial offer of $600 million. Of the total, $500 million was in loans made by the Bundesbank, with another $125 million to be sold on the German private market; Bonn would make $100 million in arms purchases, and $60 million in civil procurement was included (Lufthansa purchases of Boeing airbuses). Senator Mansfield called the bond purchases "the phoniest deal I have ever seen . . . not sharing cost but making a profitable investment."[21]

Throughout the next year plans circulated in Washington for lengthening or altering the offset arrangements, but in the end the 1969 agreement looked much like its predecessors. In the last months of the Johnson Administration, American officials pressed their German counterparts on the issue of direct support. The Pentagon calculated that the United States could save over $400 million per year in foreign exchange if the Federal Republic would assume responsibility for the salaries of German workers at U.S. bases and for other local support costs; another $30 million could be saved if the Germans began operating antiaircraft and other such facilities formerly manned by Americans.

A special American negotiator made several missions to Bonn during the winter of 1968–69, seeking a long-term solution to the offset problem. But Bonn continued to reject direct support, for the same reasons as before and with the same arguments. German officials contended that direct support was a multilateral matter for NATO, not an issue for bilateral offset discussions.

In the fall of 1968 the German Bundestag voted, after considerable debate, to buy 88 American Phantom jets, at a total cost of $500 million. That purchase would of course count under the offset agreement. The ailing German aircraft industry had objected to the purchase, and there was a controversy within Bonn about whether to commit "fresh" funds to the Phantom purchases or seek to use the money left in the Treasury accounts from previous offset agreements.[22] In February 1969 the Cabinet approved guidelines for the spring offset negotiations. Bonn would seek a two-year agreement, not a three-year pact as desired by Defense Minister Gerhard Schröder, and would cover four-fifths of the total American foreign exchange drain, with the expectation that loans would comprise more than half the total offset.

When the new Administration took power in Washington, among its first acts was the issuance of several National Security Study Memoranda (NSSM's) calling for interagency studies of both the specific question of offset and the longer-term issue of the level of American forces in Europe. Those studies examined a broad range of considerations and outlined an array of possible alternatives.

During the study and decision process, the Treasury played a weaker hand than it had in previous years. Not only was its new Secretary, David Kennedy, relatively inactive, but there was an improvement (albeit illusory) in the American balance-of-payments position early in 1969.[23] Moreover, the Treasury sought to avoid drastic actions which might destabilize foreign exchange markets in the months before the projected German upward revaluation of the *Deutsche Mark*. The State Department faced its customary quandary: its inclination was to go easy on Bonn, yet its abiding interest in sustaining the existing level of forces made it sensitive to the threat of Congressional action. Under Secretary Elliot Richardson, who made the Department's case in the National Security Council meetings on offset, argued that a new agreement should be considered by the light of other German actions in international monetary affairs. Supported by the NSC official working on offset, he suggested that the Germans be explicitly credited for actions helpful to the United States—for their assistance in the creation of SDR's, for revaluation when that occurred, and so on. Not surprisingly, Treasury refused to hear of it.

Three options were put before the President: no offset, an offset that stressed "quality" measures (direct support payments, military and civilian procurement clearly additional to that which would have occurred in the absence of an agreement); and a large offset, one that valued quantity over quality even at the cost of accepting large amounts of securities purchases. The "no offset" option was a Treasury ploy. Treasury's preference, in 1969 as in 1966, was a reduction in the force level, but that issue lay beyond Treasury's domain. But the Department calculated that an end to offset might arouse Congressional ire with the stationing to a degree which might compel substantial reduction. The distinction between the other two options was not sharp, nor was the decision between them obvious. Bonn initially appeared interested in the quality alternative but backed away after discussion of the additionality criterion. At the same time, Richardson's soundings on Capitol Hill indicated that while there was no great clamor for a troop cut, an attractive offset still would be a marginal advantage in dealing with the Senate. And it would have been hard to justify taking a 50% offset, instead of the 80% of the two previous agreements, on grounds as esoteric as "quality."

The President opted for quantity, in a National Security Decision Memorandum issued in April 1969. While the United States was to seek a better agreement, the decision explicitly favored leniency with Bonn, given that the Germans were about to begin an electoral campaign. Both President Nixon and his assistant, Henry Kissinger, were eager to maintain a "low profile" in dealings with allies and to avoid the kind of political spillover from offset which had occurred in 1966. The 1969 decision called for Washington *not* to raise the issue of direct support and *not* to seek an increase in German military procurement in the United States. The decision on offset was taken apart from any decision on the force level question; the latter was to await the study written in response to NSSM 3 on military posture. The decision, however, came soon, and the U.S. committed itself not to withdraw forces from Europe. In effect, the President had broken the link between offset and force level.

Given the President's decision, the German decision to buy Phantoms and the apparent improvement in the American foreign exchange position, it appeared that it would be easy to conclude a new agreement. But it did not turn out to be so. There was hard bargaining, both within the National Security Council Under Secretaries Committee, which was given responsibility for offset, and between the Americans and the Germans. Divorcing offset from force level could be read either of two ways: on one hand, it seemed to deny threats to reduce the troop level as a bargaining stick with Bonn; yet on the other, American officials could and did argue, both within Washington and to the Germans, that an attractive offset was all the more important lest Congress respond to a poor one by reasserting the link.

Bonn first offered $700 million per year, half for military procurement and $200 million to establish a fund which would be available to Germans who wanted to make investments in the United States (a pet project of Finance Minister Franz-Josef Strauss). Washington sought $800 million, including $400 million for military procurement and a substantial amount to purchase old Eximbank and Marshall Plan loans held by the U.S. The Treasury opposed the German proposals for civil procurement and for the investment fund; they were not matters for offset talks. The Treasury also pressed hard to have Bonn subsidize the interest rate attached to whatever purchases of securities were included in the agreement. For its part, the German government resisted the interest subsidy and was queasy about accepting the outstanding loans (both because they carried low interest rates and for technical reasons).

Washington and Bonn came together in early summer. Washington lowered its request to $760 million and accepted the investment fund, while the German Cabinet agreed to increase military procurement to $400 million, provided the agreement could run for two years. The final agreement incorporated both those figures. Bonn stopped short of a zero interest rate but did agree to a submarket rate (3.5%) and to the purchases of the outstanding loans, once the technical difficulties were worked out.[24]

For the half decade after 1970, troop stationing and offset arrangements remained remarkably stable despite a sequence of events which would have led reasonable people to predict otherwise. German elections in the fall of 1969 brought the Social Democrats to power for the first time, in coalition with the Free Democrats; former Berlin mayor Willy Brandt became Chancellor. On the other side of the Atlantic, there were major efforts made in the United States Congress to force the President to withdraw forces from Europe in 1970, 1971 and 1973. The dollar was devalued in 1971 and again in 1973, and in 1973 the Arab oil embargo and its aftermath disrupted the world monetary system to an extent the industrialized world had not seen since the 1930s. Yet none of these events produced a fundamental change either in offset or the American troop stationing. Two more offset agreements were negotiated in the usual every-other-year rhythm, and by 1976 offset seemed, if not dead, at least deeply dormant.

In 1970 Senator Mansfield again introduced his sense-of-the-Senate resolution calling for reduction, this time garnering fifty-one Senatorial co-sponsors. Within the Executive Branch a major fight appeared to be shaping up, along familiar lines. Civilian officials at Defense, hard pressed to hold down the defense budget, sided with Senate "cutters" against the Department of State and the Joint Chiefs of Staff. Studies written in response to another round of NSSM's examined troop reductions ranging from zero to 100,000, although the last option fell away early in the decision process. The full National Security Council met to discuss the issue in November 1970, and many Europeans felt reductions were imminent despite Administration pledges to the contrary.[25]

European members of NATO save France—organized into the so-called Eurogroup—began to consider ways of forestalling American reductions, at the same time as the review proceeded within the American government. Initially the Europeans split between the British, who favored improvements in European forces, and the Germans, who were prepared to make a cash payment to the United States. President Nixon himself resolved that debate, telling NATO Secretary General Brosio in September that Washington preferred European improvements to cash for itself. On the same trip Nixon pledged that there would be no "unilateral" American troop reduction.[26] Subsequently, Bonn and London divided once more: the British favoring increases in the size of European armies, the Germans calling for more jointly financed infrastructure projects. The European Defense Program (EDIP) which resulted was a compromise,[27] including both individual commitments to spend $450-500 million more on national forces over the subsequent five years and agreement to spend $420 million in joint projects to improve military communication facilities and protect air bases. For its part, Washington announced President Nixon's decision that there would be no American reductions "unless there is reciprocal action from our adversaries."[28]

The opposition in the American Congress to the existing U.S. troop level was replayed the next year, with more fervor. In May 1971 Mansfield introduced an amendment requiring the President to reduce American forces in Europe by half—to 150,000—by the end of the year. The amendment would have bound the President; it represented a break with Mansfield's previous strategy of offering only resolutions. The Administration vigorously opposed the amendment, with the White House and State Department in the van, organizing a coalition of ex-officials that included President Johnson to lobby against it. On May 20 the Senate rejected the amendment by 61-36; the Administration had received a timely boost when Soviet leader Brezhnev seemed to endorse the principle of mutual force reductions.[29]

The 1971 offset negotiations moved along tracks laid by their forebears. Washington again argued for "hard" offset and this time pressed seriously, at Treasury insistence, for measures it previously had dropped more easily: direct payments by Bonn, either via lump-sum transfers to the Treasury or through German assumption of local support costs. The Federal Republic appeared willing to go some way toward meeting U.S. demands, but the talks deadlocked over amounts and conditions. Six months after the previous agreement had expired, offset was snatched from the formal State Department-Foreign Office negotiating track by German Defense Minister Helmut Schmidt. He and his American counterpart, Melvin Laird, agreed on the $186 million program of renovating American barracks in Germany.[30]

The remainder of the 1971 agreement's provisions were less novel. About two billion dollars of American foreign exchange expenditure was covered, again about 80% of the total, and, again, about half the offset was military procurement. The continuing large size of the procurement component owed to the German decision to buy 175 more Phantom jets, at a total cost of $1.1 billion.[31] The Bundesbank agreed to purchase two billion DM (about $670 million) in Treasury securities; Bonn again agreed to a submarket interest rate and this time itself paid the interest to the Bundesbank.[32]

Nineteen seventy-three was to be the "Year of Europe" but was instead a year dominated by another war in the Middle East. What

45

was to have been a time of rebuilding the Atlantic alliance became the occasion for several prickly disputes among the allies. Henry Kissinger's speech intended to initiate the transatlantic dialogue raised for Europeans the possibility that the United States would use its military and political position to secure economic advantage. He suggested that "political, military and economic issues in Atlantic relations are linked by reality, not by our choice nor for the tactical purpose of trading one off against the other."[33] Yet the words suggested to nervous Europeans that the American government's intentions were precisely tactical.

Prior to the Kissinger speech, offset had been fed into the NSC study machinery once again. The attempt was to take another thorough look at the issue and related matters, although this time around there were several sorts of grumbles from agencies around town. First, they muttered that NSC staffers controlled deliberations, and second, the effort seemed of small consequence. No one seemed to be minding the store; the NSSM process had become mere camouflage to the serious foreign policy business which occurred only at the top of the government.

Agency positions were predictable. Treasury pressed for a larger offset and argued against the inclusion of German purchases of American securities, suggesting that only the German interest subsidy connected with the securities should count as offset. The State Department offered a single option—a new offset agreement of the customary form. There were two issues to be decided in sequence: would the United States press for new arrangements or merely renegotiate the bilateral offset accord? And if the decision were to seek new forms, would the government emphasize what Americans called "burden-sharing" (that is, European payments to relieve the U.S. of *budgetary* costs) or multilateral foreign exchange (offset) mechanisms? Kissinger's apparent preference was not to pressure the European governments, but the White House calculated— rightly it turned out—that Congressional pressures for troop reduction might mount. As in previous years, offset and its kin were ammunition for battles on Capitol Hill.

The Presidential decision, a NSDM issued in early May 1973, stressed burden sharing in substance and multilateralism in form.[34] The United States would negotiate another bilateral offset with the Germans, but would at the same time initiate multilateral discussions in Brussels. In both sets of talks, it would request that the Europeans pay the "additional" budgetary costs incurred by the

United States because the American troops were stationed in Europe rather than the United States. These costs, estimated for fiscal year 1974 at $440 million for Europe as a whole, and $310 million for Germany, were composed of such expenditures as transportation, relocation allowances and dependent education.[35]

NATO discussions had just begun, and bilateral offset negotiations had not yet formally started, when Congress turned once more to the question of American forces in Europe. In late July, Senator Mansfield renewed his call for reductions in U.S. forces abroad, this time proposing a cut of 250,000, worldwide. A provision for a forty per cent reduction in U.S. land-based forces abroad (totaling 483,000) which he tacked onto a defense procurement authorization bill was passed by the Senate, 49–46, on September 27. Later the same day, however, the Senate reversed itself, 51–44, and declined to attach the amendment to the final legislation. Then, two days later, the Senate approved a 110,000-man cut in an amendment offered by Senators Humphrey and Cranston. That provision was explicitly not directed at Europe, its number an estimate of forces which could be withdrawn from American garrisons overseas without dipping deeply into forces in Europe.

The victory for the Mansfield forces was, however, short-lived. The mandatory reduction was eliminated in a House-Senate conference on the defense bill. But the conference retained another amendment, one which had attracted less fanfare. Proposed by Senators Jackson and Nunn, its provision required the President to withdraw from American forces committed to NATO any troops whose foreign exchange costs were not offset by the Europeans. If only three-fourths of the total foreign exchange cost (estimated at $2.1 billion for fiscal year 1974)[36] were offset, only three-fourths of the troops could remain. The amendment was somewhat ambiguous, and it bore the marks of hasty drafting. Its intent was friendly to the Administration: it gave Senators something to vote for which sounded tough but was in fact far less damaging than the Mansfield amendment. Nevertheless, it was not initially regarded by much of the Administration as helpful. But so it turned out to be, paradoxically.

Washington had begun 1973 offset negotiations with Bonn in mid-September, asking for $3.3 billion over the next two-year period. The Federal Republic calculated that it could fill less than half that amount through military procurement in the United States. Bonn again parried American requests for direct, budgetary support, again arguing that it was a multilateral NATO matter and not one for

47

bilateral offset. The enactment of Jackson-Nunn switched the emphasis from burden-sharing once more to foreign exchange. But then the October war in the Middle East intervened, bringing in its trail both oil embargo and European-American discord. Offset negotiations stopped dead.

The Germans had from the beginning of negotiations resisted meeting the U.S. demand, on the ground that the *over-all* American balance-of-payments position was improving. They pointed to a 1957 NATO resolution which stipulated that member nations could ask for foreign exchange relief if they were in *over-all* deficit. Would the United States continue to demand an offset to its military deficit, the Germans asked, even if it moved into over-all surplus? The four-fold rise in oil prices only hardened Bonn's resolve, for it was obvious that the United States was better situated than its European allies to weather the foreign exchange storm (although the Federal Republic was also in good shape). The price hike raised in the United States both the anxiety that the flood of petrodollars would not be recycled to the industrial countries and the fear that a successful recycling would mean Arabs in control of major American companies; and the recycling process itself strained existing money market mechanisms. At the same time, however, the international role of the dollar probably was enhanced.

More fundamentally, in the post-1971 world of relatively flexible exchange rates, there was little economic logic to any arrangement for artificially "offsetting" any balance-of-payments "deficit." Within limits, governments should allocate resources as they see fit and let exchange rate changes take care of any balance-of-payments deficits which result. In practice, of course, particular exchange rates for dollar, pound or *Deutschemark* have retained political potency, but much less than before 1971. The political perils of running deficits (or surpluses) have lessened, and with them the need to engage allies in special measures to offset deficits.

Yet in the immediate concern with the balance of payments aroused by the 1973 embargo, offset climbed on the agenda of relations between Washington and Bonn. In January 1974 President Nixon wrote to Chancellor Brandt, requesting a resumption of the long-stalled offset negotiations.[37] Jackson-Nunn put the President under a deadline, requiring him to report to Congress on progress within ninety days after enactment, a period which ended in February 1974.

The logjam broke when Finance Minister Helmut Schmidt came to

Washington for the ill-fated energy conference in February. Paradoxically, Jackson-Nunn helped to break it. Military procurement in the United States by NATO nations clearly counted as offset in meeting the Jackson-Nunn requirement. Much of that procurement, but far from all, was made with the assistance of the United States government, and when NATO representatives in Brussels added European purchases made directly with American manufacturers to those channeled through the Defense Department, the total turned out to be larger than anyone had expected. It came to over a billion dollars a year, compared to the Defense Department figure for government-to-government sales of $350 million.

The heat was off the bilateral discussions. The large total of European procurement meant that a modest bilateral offset would suffice to comply with Jackson-Nunn. Given that target, American negotiators retreated from their earlier demands. In talking with Schmidt, Treasury Secretary George Shultz agreed to accept German purchases of Treasury securities, thereby flanking his staffers who had opposed the purchases. In September the United States government had requested an offset of over three billion dollars, but in March it accepted one of just over two billion (and one that was, in *Deutschemarks,* less than the 1971 agreement). Slightly under half the total amount was to be military procurement. Most of the rest was purchases of securities, again at a subsidized rate of interest, but some civilian procurement was included and the barracks renovation program included in the previous agreement was continued.[38]

The offset history ground to a stop during 1975 and 1976. Time and changing circumstances had eroded the premises of the original arrangements. After several years of American balance-of-payments surpluses, more and more people in official Washington began to acknowledge the force of German arguments that it made economic nonsense to offset an artificial "military deficit." As the industrial world discovered it could live with, and even like, flexible exchange rates, the whole offset exercise began to seem more and more questionable; specific aspects of previous agreements, such as the German loans to the American Treasury, appeared especially so. And if Washington were to get serious about military procurement policies to which it had given only lip service—standardization and the "two way street" of reciprocal procurement by Europe and America—then it could hardly justify the biennial practice of drumming "buy American" into German ears.

Within the American Congress pressures for a troop reduction subsided. The Jackson-Nunn Amendment was not renewed, and during 1975 and 1976 there was barely a whisper of interest in another Mansfield amendment.[39] The long war-short war debate, given form in discussion of the appropriate ratio of combat forces to supply troops, continued to result in shifting the balance away from preparation for another protracted war, another "World War II." Combat troops as a percentage of total American forces in Europe increased from 59 in 1972 to 62 in 1975, with a projected figure of 71 by 1977.[40]

The change in Congressional sentiments about troop reduction was part of a larger shift in attitudes. With the end of the Vietnam war and with other events—Soviet and Cuban involvement in the Angolan civil war, for instance—Americans and their Congressional representatives were becoming uneasy: uncertain about the United States' role in the world and mistrustful of Soviet intentions. The lack of a Mansfield amendment was one manifestation of that unease; the parades of liberal members of Congress rushing to increase the defense budget in 1976 was another. This unease gave rise to no surge of isolationism: what resulted was more a shrinking of commitments but a tightening of those that remained. During the Vietnam era, the public feeling that the United States had too many troops in too many foreign places occasionally washed across the troop presence in Europe. But with the shrinking of American commitments in the wake of Vietnam, the case became if anything stronger for retaining a strong force where America's historic commitment and sense of shared interest always had been strongest.

With less Congressional pressure and no firm deadlines, and with many American officials echoing German reluctance, neither side was in a hurry to begin discussion of a new offset agreement. Recession and inflation, the old German bugbear, made it all the harder for Bonn to contemplate another public commitment to the United States. A week before the previous agreement was to expire, Chancellor Schmidt, elevated from the finance portfolio after the surprise resignation of Willy Brandt, said of offset at a news conference: "I do not consider it a pressing problem at the moment."[41] Other German officials could see no justification at all for another agreement, and Bonn had parried a request from President Ford in May for an offset renewal. At his own press conference in September, Secretary of State Kissinger passed off offset by remarking to a German correspondent: "I think it is no secret that your Chancellor is not an unqualified admirer of offset agreements."[42]

In the summer of 1976 Ford and Schmidt pronounced offset officially dead, when they met in Washington. Their statement took explicit note of changes in both monetary structures and the dollar's strength:

> Given the recently introduced changes in the international monetary area, specifically flexible exchange rates, as well as the notably improved strength of the dollar and a more acceptable United States balance-of-payments position, the President and the Chancellor consider that the traditional offset arrangements approach has lost its relevance.[43]

Instead of offset, the allies talked of a new pattern of cost-sharing, case-by-case. For the first case, Bonn agreed to pay sixty percent ($68 million) of the cost of building a base in north Germany for the recently arrived American brigade. By all the signs of 1976, offset would be permitted to rest in peace. Senator Nunn had reacted to Schmidt's comment the previous June by insisting on the old offsets-for-military-deficits formulation and by threatening to introduce legislation to compel an offset or force a troop reduction; he raised the issue again in the late winter of 1976. But nothing came of either initiative. If the balance-of-payments logic which implied an end to offset was not necessarily as compelling to the American Congress as to the Executive Branch, that logic still seemed sufficient to put the traditional offset formulation beyond revival as a political issue.

The foregoing overview can do no more than suggest the continuity in outcomes reached by the allies with respect to offset and force level. It contains only hints about why given outcomes ensued. To address that question, I turn to an examination of the politics and policy-making within the allies and of the interactions between them, concentrating on the instance of 1966–67. That discussion begins with Bonn.

NOTES TO CHAPTER II

[1]For accounts of the Anderson mission, *see* the *New York Times,* November 22–27, 1960. For the total of occupation costs, *see* Horst Mendershausen, *Troop Stationing in Germany: Value and Cost,* RM-5881-PR (Santa Monica: The Rand Corporation, 1968), p.44.

[2]For a description of the 1961 agreements, *see* the *New York Times,* October 24–25, 1961. U.S. foreign exchange expenditures in Germany from mid-1961 through mid-1967 (fiscal years 1961 through 1966) totaled $3.6 billion.

U.S. Forces in Europe, Hearings before the Subcommittee on Arms Control, International Law and Organization of the Senate Committee on Foreign Relations, 93 Cong., 1 sess.(1973), p.333. [Hereafter cited as *U.S. Forces in Europe (Senate, 1973).*] Former Finance Minister Strauss calculated German offset payments during the same period at 15.4 million DM ($3.9 billion). *Neue Zürcher Zeitung,* March 1, 1967.

[3]The texts of German-American agreements originally were secret, but Anglo-German accords were made public. *See Agreement between the Government of the United Kingdom ... and the Government of the Federal Republic of Germany for Offsetting the Foreign Exchange Expenditure on British Forces in the Federal Republic of Germany,* Bonn, July 27, 1964, British Treaty Series No. 58; and *Protocol for the Extension and Modification of the Agreement of 27 July 1964,* Bonn, July 20, 1965, British Treaty Series No. 63.

[4]$1.7 billion of gold was sold in 1965. $.6 billion in 1966. Department of Commerce, *Survey of Current Business,* June 1967. Under Secretaries Katzenbach and Deming estimated the deficit due to Vietnam at about a billion and a half dollars for 1967. *See* Mendershausen, cited above, p.97.

[5]More will be said on the NATO crisis in subsequent chapters. For an account of deliberations leading up to the creation of special drawing rights (SDR's) in 1967, *see* Stephen D. Cohen, *International Monetary Reform, 1964–69: The Political Dimension* (New York: Praeger Publishers, 1970).

[6]The United States' position as expressed in the letters of understanding signed by the two men was that the U.S. would reduce to the level covered by German offset. For an account of that meeting, *see* a column by Robert Kleiman in the *New York Times,* June 6, 1966. For a description of ensuing events, *see* an article in the same paper, July 11, 1966.

[7]June 2, 1966. 15,000 specialists had been transferred just prior to McNamara's meeting with von Hassel. In all, 30,000 men were moved during 1966, but apparently half were quickly replaced. Nevertheless, some deterioration in the *quality* of the American garrison did occur and did receive critical attention, both in the U.S. and in Germany.

[8]He did so in a speech before the Bundestag on July 1, indicating that $782 million in orders had been placed and another $428 million earmarked. *New York Times,* September 26, 1966.

[9]Reported in the *New York Times,* June 15, 1966.

[10]The Erhard letter is mentioned in Walt W. Rostow, *The Diffusion of Power: An Essay in Recent American History* (New York: The Macmillan Company, 1972), p.396.

[11]For general accounts of the visit, *see* the *New York Times,* September 26–28, 1966; the last of those issues contains the communiqué signed by the two chiefs of state. For reactions to the visit in the German parliament, *see Deutscher Bundestag* (proceedings), 5th Period, 6th sess. (October 5, 1966). The Bundestag debate is also covered in the *New York Times* of October 6.

[12]McCloy's charter is described in an article in the *Washington Post* of October 30, 1966.

[13]In testimony before Congress in April 1967, just at the time the Trilaterals were concluding, McNamara stated his belief that a cut of two divisions would be militarily acceptable. He was, however, opposed by the Joint Chiefs

of Staff, who wanted no reduction. For a reference to McNamara's remarks, see *United States Security Agreements and Commitments Abroad, Pt.10: United States Forces in Europe,* Hearings before the Subcommittee on United States Security Agreements and Commitments Abroad of the Senate Committee on Foreign Relations, 91 Cong., 2 sess. (1970), pp.2068,2250.

[14]American deliberations and their results are discussed in general terms in the *New York Times,* February 24 and March 4, 1967; and in the *Washington Post,* March 4, 1967.

[15]The letters agreed to on April 28 were not released, but the basic contents of the agreement were made public in a State Department press release on May 2nd and in the simultaneous publication, by the Treasury and the Federal Reserve, of correspondence between the two countries.

[16]Quoted in the *New York Times,* May 3, 1967.

[17]*See* reports in *ibid.,* July 12 and September 12, 1967.

[18]In a statement on January 1, printed the next day in *ibid.*

[19]Mendershausen, cited above, p.108. The total for fiscal years 1968 and 1969 was $371 million. *U.S. Forces in NATO,* Hearings before the House Committee on Foreign Affairs and its Subcommittee on Europe, 93 Cong., 1 sess.(1973), p.324. [Hereafter cited as *U.S. Forces in NATO (House, 1973)*.]

[20]The Army component of the redeployment, REFORGER, involved about 28,000 men; the Air Force portion, dubbed CRESTED CAP, about 3400. The first yearly exercise was to occur in the fall of 1968 but was delayed to the fall of 1969 for reasons of cost and because the brigades were well below strength. *New York Times,* September 17, 1968. Subsequent exercises took place in 1970, 1971 and 1972.

The redeployments have been criticized for producing much less than the anticipated foreign exchange savings. *See,* for example, Timothy W. Stanley, "Mutual Force Reduction," *Survival,* XII, 5 (May 1970), 157. The Defense Department, however, estimated the savings at $93.2 million per year, well within the range of Secretary McNamara's original projections. *The American Commitment to NATO,* Hearings before the Special Subcommittee on NATO Commitments of the House Committee on Armed Services, 91 Cong., 1 and 2 sess.,(1971–72), p.14963.

[21]The securities again carried market interest rates—between 5.20 per cent and 6.23 per cent for those purchased by the Bundesbank, and 6.25 per cent for those purchased by the private banks. *U.S. Forces in NATO (House, 1973),* p.323. The inclusion of the airbus purchase was due to special circumstances. Lufthansa previously had contracted for the planes and had received a credit from the American Export-Import Bank. In the offset negotiations, the German government agreed *not* to use that credit. *See* the *New York Times,* June 15, 1968, for a description of the agreement, and *ibid.,* August 19, 1968, for the Mansfield quotation.

[22]*Ibid.,* October 25, 1968.

[23]The figures, on the official reserve transaction basis, were +4.6 billion dollars for the first quarter of 1969, and +4.9 billion for the second quarter (seasonally adjusted annual rates). *Economic Report of the President* (Washington, 1970), p.277.

[24]The 1969 agreement won the competition for complexity hands down: $800 million for arms procurement; $250 million in loans made by the

German government (10-year duration, at 3.5 per cent), $118.75 in purchases by Bonn of outstanding Eximbank and Marshall Plan paper (at 4–5 per cent); the creation of a $150 million fund to encourage German investment in the United States (8-year duration if unused); $43.75 million in advance repayments of German debts; and $32.50 million in relief given the U.S. on interest payments for German accounts held with the Treasury. In addition, $125 million in German civilian (government) procurement was included—for enriched uranium, railroad couplers and parts for a German-built airbus—although apparently only the uranium purchase materialized. *See U.S. Forces in NATO (House, 1973),* p.322; Federal Republic of Germany, Press and Information Office, *Mitteilung an die Presse,* July 9, 1969; and *Handelsblatt,* March 10, 1971, for details of the agreement.

[25]Disputes inside the Administration are described in an article by Chalmers Roberts in the *Washington Post,* November 12, 1970, and in accounts in the *New York Times,* January 21, February 4, and December 1 and 25, 1970. For a list of the first NSSM's issued in the Nixon Administration, *see* John P. Leacacos, "Kissinger's Apparat," *Foreign Policy,* 5 (Winter 1971–72), p.27.

[26]For reporting on the Nixon trip, *see* the *New York Times,* September 5 and 9, 1970.

[27]*See The Economist,* December 5, 1970, and Federal Republic of Germany, Press and Information Office, *White Paper 1971–72: The Security of the Federal Republic and the Development of the Federal Armed Forces* (Bonn: Press and Information Office, 1971), p.19. [Hereafter cited as *German White Paper.*] The compromise was facilitated by Anglo-German negotiations over a new offset arrangement. Those negotiations proceeded simultaneously with the Eurogroup discussions and were concluded early in 1971. Bonn agreed to pay London a lump sum of 110 million *DM* per year for five years. *Exchange of Notes between the Government of the United Kingdom . . . and the Government of the Federal Republic of Germany for Offsetting the Foreign Exchange Expenditure on British Forces in the Federal Republic of Germany,* Bonn, March 18, 1971, British Treaty Series No. 41. In effect, Bonn financed British participation in EDIP. The Germans were willing to let the British play Europeans with German money once but were unwilling to make the practice a habit.

[28]Reported in the *New York Times,* December 4, 1970.

[29]*Ibid.,* May 12, 13 and 20, 1971. NATO had proposed mutual and balanced force reduction (MBFR) negotiations at its Ministerial Meeting in Iceland in June 1968.

[30]Treasury opposed the barracks deal, for good foreign exchange reasons which will be discussed later. For an example of the use of the program in argument before Congress, *see* the statement of Under Secretary of State William Casey in *U.S. Forces in NATO (House, 1973),* p.320.

[31]*New York Times,* June 25, 1971; *German White Paper,* p.145.

[32]The agreement was expressed in *Deutsche Marks* (6.650 billion in total), so the February 1973 devaluation increased the dollar values somewhat. The interest subsidy ($31 million) was designed to pay the interest for two years; it was money from offset deposits accumulated in the U.S. Treasury under previous agreements. *U.S. Forces in NATO (House, 1973),* pp.320–24.

[33]A transcript of Kissinger's speech is printed in the *New York Times,* April 24, 1973.

[34]The decision contrasted with the emphasis in the President's foreign policy report, issued about the same time, on the balance-of-payments consequences of the U.S. stationing.

[35]*U.S. Security Issues in Europe: Burden Sharing and Offset, MBFR and Nuclear Weapons,* A Staff Report for the Subcommittee on U.S. Security Agreements and Commitments Abroad of the Senate Committee on Foreign Relations, 93 Cong., 1 sess.(1973), p.8.

[36]*Report by the President on Implementation of the Jackson-Nunn Amendment,* May 16, 1974.

[37]The Nixon letter is discussed in an article by Craig Whitney in the *New York Times,* February 5, 1974, and also in *Welt am Sonntag,* February 17, 1974. There was considerable newspaper reportage on the negotiations, particularly in German papers. *See,* for example, another article by Whitney in the *Times,* February 8; and articles in *Handelsblatt,* September 18 and November 8, 1973; and in *Frankfurter Allgemeine Zeitung,* February 8 and March 12, 1974.

[38]The details of this agreement were made public immediately, in a Department of State press release, April 25, 1974. For reports on the final stages of negotiations, *see* an article by David Binder in the *New York Times,* March 20, 1974; and articles in the *Frankfurter Allgemeine Zeitung,* February 21, March 26 and April 5, 1974; and in *Neue Zürcher Zeitung,* March 23, and April 27, 1974.

[39]*See* Philip Williams, "What Happened to the Mansfield Amendment?" *Survival,* XVIII, 4 (July/August 1976), pp.146—53.

[40]Pentagon figures, cited in the *International Herald Tribune,* February 3, 1975.

[41]Two years before, while serving as Finance Minister, Schmidt had labeled offset "blackmail . . . Either we pay or the Administration withdraws troops. It can only end badly." Both quotations appear in the *New York Times,* June 26, 1975.

[42]For newspaper reportage of dealings between Washington and Bonn, *see* the *Washington Post,* September 8 and 10, 1975. Kissinger's statement appears in the latter.

[43]Quoted in the *International Herald Tribune,* July 19, 1976.

CHAPTER III: BONN

WHAT moved officials in Bonn, like their counterparts in Washington, were considerations based on their own internal politics. Certainly, actions taken by one nation affected the decisions of the other. Of that fact officials in Bonn, especially, had no doubt. Yet the governmental establishment labeled in shorthand "Bonn" was no monolith; nor were its reactions to American actions automatic. The Federal Republic's actions were constrained by domestic politics given form in bureaucratic divisions and parliamentary procedures, and by the nature of relations among the officials who presided over the governmental creature in Bonn.

The nature of the constraints differed during the several intervals in the 1966–67 history: the months preceding the visit of Chancellor Erhard to Washington, in September 1966; the interval between the visit and the collapse of the Erhard government in November; and the period from the formation of the Grand Coalition government through the conclusion of the Trilateral Negotiations, in May 1967. These three intervals will be taken up in turn. While the state of deliberations in Bonn altered from one period to the next, there were consistent threads. Some of these continued to be characteristic of the German approach to the issues of offset and troop level long after the Trilaterals were over.

Even the broad outlines of German politics and government are unfamiliar to most Americans, not least to their elected and appointed officials. Bonn is, in common perception, an amalgam of images inherited from older German governments, located in Berlin, not Bonn—the democratic instability of Weimar and the despotic authoritarianism of the Third Reich—all overlaid with a sense of the Federal Republic's newness. Federal German governance mixes federalism with parliamentary form with chancellor government in a way that frustrates analogy to models rooted in the experiences of Washington or London or Paris under de Gaulle.

The political center of the federal government is familiar enough: a figurehead president with leadership responsibility vested in a prime minister, by German custom denominated "chancellor." That semantic difference is suggestive, for the chancellor is no mere *primus inter pares*; his paper powers are impressive. He alone carries the flag of government in the principal house of parliament, the Bundestag. His cabinet ministers are drawn from the Bundestag, but he appoints them, reorganizes their ministries and has the power to issue them binding policy guidelines *(Richtlinien der Politik)*.[1] Even a chancellor with a thin majority in the Bundestag has little fear of being thrown from office in mid-term, for he can be ousted only by a so-called "constructive" vote of no-confidence. An opposing party or coalition must be able not only to defeat him but simultaneously to elect a successor.

The authority of the chancellor, embedded in German Basic Law *(Grundgesetz)*, became a matter of routine practice and common expectation during the long tenure of the man who first occupied that position, the father of the Federal Republic, *Der Alte*—Konrad Adenauer. Adenauer could play in the late 1950s with the idea of having himself elected president, only deciding not to after he concluded that he could not convert it into an office with more authority than that of the chancellorship. Adenauer's successors, and especially the man who immediately followed him in the Palais Schaumburg, Ludwig Erhard, would be judged against his incumbency.

Yet much of the apparent power of the chancellorship owed to Adenauer's personal force, not to the structure of government. For the Federal Republic's allies to conceive of the Bonn government by light of Adenauer's tenure was to risk serious error, especially in 1966 when the Chancellor was a man with nowhere near Adenauer's personal force or party standing. The federal structure meant that politicians on the way up or those who had lost in internal power struggles need not bide their time or lick their wounds on the back benches of the Bundestag; they had the alternative of seeking power and prominence in state (*Länder*) governments. The structure of the central government meant that the upper house of parliament— the Bundesrat—composed of representatives from the states, was not normally a force in foreign affairs but acquired indirect influence through its effective veto power over tax legislation, and hence budgets.

In 1966 the Bonn machine was presided over by the coalition that had ruled the Federal Republic virtually since its formation. The senior partner was Erhard's Christian Democratic Union (CDU), a mildly conservative aggregation of regional political barons and interest groups. The "union" in place of "party" in its title was apt, for the CDU's fragments had been held together for many years as much by Adenauer's force as by a common ideology. For Bundestag purposes, the CDU formed common front with its Bavarian associate, the Christian Social Union (CSU). The CSU tugged at its partner from the right on most domestic issues and was more tempted by nationalistic postures in foreign relations. The mutual dependence of the two parties was easy for neither. While the CSU organization and its preeminence in Bavaria made it vital to the CDU for national purposes, those same attributes made it a force to be reckoned with in fraternal debates. CDU chancellors from Adenauer onward lived with the menacing presence of CSU boss Franz-Josef Strauss, whether he was in the cabinet or out.

Cabinet-building became a work of art for the CDU, even in the rare intervals when the CDU-CSU majority in the Bundestag permitted them to govern alone. CDU cabinets represented delicate balances of different religions, regions, interest groups and political hues. The constraint implied by those balances operated even on Adenauer. A reduced margin of victory in the 1961 elections compelled him to re-establish the coalition with the Free Democratic Party (FPD); he was also forced to give the position of foreign minister to Gerhard Schröder, a Protestant and a man inclined to look to transatlantic ties, in place of von Brentano, a Catholic Europeanist and faithful Adenauer disciple.[2] When the Social Democratic Party (SPD) became the senior partner in ruling coalitions, it did not find it much easier to assemble cabinets than had the CDU, although in the

SPD's case the characteristics to be balanced were ideology and age more than region or religion.

The Free Democratic Party (FPD), heir to the prewar liberal legacy, was the junior partner in the long string of conservative coalitions. Its adherents, about ten percent of the electorate, possessed little common ideology, were drawn initially to the party by distaste either for the mixing of politics and religion in the CDU/CSU or the collectivist tendencies of the SPD. During the liberals' period of token opposition to the Grand Coalition (1966–69), the party's left wing wrested control from the more conservative wing. That made possible the ruling alliance with the SPD from 1969 onward, but the cost was high. The party lost roughly half its vote to the CDU and lived in constant fear of extinction, for no party which receives less than five percent of the vote can be represented in the Bundestag.

The opposition party in 1966, the Social Democratic Party (SPD), alone of the three parties, traced its ancestry directly to a prewar party. Its march to power in 1969 was a long one; its course took it from strident opposition to "loyal" opposition, with a dramatic change of party platform in between. In the early years of the Federal Republic, it offered the voters socialism domestically and rigid nationalism internationally—including hostility to alliance with the western powers and to rearmament, and opposition to European integration. Tarnished by the success of CDU free market economics and tarred by its opponents with the epithet of unfitness to govern, the SPD earned for itself severe electoral defeats in 1953 and 1957. In the Godesberg Program of 1959 and in actions during the following year, the party reversed course, abandoning its dogmatic commitment to socialism and declaring its willingness to accept the political and military arrangements of western alliance. In the next decade, its share of the electorate grew steadily. By 1969 it received over forty percent of the vote, virtual equality with the CDU/CSU.

The governmental creature over which Ludwig Erhard presided in 1966 was not, even in formal structure, the well-oiled machine it had often seemed during Adenauer's long tenure in office. For Americans to behave as though it were was a serious mistake in itself, quite apart from the weaknesses that derived from Erhard's personality, not his position. As Chancellor, Erhard had to deal with ministers he could fire and to whom he could issue binding policy guidelines, but whom he could not compel to take specific actions in particular instances. And he had to confront powerful barons in other places: his

59

coalition's parliamentary leaders, for instance, or the independent central bank, the Bundesbank. The SPD could not threaten his government's survival—only events within his coalition could do that—but it could harass and delay his legislation through the Bundestag committees that were becoming, in 1966, less like their British counterparts and more like committees of the American Congress, a trend that accelerated during the Grand Coalition government. An observation made by two German observers, whose vantage point was the period of the Grand Coalition, holds for other governments in Bonn as well, none more than Erhard's:

> ... the federal government ... consists of a plurality of semi-independent actors. The chancellorship does not provide the unifying potential of the American presidency; ministers are political power centers with their own parliamentary base, rather than "secretaries" assisting the President in the execution of his own program.[3]

For the officials who composed that government in Bonn, the alliance with Washington was a matter of postwar necessity, not of long friendship and wartime collaboration, or of ties of history and language. The American link, and the priority assigned to it, became second nature, easy enough in a time of economic boom and so long as there was neither a "Europe" with which to cooperate nor Frenchmen tugging hard at German sentiments. Offset was a symbol of the alliance, military and economic cooperation for political purpose, something Germans had agreed to initially because Americans desired it and because the cost of agreeing was low. When fulfilling agreements became harder, Bonn tried to do so in order to sustain the symbol. No segment of German officialdom—save perhaps parts of the Defense Ministry—had an interest in offset for its own sake. Rather the accords were proof that the Federal Republic was willing to do more than its share not only in maintaining the alliance but in meeting the desires of its recently found allies.

I. PRELUDE TO THE ERHARD VISIT

What factors combined to make the offset issue so important for Erhard and why was the unhappy outcome of the visit to Washington so disastrous for him? That question brings in train others, more specific: given the importance of offset, why was the Erhard government so ill-prepared on that score when he arrived in Washington, so unwilling to engage in dialogue with the Americans in the month before? The answers to both questions lie in the context surrounding the offset issue in Bonn and the form its management took in the German government.

Context of Offset

Five aspects of the context in which offset fell are important. Context had both external and internal consequences; it affected both the form the issue took and the way it was dealt with inside the German government. On one hand, the range of options was limited and deadlines were imposed; on the other, the pattern of the internal debate was altered, with various participants advantaged or hampered. Two related aspects of the context stand out: the 1966 "recession" in Germany; and the decline in Erhard's popularity and capacity for governance caused partly, but not exclusively, by the economic downturn.

Economic Problems. Germany's economic boom began to taper off noticeably in 1966, a serious problem for any government, no doubt more serious for Erhard, the creator of the German "miracle." Erhard, portly and professorial, had been tabbed by the victorious allies as a central figure in the postwar reconstruction of the shattered German economy. He had become a politician more by accident than by design, not even formally joining the CDU until 1963. GNP, which had risen 5.3% in 1965, rose only 2.4% in 1966 (and only 1.1% in 1967). Unemployment rose, and tax revenue lagged behind spending.[4]

Keynesian economics came late to the Federal Republic, for two reasons. The first was the success of the Adenauer-Erhard free market economics of the 1950s, which created a presumption against government controls and tinkering of all sorts. Free market principles were at the heart of the rhetoric of a "social market economy" which was given lip service by all political parties. Karl Schiller, the SPD's foremost economic figure, resigned from the Cabinet and left his party in 1972 rather than accept modest government controls on international currency speculation.

A second reason for the persistence of liberal economic orthodoxy was the hyperinflation of the interwar period in Germany. That created a deep and abiding fear of inflation and made balanced budgets an article of faith, especially for the CDU. Throughout the 1950s and into the 1960s, the Federal Republic maintained balanced government budgets, with export earnings and balance-of-payments

61

surpluses feeding the economic boom. Yet by 1966 Erhard's brand of liberal economics was becoming more and more inappropriate. His government played with equivalents to deficit spending, but the fiscal function of government spending was not formally recognized until the Economic Stabilization Act of 1967. And even then fiscal policy was limited to the voluntary coordination of federal, state and local budgets.

Erhard's economic stabilization program concentrated on balancing the budget. That program confronted the political obstacles inherent in whittling down social programs. Those problems were compounded because many of the increases in social spending were automatic. Limiting them meant changing as many as thirty laws and, perhaps, amending the German constitution, all measures which had to be maneuvered through a Bundestag in which Erhard's government depended on the support of its junior coalition partner, the Free Democratic Party (FPD). From this context came the Chancellor's letter to President Johnson of July 5, 1966, noting the difficulty of meeting existing offset commitments and suggesting the possibility of crediting nonmilitary purchases as offset.

Erhard's Decline. The decline in Erhard's popularity and capacity for leadership was evident throughout 1966. Never considered decisive, in a political system accustomed to the strong hand of *Der Alte*—Adenauer—Erhard suffered by comparison to his predecessor. (Adenauer had, in fact, maneuvered in 1963 to deny Erhard the chancellorship and continued to hold the post of party chairman until March 1966, on the transparent rationale that Erhard had no time for both jobs, in order to prevent Erhard from obtaining it). Erhard's somewhat woolly personality, baroque manner and lack of political acumen provided abundant opportunities for his enemies within the CDU. The "recession" further weakened his position.

Several benchmarks in Erhard's decline were visible well before his visit to Washington. In the 1965 national elections, the CDU/CSU union nearly regained the absolute majority in the Bundestag it had lost in 1961. Yet the elections were followed by protracted negotiations over the formation of a new coalition government. Erhard's inability to control the intraparty jockeying was both a sign of and a contributor to the weakening of the Chancellor's position. Franz-Josef Strauss threatened to withdraw his Bavarian Christian Social Union from its traditional association with the CDU and form a national party, and there was talk within both parties of a grand coalition with the SPD.[5] In the end neither possibility materialized, and the governing coalition with the FPD was reformed. Vote totals registered in state (*Länder*) elections in 1965 and 1966 by the right-wing National Democratic Party (NPD) were widely interpreted as a symptom of eroding authority in Bonn.

The outcome of the June 1966 elections in the important state (*Land*) of North Rhine-Westphalia was a still more significant measure of Erhard's decline. The CDU had held virtually unbroken control of the *Landtag* (state parliament), but the SPD won the June elections (and nearly achieved an absolute majority), despite intensive campaigning by the Chancellor. Since many of Erhard's enemies within the party had tolerated him only because of his utility as a vote-getter—he was referred to as the electoral "locomotive"—the loss was a serious personal blow to him.[6]

The Status of French Forces in Germany. When the French withdrew from the integrated NATO military command, there remained the testy problem of what to do with the 70,000 French troops remaining on German soil. Initially, many in official Bonn were tempted to vent their pique by insisting that the troops leave. Officials in both Bonn and Paris eventually agreed that the troops should stay, but agreement on a legal basis for the stationing was hard to come by.

Within Bonn the dispute reopened a schism that had been just beneath the surface of German foreign policy-making for years: the conflict between the "Gaullists" and the "Atlanticists." Adenauer was counted in the former group in 1966, along with Strauss, Bundestag President Gerstenmaier and CSU foreign policy expert von Guttenberg. While chancellor, Adenauer, a lifelong francophile, had artfully straddled the fence between Paris and Washington, most often siding with the latter in a pinch. However, Adenauer had been tempted by France, not just as a partner in European integration but as an alternative to the United States, even while John Foster Dulles was still Secretary of State.[7] In 1966 Adenauer's general opposition to Erhard provided another reason for siding with the "Gaullists." That group had become disenchanted with American policies and was inclined to be sympathetic to de Gaulle's vision of an independent Europe (though not necessarily to the specifics of the General's plan). The "Gaullists" in Bonn conceded precedence to the Federal Republic's ties to Paris over its alliance with Washington. For instance, Strauss and the CSU opposed the American proposal for a NATO multilateral nuclear force (the MLF).[8]

By contrast, the "Atlanticists"—Erhard, Foreign Minister Schröder and Defense Minister von Hassel—regarded Bonn's connection to Washington as vital. The Federal Republic sided with the United States in a series of Franco-American disputes, and President Johnson's decision at the end of 1964 to sink the MLF was a source of considerable embarrassment to Erhard. While Adenauer had managed to strike a balance between the requirements of Bonn's two principal alliances, it was Erhard's failing that he maneuvered the Federal Republic into a position of open and apparent dependence upon the United States.

The debate between Gaullists and Atlanticists was played out almost entirely within the CDU/CSU: both the SPD and the FPD gave passive support to Erhard's Atlanticist policies. Paradoxically, it was the Gaullists who flirted with the idea of a grand coalition with the SPD in 1965, even though they opposed the thaw in relations with Eastern Europe, a policy that found favor with the Atlanticists, the SPD and the FPD. Conflicts within the CDU/CSU were rooted as much in competitions for personal power as in ideological differences.

In negotiations over the status of French forces, Schröder was inclined to take a hard line with the French (a position the American State Department initially supported). He opposed Paris' suggestion that the French troops revert to the residual occupation status conceded them by 1954 treaties. Schröder argued in May that he had "no intention of giving forces stationed in Germany but not integrated in NATO the same rights as integrated forces."[9] Schröder's preference was accepted by Erhard, adopted by the Cabinet on April 6 and embodied in a German note to France, May 4.

Strauss vigorously attacked the government position. He met with Erhard to express his position and maneuvered to passage at a CSU meeting a resolution opposing "any policy which plans or provokes the elimination of French troops from German soil."[10] Adenauer campaigned against the Schröder line, and CDU Bundestag leader Barzel publicly separated himself from it.

A satisfactory solution finally was reached, but the dispute outlived the Erhard government. Erhard himself seemed to back away from the Schröder line almost as soon as he had acquiesced in it. In a handwritten note to de Gaulle in late May, Erhard suggested formation of a Franco-German commission, at the same time making clear to the Bundestag that he wanted the troops to stay.[11]

An interim agreement was reached, allowing the July 1 French deadline to pass without a hasty withdrawal. On a French initiative, talks began between the Supreme Allied Commander in Europe, Lemnitzer, and the French commander, Ailleret. Bonn and Paris exchanged letters setting forth a general basis in late December (a plan which apparently had been tentatively agreed upon when Erhard met with de Gaulle the previous July), and left it to the military commanders to work out the details.[12]

"Starfighters" and Defense Ministry Problems. The Federal Republic experienced a string of tragedies with the American-made F-104G Starfighter, the plane it had selected as the cornerstone of its new air force. Sixty-six planes (in a fleet of 700 planes) had crashed through 1966—10 in the first half of 1966 alone—and 38 pilots had perished. More than one air force chief of staff lost his job over the Starfighter crashes. These tragedies with the most visible of German procurements from the U.S. certainly contributed to an unwillingness, at least among the general public, to spend increasingly scarce resources on more American arms. German officials had difficulty, both in 1966 and later, responding to a public opinion that the U.S. was using offset to sell Germany unneeded arms.[13] The bargaining form of negotiations risked misperception on both sides of the Atlantic. Bonn needed simultaneously to convince the Americans that it was making a large sacrifice and its domestic audience that it was yielding little.

Against the backdrop of Starfighter disasters came a more specific Defense Ministry "management crisis" in August, prior to Erhard's trip to Washington. Two of the highest ranking German officers, including the Inspector General (chief of staff), objected publicly to a Ministry plan to allow soldiers to join labor unions. They were dismissed by von Hassel. SPD leaders in turn called for the Minister's resignation. The episode added another item to the Chancellor's heavy plate of political woes and diminished von Hassel's own credibility and authority.

British Offset. London's offset problem will be discussed in more detail later, but it formed an important part of the context surrounding German dealings with Washington. The British threat in July reversed the customary German order of dealings: Bonn preferred to work out an offset with the U.S. first. German officials tended to place a lesser value on the presence of the British troops than the American. There was much grumbling about their cost and the high ratio of local employees to British soldiers. What the Germans had not yet realized was the extent to which decisions in London and Washington were linked: even if the British troops were worth little, should they be reduced it would be more and more difficult for Washington not to follow suit. When President Johnson proposed converting the

Anglo-German offset commission into a trilateral group, in a late August letter to Erhard,[14] the Chancellor resisted. Foreign Minister Schröder urged that response on Erhard, arguing that in the trilaterals Bonn would be confronted by two pleaders simultaneously and that it should, in any case, strike a bargain with the Americans first.

Management of Offset

The economic puzzle confronting Erhard made it important for him to resolve the offset problem; other elements in the context within which the issue arose suggested that it would be difficult for him to do so. Yet those factors are but partial explanation for German actions in August and September 1966. If the Germans did not understand what was going on in Washington, why not? Why had no coherent approaches been formulated or broached with the Americans? The form of the handling of the issue in Bonn seems at the heart of the answer. One aspect of German management found its parallel on the American side, as will be seen later: in both governments the handling of offset had become embedded in particular routines, procedural "channels" from which it was not easily dislodged—at least in time. The second, critical aspect of German management was Erhard's own personality and his approach to the issue.

The Offset "Channel." Up to the Erhard visit, offset was a military sales matter for the U.S. For the Germans it was a military procurement matter, hence an issue of the defense budget. It was dealt with, day to day, by the Procurement and Budgets Departments of the Defense Ministry. As the economic situation tightened, the Finance Ministry, especially its Budget Department, became more and more involved, but its encroachment was resisted by Defense. Significantly, offset was not yet regarded as "political" and so the Foreign Office paid minimal attention to it.

Within the Defense Ministry, at Hardthöhe outside Bonn, there were signs of ambivalence about offset even in 1966, and that ambivalence increased with time. The men who handled offset routinely—officials at about the level of American assistant secretaries (*Ministerialdirektor*)—had, like their American counterparts, dealt with the issue for years. They tended to regard the German commitment as firm. But the Bonn government regarded German rearmament as basically complete, although there were, of course, military officers who readily seized American offers of fancy new weapons. And German offset accounts in Washington were a handy receptacle for procurement funds which could not be spent in the year appropriated. Money could be deposited for later use, not returned to the federal treasury and thus lost to the Defense Ministry.

Yet even procurement officials began to have second thoughts as the European arms industry grew more sophisticated, and offset arrangements began to compete with giving orders to domestic firms or spurring European cooperation. In the first years of offset the Defense Ministry had been happy enough to spend its own procurement funds on purchases under offset. After 1966 it began to request additional appropriations to fulfill offset commitments. It lost that battle, but for several skirmishes, to the Finance Ministry. There is some evidence that by 1966 the men who handled offset for Defense were becoming isolated within the Ministry, viewed as members of a transnational cabal.

Budget stringency gave the Finance Ministry an entry to the issue. To the extent it was involved it acted like finance ministries everywhere, opposing expenditures on offset, insisting, in 1966, that Defense would have to take its budget cuts like all the other agencies. For Finance, offset wore strictly a budget face. The German constitution gives the finance minister a strong role in the budget process: if he opposes a particular expenditure, he can be overruled only if his chancellor makes the issue a matter of basic government policy— "guideline" status, so-called—the chancellor's prerogative. However, Dahlgrün, the Finance Minister in 1966, was not a strong figure in Cabinet. By custom, the CDU gave the Finance portfolio to its junior partner, the FPD. Dalgrün belonged to the right wing of a deeply divided FPD. That and temperament relegated him to an inactive role.

Differing agency perspectives and little coordination among them made Bonn's pronouncements on offset indecisive and often contradictory. Under the pressure of the McNamara threat, Defense Minister von Hassel consistently asserted that Germany would meet its commitment through June 1967 (the end of the offset agreement then in force.) Official government spokesman von Hase did likewise. At about the same time, however, the Finance Ministry issued a report calculating the German "shortfall" in purchases at $375-500 million.[15] What the U.S. was treating as a firm obligation, the German Defense Ministry believed was a commitment, and the Finance Ministry conceived of merely as a goal.

Part of the confusion stemmed from the omission of a customary German reservation from the offset agreement concluded when

Erhard met Johnson in Texas, in December 1963. Offset agreements were informal: first oral, then Memoranda of Understanding agreed to by the two defense ministers. Before the Texas meeting, the Germans always had insisted on the inclusion of language stipulating that the actual amount of offset depended on German military planning, the country's financial situation, and domestic and foreign economic developments.[16] The omission of that reservation permitted the U.S. to consider the agreed amount as a firm commitment— McNamara apparently used the Memorandum of Understanding on von Hassel—while the Germans, especially the Finance Ministry, still could feel that the amount was an "expectation," not an obligation.

Bonn's problem was made worse by weaknesses in the agents of coordination at the center of the German government. The Budget Department of the Finance Ministry had a staff of several hundred and a role akin to that of the American Office of Management and Budget (OMB). But its coordinating was budgetary; in 1966 that meant paring down expenditures to match revenues through separate negotiations with various ministries. Conceiving of the foreign policy effects of budget decisions, let alone worrying about those effects, was not Finance's business.

The Chancellor's Office would have seemed the likely place for budgets and foreign policy to cross, the place where alarms would have sounded and strategies been conceived. In the event, however, it was not. In 1966 the Office more resembled the small secretariat it had been in the first decade of the Federal Republic than the large (400 people) operation it became by the early 1970s. Moreover, the Office was organized with divisions paralleling ministries. If the Foreign Office was not seized of the offset problem, it was unlikely that those who carried the foreign policy brief in the Chancellor's Office would be either, especially without some signal from the Chancellor. Even after it had become large, the Office remained much more a place where conflicts were brokered among interested ministries than a home for policy planning across ministries. Both the Grand Coalition and the SPD government tried to give the Office that latter function; the first attempt, in 1967, was halfhearted, while the second, a serious effort by the SPD in 1970, brought down a reaction from the ministries that destroyed the new mechanism.[17]

Various proposals for new forms of offset circulated in Bonn throughout 1966. But in the absence of a means of generating a coordinated, high-level review of offset in the light of the budget, these ideas never intruded on the offset "channel," were isolated ideas rather than government policies and never were pressed hard on the Americans. U.S. officials on the American offset "channel" could, and did almost ignore them. Erhard mentioned to Johnson switching some offset funds to joint space projects, in December 1965, and the same idea was proposed later by German Science Minister Stoltenberg, but little was heard again of the idea. Bonn had long wanted to count some nonmilitary purchases by government agencies under the offset agreements, as was the practice in the British accords. In 1966 there was a specific proposal for Lufthansa purchases of Boeing aircraft. That proposal, however, also disappeared quickly; by June von Hassel told the Bundestag only that he hoped the proposal might be accepted under the next agreement.[18]

Another Erhard attempt to escape his offset bind foundered on a combination of institutional separations in the German government and lack of advance planning. There was talk in Bonn at least as early as May of some form of Bundesbank assistance in meeting the offset commitment.[19] But the Bundesbank was and is formally separate from the central government and jealous of its independence. Bank President Karl Blessing was approached before Erhard's trip with a vague proposal something like what eventually emerged from the Trilaterals—Bundesbank purchases of nonconvertible U.S. Treasury securities in lieu of arms purchases. He was, however, reluctant on solid bankerly grounds. He argued that it was improper, perhaps illegal, for the Bank to hold its assets in a form as illiquid as nonconvertible securities, and that in any case he would be hard pressed to secure the necessary approval from the Central Bank Council, the Bundesbank's governing board.

The Chancellor's Approach. Offset was entrenched in the Defense Ministry channel, but there is no doubt that the Chancellor could have snatched it out. He might have set his government to work on a systematic review of the situation and remedies. His July 5th letter put offset at the top of the agenda for his meeting with President Johnson in September. Erhard knew that the issue and the outcome of the visit were important to him, and he said as much to the press shortly before he left for the U.S.[20] Yet he set no working groups to the study of alternatives, avoided all American attempts to begin a lower-level dialogue and was uninterested in proposals from his own ministries. He held the issue close to him. An issue which had resided in the middle of German officialdom passed straight to the top of the government, and disappeared.

The Chancellor arrived in Washington prepared only to make a vague appeal for relief from the existing German offset commitment. (He had been seen off at the airport in Germany by the youth choir of a moral rearmament group. Their musical choice, ironically, was a popular song whose refrain was "You can't have freedom for nothing.") What proposals the Germans made in Washington were worked out there by senior Defense and Finance ministry officials while their Chancellor was sightseeing the day before official activities began.[21]

Inside the German government all was drift and indecision in the summer and fall of 1966. Erhard had been talking of a sweeping Cabinet reform for months, but when the government reconvened after the August holiday the Chancellor did not act. Several of his senior aides urged him to postpone his trip to Washington until the Cabinet was rebuilt but Erhard refused.[22] Many legislative proposals which were crucial to his economic stabilization program were slow in reaching the Bundestag. CDU Bundestag leader Barzel talked publicly of Erhard's ouster and Bundestag President Gerstenmaier declared his willingness to become Chancellor, should his party call upon him. By the time of Erhard's visit to Washington, members of the German delegation were muttering openly to their American counterparts that the government was in desperate shape but not to worry, for it would be replaced soon. They no doubt got more than they bargained for with the formation of the Grand Coalition!

Bonn displayed only a vague understanding of the Washington politics of offset. Of that more will be said in chapter V. German officials held contradictory conceptions of events in Washington. So far as I can tell, the Chancellor's Office made no attempt to seek for information which might have resolved the contradiction. On the one hand, McNamara was viewed as firmly in command, holding the President at his mercy. The Defense Secretary was vilified in a series of German editorials through the summer, in which he was portrayed as an eager arms salesman, ready to put the health of the U.S. munitions industry above German-American relations.[23] On the other hand, there was a tendency, one also reflected in official statements, to separate McNamara from Rusk and to assume that eventually the latter would intervene with the President to rescue the situation, breaking the link between offset and troop level. In a press bulletin of June 15, for example, government spokesman von Hase interpreted a joint Rusk-McNamara press conference staged the previous week in Washington as evidence that the link was not official American policy. Defense Minister von Hassel, however, told the Bundestag in July that the American position was firm, that while there was no formal link, the link did exist "in the American administration, in the White House, in the Department of State, in the Pentagon and above all in the press."[24]

Offset advice served up by subordinates was dismissed by the Chancellor, or never reached him at all. Whatever Foreign Office analyses were performed seldom were pressed on the Chancellor. In the last months of the Erhard government, communication between the Palais Schaumburg and the Foreign Office was handled by Erhard's closest advisor and longtime friend, Ludger Westrick, the Cabinet-rank chief of the Chancellor's Office. But Westrick held information close to him, leaving subordinates charged with responsibility for defense and alliance matters to rely on personal contacts with the working levels of the Foreign Office to find out what was afoot.

If Foreign Office cables seldom moved downward from Westrick, still less often were they put before the Chancellor. Erhard was not a reader, instead preferring to be informed through oral briefings. In matters of foreign affairs, he often came to those briefings woefully lacking in background. By 1966 Erhard was sixty-nine and growing deaf.

Ludwig Erhard had been an adept Economics Minister. That record and the association he thus acquired with the remarkable postwar recovery of the West German economy made his career as a politician. It was ironic that just as economics made Erhard's political career in the 1950s, so also was economics his undoing as Chancellor in 1966. The German economic problems of the mid-1960s did not yield to Erhard's brand of liberal economic management that had been so successful a decade earlier; his inability to cope with those problems, more than any other factor, brought about Erhard's downfall in 1966. Yet he had always been out of his depth as Chancellor, both as a politician and as the governor of an official machine that had grown more cumbersome and fractious since the early days of Konrad Adenauer's tenure.

Moreover, the Economics Ministry backgrounds of the Chancellor and Westrick disadvantaged them in a specific way as they faced Washington in the summer of 1966: the officials at the top of the American government were as strange to them as vice versa. They

71

had at hand no easy, confidential means of probing Washington's intentions. They were dependent on formal, and potentially leaky, channels of communication.

By sometime in the first several weeks in September, officials in the Budget Department of the Finance Ministry came to fret about the visit and began to work on offset proposals with Defense Ministry colleagues. However, Dahlgrün, the Finance Minister, could not or would not press those proposals on Erhard and refused to request that the assistant secretary of the Budget Department be included in the official delegation to Washington. Defense Minister von Hassel, never a decisive Cabinet officer, was by September under attack himself and was in no position either to press for German compliance with the existing agreement or to engineer a new policy.

Given the lack of preparation anywhere in Bonn for offset discussions in Washington and the chaos around Erhard, there are indications that senior Germans did not realize themselves until the last minute just how serious was their budgetary plight. Still, Erhard's basic attitude to the visit was decided—and known to Washington—at least several weeks before he departed. He would ask for a stretch-out of the existing commitment coupled with a reduction in future offset (the two measures together obviously amounted to a reduction in the existing commitment). The appeal would be personal, politician to politician.

Westrick counseled against the approach. His argument was not based on any sophisticated analysis of the American government, although it turned out to be correct for Bonn's purposes. Rather it was yet another variation of the "McNamara-in-the-saddle" vision of deliberations in Washington: however friendly the President might be, there was no way around McNamara. Westrick was about to leave government and had not intended to accompany the official party to Washington. He changed his mind at the last minute, convinced by federal President Lübke that the Chancellor would need help in Washington.

The role of the Foreign Office, and of its minister, Gerhard Schröder, remains unclear. By what information is available the Foreign Office played a minimal role in offset deliberations, even in the weeks immediately preceding the visit to Washington. Its operating bureau which later handled offset—the Department for Foreign Economic Policy—was not a party to discussions of offset. In Bonn issues ran through channels that were deep and separate. Even in Washington amidst a summit conference, the ministry that sought to rescue the situation was Defense, not the Foreign Office. Cables from the German embassy in Washington, if helpful, probably did not reach the Chancellor. The German ambassador, Heinrich Knappstein, did request an appointment with Erhard to express his opposition to the Chancellor's intended course of action, on an argument which apparently mirrored Westrick's. But Knappstein was thought to be of little account by Washington officials, hardly the man to choose to carry signals to Erhard. Perhaps his warning was discounted similarly in Bonn.

For his part, Schröder argued against the suggestion of the trilaterals but seems not to have taken a firm position in the days immediately before the visit. Whether his passivity resulted from ignorance of events in Washington, deference to other Cabinet colleagues or design (Schröder long had coveted the Chancellorship), I do not know.

In any event, Erhard believed the offset issue was one which could be settled easily once he sat down with Johnson. The evidence is fragmentary but compelling: *Erhard placed tremendous faith in his personal relationship with the President* and assumed that the friendship was a kind of capital which could be spent to solve his political problem. Erhard and Johnson shared a liking for face-to-face dealings. They seem also to have shared a sincere mutual affection. (That was not true of Johnson's relations with other western heads of state, though all were recipients of his fabled charm.) Unlike the President, however, the Chancellor lacked the politician's sense of what lay behind the gestures of friendship. He apparently likened affection between leaders to common friendship, assuming it would translate directly into assistance in time of need. That was his error, a serious one, perhaps fatal.

Several Erhard remarks made in 1964 after a visit to the United States are suggestive of his feelings about Johnson and of the stock he put in their relationship: "He likes *(liebt)* me and I like him. . . When two men are so similarly structured, that is also a political factor."[25] For Erhard, the pilgrimage to Washington was not only a practical necessity but also, apparently, a source of sincere pleasure. He came to the United States six times between November 1963 and September 1966, while Adenauer had come only ten times in the decade between 1953 and 1963.

Erhard's desire to personalize his relations with foreign countries ran through his relations with other national leaders. When he met with de Gaulle in early 1965, he insisted that the two meet alone. He was ill-prepared for the encounter. The General lashed out at the MLF proposal, threatening a break in Franco-German cooperation if Bonn persisted in entertaining the MLF. Erhard, taken by surprise, apparently reversed course abruptly. It took a strange coalition of CDU ministers and SPD parliamentarians to quell the row which ensued.

By the time Erhard came to Washington he was a desperate man, fighting for his political life. Insofar as he was making calculations about Washington, he must have assumed that any attempt to solve the offset problem through Rusk in the time before the visit would eventually founder on McNamara's firmness. Any attempt to operate beneath the Defense Secretary also would fail. Initiating a low-level interchange was, moreover, not the way Erhard operated. Besides, it appeared futile and might have seemed dangerous to boot, for if discussions leaked, that would only have provided grist for the Chancellor's political opponents. Even the August change in American policy and the appointment of McCloy seemed not to offer Erhard a way out. He needed a resounding "victory," not a negotiated settlement, and he needed it soon. Summitry seemed the only possibility.

II. THE FALL OF THE ERHARD GOVERNMENT

On the face of it, the fall of Erhard was for the United States, if not a disaster, then at least a serious blow. Whatever its internal difficulties, the Erhard government was committed almost above all else to maintaining tight links to the United States and it had pledged to increase Germany's contribution to NATO. A senior American official was quoted in July 1966 as asserting that "we couldn't possibly get any better than Erhard, Schröder and von Hassel."[26] And the new German government began in the same mood as the old one ended, irritated at and slightly suspicious of the U.S.

How important to Erhard's demise was the courteous drubbing administered to him in Washington? In my judgment, the offset outcome was the proximate cause of Erhard's downfall, perhaps not the essential cause and surely not the only cause. It was an occasion, a final straw. Events in Bonn after September were so tangled, and so many purposes were at play in German politics, that Washington escaped complete blame for Erhard's end. But to say that Erhard likely would have fallen even had there been no offset dispute does not diminish the importance of the visit. It might have been many months before the next government crisis arose in the Federal

Republic. And in any event, German-American relations did not need to bear the burden of presumed American complicity in Erhard's downfall.

Judgments about whether Washington should have altered its actions in order to assist Erhard turn on American goals and on how predictable were the consequences of U.S. actions. (The issue of whether the United States government *could* have changed course, in August and September 1966, rapidly enough to suit Erhard's purposes is at the center of chapter VI.) Both goals and predictions were contested matters in Washington.

Assessing American actions is made harder because the way in which official Washington viewed a given eventuality changed over time. What Washingtonians feared in prospect, they often applauded after the fact. State Department officials and their colleagues in 1966 took it for granted that Bonn would be ruled by CDU governments. Those governments were familiar, if only relatively so, and predictable; their acquiescence in Washington's plans could be assumed. By contrast, the prospect of governments in which the SPD would participate, or even predominate, disrupted happy assumptions and threatened disharmony in the German-American alliance. A decade later, Washington's view no doubt is almost exactly the converse: SPD governments appear stable and cooperative in comparison to the prospect of governance by a CDU in which the right-wing is increasingly assertive.

Washington's worries about a grand coalition (or an SPD government) in 1966 were excessive. That became clear fairly quickly. The substance of Bonn's approach to Washington was little affected by the change of government. The Grand Coalition did not fulfill Erhard's pledge to increase Germany's military commitment to NATO, but Erhard himself would have been hard-pressed to make good on that promise. Although the conduct of German-American relations was made more difficult for Washington by Kiesinger's need to sound a bit "Gaullist," that need derived not from the participation of the SPD but rather from Strauss' reentry to the Cabinet and the influence that was conferred on the "Gaullist" right of the CDU/CSU.

Offset, Tax Increase and the Fall of Erhard

The chronology of Erhard's fall can be related quickly. While in Washington the Chancellor had agreed, reluctantly, to the idea of the trilaterals: converting the Anglo-German offset commission into a tripartite group with a mandate not only to study finance but also to undertake a sweeping review of NATO capabilities and strategy. Erhard returned to Bonn a dispirited man. He felt he had been, in Westrick's word, "deceived" by Washington. When he arrived the Chancellor was subjected to a barrage of criticism in the Bundestag. He was scored by the SPD for having reaffirmed commitments in Washington of which Bundestag members never had known details. And other SPD parliamentarians voiced the fear that the Trilateral experience would become an institutionalized NATO "directorate."[27]

Erhard pressed his stabilization program but could not maneuver the necessary budget economies through his Cabinet. He then turned to tax increases in an effort to finance an estimated budget deficit of one billion dollars.[28] It was Erhard's proposal to raise several consumer taxes that finally provoked his downfall. The Cabinet reached a compromise on October 26, but the four FPD ministers were compelled by their parliamentary party to repudiate that compromise the next day and leave the government. With the FPD departure, Erhard lost his majority in the Bundestag and was left at the head of a minority government.

The conjunction of offset failure in Washington and a tax increase was at the least disastrous symbolism: having failed to win offset relief from his American "friends," Erhard was forced to levy additional burdens on his own people. That relation obtained whether or not the tax increase actually might have been avoided had Erhard's offset desires been met by Washington. The sums of money involved seem trivial now but were not then. Moreover, the "shortfall" in German arms purchases under the existing agreement, $900 million, was suggestively close to the projected German budget deficit. After the Chancellor's visit to Washington, Bundesbank President Blessing apparently agreed to the Bank's portion of the package which had been worked out in Washington. But he conditioned his acquiescence on Erhard fulfilling his portion of the package. That required the Chancellor to draw an additional $250 million for offset from the federal budget.[29]

The Formation of the Grand Coalition

When the Free Democrats left the governing coalition, three future governments were possible: the CDU-CSU/FPD coalition might have been reestablished, quite likely with a new chancellor; a "mini-coalition" of the SPD and FPD might have been formed; or a grand coalition of the CDU-CSU and SPD might have been established. In retrospect it is simple to explain why the Grand Coalition in fact emerged; in prospect that eventuality might not have been so obvious.

The formation of a new CDU/FPD coalition was not, on the face of it, implausible. After all, the FPD had left and rejoined the government several times, most recently in 1962 during the *Spiegel* affair. In 1962, Franz-Josef Strauss, then Defense Minister, ordered government agents to search the offices of the popular magazine, *Der Spiegel,* and to arrest several magazine staffers, on flimsy charges. Strauss left office in the ensuing scandal, and after his departure the FPD ministers reassumed their portfolios. Two factors, however, distinguished 1966 from previous episodes. The FPD pullout appeared to be the result of commitment to change in government, not mere pique. Dissatisfaction with the pace of *Ostpolitik* may have been at the root of FPD unhappiness. The tax issue served as a convenient pretext; the fact that the FPD cabinet ministers initially agreed to a compromise on the tax issue is indicative of that.

Whatever slim chance there was of a new CDU/FPD government vanished when the Chancellor refused to resign immediately after his government collapsed. He was permitted that luxury by the provision of the German constitution which allows only so-called "constructive" votes of no confidence: the Chancellor's fate hinged not on whether his government commanded a Bundestag majority but rather on whether another coalition could elect its own chancellor. Erhard wanted to remain in the Palais Schaumburg, and the CDU at first saw little chance of an SPD/FPD coalition.

A "mini-coalition," however, was not entirely out of the question. FPD leader Erich Mendes had declared himself publicly in favor of the possibility, and the platforms the two parties drew up during negotiations looked quite similar.[30] There were good reasons for both parties to want to rule: the SPD was eager to eradicate finally its image as an "irresponsible" party not suited to governance; and the FPD had reason to fear that any grand coalition would change the electoral law, extinguishing third parties. On November 8, the SPD and the FPD did join together in a motion to request a confidence vote. The vote, while not binding on Erhard, was nonetheless a powerful symbol, one not lost on the CDU.

Yet the apparent similarity of the SPD and the FPD platforms was misleading, masking differences between the parties over economic policies. And the FPD itself was deeply divided. Sixteen of its 42 parliamentarians opposed joining forces with the SPD to request a confidence vote. In the end the mini-coalition was ruled out by the slimness of the majority it would have possessed (six votes). SPD leaders, eager as they may have been to be the principal coalition partner, were not willing to invest their first chance at power in such a dubious venture.

Once it was clear that FPD would not rejoin a CDU/CSU government, the grand coalition was the most likely possibility. The CDU feared its centrifugal tendencies—so obvious in the previous months of machinations—would be abetted by a period out of power, spelling disaster for the party. The SPD/FPD alliance in the confidence vote motion was alarm enough for CDU leaders to induce them to force Erhard out (with a promise, never heard of later, that he would be allowed some voice in the choice of a successor). The CDU executive committee named four men as chancellor candidates: Rainer Barzel, the CDU parliamentary leader who had been campaigning for Erhard's ouster; Eugen Gerstenmaier, the Bundestag President; Schröder; and Kurt-Georg Kiesinger, then minister-president (premier) of Baden-Wuerttemberg, who had been chairman of the Bundestag foreign affairs committee a decade earlier before abandoning Bonn for state politics. Kiesinger was elected after obtaining the support of the CSU, thereby ensuring that Strauss, the CSU party chief, would be a prominent member of any new government involving the CDU.[31]

The SPD was forced, somewhat reluctantly, to the realization that a coalition with the CDU offered it the best prospects. Party leader Herbert Wehner had broached the idea of a grand coalition as early as 1962. Yet there was considerable opposition to it within the party: some members objected to the idea in principle, while some wanted no part of a government including arch-enemy Strauss. About one-fourth of the SPD members of the Bundestag defected from the party line in the formal vote establishing the new government. The Christian Democrats made the coalition more palatable to the socialists by accepting the main planks of the SPD platform and by conceding the SPD nine of nineteen ministries.[32]

There could be no doubt that the new government would regard the U.S. differently than had the old, and that the difference would be reflected in offset dealings. Willy Brandt of the SPD replaced the "Atlanticist" Schröder at the Foreign Office. Kiesinger—a one-time member of the Nazi party and junior official in Ribbentrop's Foreign Office, his patrician good looks and manner belying his middle-class,

Swabian origins—owed his election to the chancellorship to the "Gaullists." Their leader, Strauss, returned to the Cabinet, taking the Finance portfolio. The new Chancellor separated his government from its predecessor, at least in tone, in his first policy speech. He stressed the importance of Germany's alliance with France:

> The European peace order desired by East and West is unthinkable without a close and trusting relationship between Germany and France. . . . Together with France . . . we regard a solid alliance between . . . the nations of Europe and the United States as indispensable. . . . We refuse to be talked into the false and dangerous alternative of choice.[33]

Implications for Offset Handling

The disastrous outcome of Erhard's visit to Washington accomplished what had not occurred before: offset was lifted from its Defense Ministry "track." At a long Cabinet meeting on October 12, Karl Carstens, the State Secretary[34] in the Foreign Office, was selected as German delegate to the Trilaterals. As a response to fears expressed in the Bundestag that the Trilaterals would become a "directorate," Carstens was dispatched to Paris before the first Trilateral meeting, October 20 in Bonn. Germany decided to press for the inclusion in the meetings of Manlio Brosio, the NATO Secretary General, as a representative of the smaller NATO members.

Offset had been a military procurement issue with budgetary overtones; after the Erhard visit it became an issue of high politics, with a budget face. The Foreign Office was given, and retained, negotiating responsibility. Within the Foreign Office the issue was delegated to the Department for Foreign Economic Policy, and the assistant secretary of that Department became the State Secretary's principal aide. The Finance Ministry role was enhanced; within the ministry, offset continued of course to be handled by the Budget Department. Bureaucratically, the Defense Ministry was the principal "loser." Offset continued to be handled as a procurement matter, but those decisions became only pieces of policy and not crucial pieces at that. In addition, military officers on the Inspector General's staff (the joint staff) participated in the working groups established during the Trilaterals.

The Erhard visit and subsequent change of government produced caution and delay in the German approach to the Trilaterals: caution first because the issue remained explosive during the closing days of the Erhard government, then caution and delay because lower-level German officials acted in the absence of official policy until the Kiesinger Cabinet had time to come to grips with the issue. German negotiator Carstens made it clear at the second Trilateral meeting, November 9–10, that the change of government in Bonn would delay the negotiations.

III. OFFSET AND THE GRAND COALITION

Bonn's offset actions after the formation of the Grand Coalition depended on the combined outcomes of political processes at two levels: high-level bargaining among members of the Coalition and the interactions of the bureaucracies those leaders sat atop. The Grand Coalition of course had a huge majority in the Bundestag; all disputes were "family" fights. The constraints were those imposed by coalition government. They were, in the case of the Grand Coalition, serious ones because the political bedfellows were so strange. Producing an acceptable outcome to the Trilaterals necessitated, on the German side, pulling big enough amounts for offset from the federal budget and including the Bundesbank to participate in the agreements. Neither was easy. Yet while the Kiesinger government confronted special difficulties in reaching offset decisions, the pattern of German decision-making in 1967 resembled Bonn's approach to the issues of offset and force level in later years.

Agency Positions

Various parts of German officialdom, like their Washington counterparts, viewed the issues from perspectives which changed little over time. The interaction of those conflicting views—their aggregation into official German policy—was less consistent, but only slightly so. This section provides a look at those various positions and at the relations among them, concentrating on the period of the Trilaterals but drawing comparisons to later episodes as well.

Foreign Office. The Foreign Office continued to hold official negotiating responsibility for offset under the Grand Coalition. State Secretary Georg Ferdinand Duckwitz replaced Carstens (who followed Schröder to the Defense Ministry) as German delegate to the Trilaterals. The Foreign Office continuity was a product partly of logic, partly of politics. Schröder, who had been forced to relinquish the Foreign Office portfolio to Brandt of the SPD, apparently felt that if the socialists got the ministerial plum they should also take the political pit, offset.

The Foreign Office acted as the convener, the solicitor of other agency positions and, to an extent, the mediator of those views. It took no firm view on the merits of various forms of offset, rather its independent stakes went to preserving good relations with German allies and insuring that actions taken in offset deliberations were consonant with general German foreign policy. That made the Foreign Office quick, in 1967 and later, to applaud any German offer agreed upon by the other ministries, especially Finance and Defense, and acceptable to the Americans, so long as the offer did no brutality to other important foreign policy considerations of the Federal Republic.

Retaining a large number of American troops in Europe was a basic tenet of the Federal Republic's foreign policy long before 1967, and it remained so after the SPD/FPD government replaced the Grand Coalition in 1969. The troops were, for Erhard, visible sign of the alliance which was an article of faith; they were no less important to Willy Brandt. For him, they stood as a symbol of Germany's "anchor" in western alliance as Bonn began in earnest the delicate process of seeking better relations with its eastern neighbors. Bonn's agreement in 1971 to increase offset, despite dissent within the government, suggested that the Federal Republic was willing to pay a high price to cement that "anchor" at a time when *Ostpolitik* was arousing some controversy.[35] So long as offset was perceived as one means of undercutting criticism directed at the size of the United States force in Europe by members of the American Congress, no Foreign Office official was moved to question the necessity of providing offset in some form.

Twice, in 1971 and 1974, offset deliberations in Bonn were pulled from the control of the Foreign Office. Each instance provoked initial dismay in the agency, but each ended in acceptable outcomes. While Foreign Office professionals might mutter about the breaches of form, they were forced to acknowledge the results. Both times the interventions were those of Helmut Schmidt. In 1971, as Defense Minister, he played on his expertise in defense matters, his strong position in the Cabinet and his close relations with Chancellor Willy Brandt to obtain charter for an attempt to break the German-American deadlock. That he did, in discussions with his American counterpart, Defense Secretary Melvin Laird. In the last months of the Brandt government, in 1974, he intervened again, this time while

81

holding the Finance portfolio. Again he worked out a solution in private meetings with his American opposite number, in this instance Treasury Secretary George Schultz.

Finance Ministry. The Finance Ministry's primary interest in offset continued to be budgetary, and its Budget Department remained the Ministry's operating agent. It behaved like good finance ministries everywhere, as the guardian of fiscal responsibility, all the more so in a Germany where inflation was anathema. It opposed spending money on offset, especially increasing other ministry budgets in order to meet offset commitments.

Shortly after the Grand Coalition assumed power, the Cabinet decided on a program of budget-cutting measures (*Sparmassnahmen*), and it was clear that the defense budget would have to take its reductions with the rest. Strauss and Schröder, party rivals and old foes in disputes between "Gaullists" and "Atlanticists," clashed over that and tangled again later in the spring of 1967 over military procurement in Britain. The latter dispute followed a pattern which became customary in Bonn: if Defense were to be called upon to fulfill part of the offset agreement through procurement in Britain, then Schröder wanted the defense budget increased by the amount of that procurement. By contrast, Strauss insisted that purchases be made from the existing defense appropriation.[36] Strauss won that round, and the Finance Ministry generally prevailed in such disputes. Additional money was appropriated to fulfill offset commitments in only two cases: to provide interest subsidies on loans to the U.S. Treasury, in the 1969 and later agreements[37]; and to finance the barracks rehabilitation program, in 1971 and 1974.

The Finance Ministry hierarchy of preferences among forms of offset derived directly from its preoccupation with the budget. Loans made by the Bundesbank, or any other scheme involving only the management of German foreign exchange reserves, clearly were the most painless way to meet an offset commitment. Procurement in the U.S., either of civilian or military goods, ranked second, provided purchases were made from ministry funds which previously had been budgeted. When Washington began to demand submarket interest rates (on securities purchased either by the Bundesbank or by the federal government), the Finance Ministry first opposed the arrangement—interest subsidies cost budget money—but later shifted position. The subsidies provided "leverage": Germany could provide much offset "coverage" to the American balance of payments with fairly modest budgetary expenditures on its part.

Providing direct payments in support of American forces was, of course, a distant last among Finance Ministry preferences. What other Germans opposed for moral or political reasons, Finance opposed for *its* reason: direct support cost money. When direct assistance was finally offered, reluctantly, in 1971, the amount was small. Finance apparently insisted that since direct support saved the United States both budget and foreign exchange, it should count in offset agreements more heavily than other forms, either by multiplying the dollar amount Germany was prepared to offer by two or three or by reducing the total offset to less than 80% of the gross American foreign exchange expenditures.[38] Later in 1971, when the direct support offer was in effect captured by the Defense Ministry for the barracks program, there is some evidence that Finance joined the American Treasury in opposing the deal. As long as budget money was to be spent, Finance may have preferred spending it in a way which gave direct, immediate assistance to the American balance of payments—for example, by paying salaries of German civilians working at American bases. On the other hand, agreeing to pay salaries or other support costs would have committed the Ministry to underwriting costs which could only go up and would have involved it in the uncomfortable process of auditing U.S. expenditures.

The Economics Ministry played a minor role in offset deliberations. Before 1969, the monetary division was part of the Ministry, and its representatives took part in negotiations with the Bundesbank. A year after the SPD/FPD government took power, Finance and Economics were fused (with SPD finance expert Karl Schiller as Minister), and when the two were separated again, the monetary division stayed at Finance. Economics, however, retained at least a formal part in offset discussions. Its representatives were included because its minister sat on the Security Council, the Cabinet committee which dealt with offset. In later negotiations, Economics officials lobbied for the inclusion of civilian procurement in offset accords.

Defense Ministry. Formal responsibility for offset within the Ministry continued, until 1970, to reside in the Procurement Department. The Department's approach to offset remained ambiguous. On one hand, it was responsive to the necessity of providing offset. U.S. weapons often were the technically most advanced available, hence attractive to the military commanders the Department served. On the other hand, purchasing in the United States inhibited the growth of domestic arms production capability and competed with European cooperation in procurement. In 1967, Bonn's determination to curtail

83

procurement in the United States was stiffened by domestic arms producers.[39] Later on, in the late 1960s and early 1970s, when the Federal Republic placed large orders for American F-4 Phantom fighters, it insisted that the deals include sizeable subcontracts for German firms. At the time of the 1971 offset negotiations and later, Bonn officials expressed the worry that large F-4 purchases coupled with shrinking procurement budgets would mean fewer orders for the MRCA, the fighter plane developed jointly by the Federal Republic, Britain and Italy.[40]

Senior Defense officials, like their Foreign Office colleagues, were attentive to offset because of the need to stem American troop cuts. Schröder, for example, was considerably more enthusiastic about offset as Defense Minister in 1967 than were his fellow Cabinet members.[41] To the men who governed in Bonn, American troops were more valuable than German ones on two counts. First, to Germans who were understandably appalled by the prospect of a conventional war fought on German soil, *deterrence* was what mattered above all else. And deterrence, to officials in Bonn, meant *nuclear* deterrence, provided by the United States. The troop presence was—and continued to be—perceived as the link to that deterrent, as the earnest of the American commitment to the nuclear defense of the Federal Republic. The more troops, the more sure and credible was the American nuclear response. For that purpose, American troops in the U.S. which could be rapidly returned to Europe would not serve. Only troops in place on German soil would.

Second, even for the purposes of conventional defense, German soldiers could not easily replace Americans who departed. Increasing the size of the Bundeswehr was difficult economically and, moreover, provoked opposition from the German political left. And it raised the specter in Europe of a NATO in which Germany would be predominant.

When Helmut Schmidt took the Defense portfolio in 1969, he created a Planning Office, responsible directly to the minister and state secretaries, as a source of strategic and politico-military advice. The Planning Office was given Ministry responsibility for offset. It reflected Schmidt's view that any *budget* money spent on offset should purchase an increase in *defense* capability. That perspective made it an advocate of the barracks program, both in 1971 and in 1974, after Schmidt had moved to Finance. Rather than merely replacing American expenditures, the program offered promise of improving the morale of American troops and upgraded facilities which German soldiers might one day use.

Bundesbank. The German Bundesbank was crucial to the 1967 negotiations but less important as a direct participant afterward. Yet the outcome of the 1967 negotiations meant that offset was much less a matter of defense budgets and procurement for the Federal Republic and much more a piece of general balance-of-payments dealing between Bonn and Washington. Offset was affected by, and in turn influenced, Bonn's decisions in the realm of monetary policy— interest rates, the value of the *Deutschemark,* the form of Bundesbank holdings of foreign reserves; many officials other than the chancellor had a claim to participate in those decisions or could take actions which shaped them—Bundesbank officers and Cabinet ministers with economic briefs. For instance, Bonn often made the argument that it was being asked to "pay" twice, first through general currency policy and then through offset: when the Federal Republic revalued the *Deutschemark,* usually after pressure from its allies (or when the United States devalued the dollar), that provided general assistance to the American balance of payments by making German exports to the U.S. more expensive and American exports to Germany cheaper; but it also increased the dollar cost of maintaining American troops in Germany, with the Federal Republic then asked to offset that higher cost the next time around.

Relations between the federal government in Bonn and the Bundesbank in Frankfurt were nearly those of sovereign powers, especially in 1966 and 1967. Foreign Office and Finance Ministry officials made many missions to Frankfurt in search of assistance from the Bank, and Bank President Blessing was invited to several Cabinet meetings in the spring of 1967. The Bundesbank's position during the Trilaterals remained much the same as it had been during the Erhard period, consistent with good central bank practice. It sought to preserve maximum flexibility in the management of German foreign reserves. That made it reluctant to become involved in offset at all, and slow to agree to the purchase of Treasury securities or to respond to the American suggestion of a gold pledge. In 1967 the Bundesbank apparently rejected a British suggestion that it buy twenty-five-year sterling bonds because the bonds were too long-term a commitment, hence too inflexible.[42]

To the Bundesbank, moreover, buying securities—American or British—was unattractive on precisely the grounds that made it attractive to the federal government: it replaced what otherwise would have been budgetary expenditures and thus smacked of financing a federal budget deficit, from which the Bundesbank was prohibited. The gold pledge was less of a problem, since the Bank had little intention of making direct claims on the American gold stock in any case. Still, admitting publicly to having circumscribed its options was uncomfortable.

The nature of dealings between the federal government and the Bundesbank was reflected in details of the Trilateral outcome. To Foreign Office negotiators, the gold pledge was of little account, since from their point of view it appeared to make little difference in German behavior. They left the Bundesbank to work it out with the Americans. The Bank promise was worded cautiously, reflecting professional conservatism and some ambiguity in existing Bank practice. While the Bundesbank had not purchased gold directly from the U.S., it had acquired some American gold indirectly, through the IMF or other international sources. Blessing's letter containing the pledge said that the United States could be "assured also in the future the Bundesbank intends to continue its practice of not converting dollars for gold."[43]

With respect to the securities purchase, the German Foreign Office and the American State Department cared mostly about the total amount, and let their Finance and Treasury colleagues specify the exact terms. That nuance also made a difference. While the securities were essentially nonconvertible, they were not completely so and could be redeemed "in the event of a sustained decrease in the reserves of the Bundesbank" which carried the total below a specified level. Redemption did occur in 1969 following the revaluation of the German mark, to the consternation of several U.S. senators following the issue.[44]

Two other parts of the governmental establishment in Bonn lay astride the Federal Republic's policy-making with respect to offset and force level:

Security Council. Most offset decisions were taken not by the whole Cabinet but by a committee, the Security Council, chaired by the Chancellor and composed of the Foreign Minister and the Ministers of Defense, Finance and Economics. Like the other Cabinet committee chaired by the chancellor, the Security Council functioned as a high-level coordinating committee, an "inner" Cabinet where sensitive political issues could be discussed without by-standers and away from the parochial interests of department heads.[45] With regard to offset, the Council somewhat enhanced the influence of the Economics Minister, but chiefly it served to narrow the arena in which final decisions were taken. Decision-making could be restricted to ministers with direct interest, not delayed by debate among ill-informed members of the full Cabinet. In 1969, for example, senior civil servants negotiating for the Federal Republic cleared an offset package with their respective ministers by telephone from Washington.

In 1967 and later, the Security Council had little staff or institutional force of its own, by contrast to the creature with the same name on the other side of the Atlantic, particularly in the first years of the Nixon Administration. In the early 1960s, Heinrich Krone, a senior civil servant with close ties to Adenauer, attempted to build up the Council staff as a counterweight to the power of the "Atlanticist" Schröder. However, that effort ended with Krone's departure from government in mid-1966.

German negotiators customarily operated under tight instructions. They were given only small margins with which to sweeten a German offer; once that margin was exhausted, the issue returned to Cabinet or to the Security Council. In 1971, for example, the German negotiator ran to the end of his margin in discussing the offer of direct support, and the matter returned to Cabinet at least once. Or in 1967, the Germans pressed, on Cabinet instruction, for the inclusion of civilian procurement under the offset agreement. When the Americans held firm, negotiator Duckwitz returned to Cabinet for further guidelines.

Chancellor's Office. The Chancellor's Office is the chancellor's mechanism for policing the ministries, for attempting to insure that implementation is faithful to Cabinet intent. As in other European capitals, the Office has expanded faster than the central government as a whole, reflecting a desire to make the state bureaucracy more responsive to the desires of the government's center. Since 1967, chancellors have also used the Office as a place from which to conduct particular foreign policies when the issue—relations with Eastern Europe, for instance—is regarded as sensitive and when, perhaps, prevailing attitudes of Foreign Office civil servants would make their execution of a new policy suspect.

During offset deliberations in Bonn, the Chancellor's Office carried his personal brief, assuring that discussions reflected his perspective. For example, while various ministries objected to making direct payments to the Americans because doing so was improper or cost money, the Chancellor's Office during the Brandt government worried about the reaction of the left wing of the Chancellor's party, the SPD. The perspective of senior aides inside Palais Schaumburg was much like that of the Foreign Office: offset deliberations in Bonn and negotiations with the Americans ought to be as frictionless as possible. To that the men around the Chancellor added a corollary: German deliberations over offset should be kept from public view to the extent possible.

Willy Brandt conducted his *Ostpolitik* almost exclusively from his own office, leaning on the advice of Egon Bahr. In the first months of his government, Chancellor Helmut Schmidt displayed an eagerness to be his own foreign minister for a wide range of issues, no doubt for reasons of his own experience and because of the greenness of the man who formally held the Foreign Office portfolio (and who was, following the custom of the Socialist-led coalitions, the leader of the junior coalition partner, the FPD). In both cases, Foreign Office professionals disapproved of the loss of power and of the untidiness of the process but probably, on balance, approved of the results.

Yet in his tenure as Chancellor, Brandt evidenced no desire to pull offset deliberations close to him, quite the contrary. In part, adequate machinery for handling the issue had grown up over the years, both in Bonn and between the two allies. More important, however, was the lesson Brandt apparently drew from Erhard's downfall: there was no political profit in offset and much danger, so that it was better to avoid too close a personal identification with *that* potential land mine.

Context of German Decision-Making during the Trilaterals

Against the foregoing paragraphs of background, this section and the next sketch what transpired in Bonn in the spring of 1967, in the months leading to the conclusion of the Trilateral Negotiations. Like the context of German deliberations during the Erhard government, the context of offset decision-making during the Grand Coalition government affected both the pattern of internal discussion and Bonn's approach to the Americans. Two elements were predominant:

Defense Budget. Internal debate over the size of the 1968 defense budget paralleled that with respect to offset. When the Grand Coalition began its effort to balance the budget, the defense budget was an obvious target for reduction. But Schröder opposed any cuts, and the ensuing fight over both the size and form of reduction pitted him against first Strauss and then Kiesinger. The dispute continued throughout the spring as offset deliberations proceeded. Schröder ultimately lost, when Kiesinger and Strauss carried the Cabinet with them. In July, it was decided to reduce the budget from 19.4 billion *DM* in 1967 to 18.5 billion in 1968. (By contrast, the Erhard government had projected a rise to more than 20 billion for 1968.) The cut was disguised by taking a billion *DM* of funds appropriated in 1966 and 1967 which remained unspent in U.S. Treasury accounts and adding that billion to later budgets. Thus, "money available for military expenditures" could be shown, for allied consumption, to go in the proper direction—up.[46]

Schröder took his opposition outside Cabinet. He countered the decision by sending a telegram to the German ambassador in Washington instructing him to warn the Americans that the Bundeswehr would be thinned by 60,000 men (to 400,000). Schröder's move was more political than military. There was, to be sure, a serious debate over military strategy. Schröder preferred to reduce the size of the army and keep procurement up, while Kiesinger and others in the government regarded it as necessary for alliance purposes to maintain the size of the Bundeswehr, even at cost to procurement budgets.[47] Schröder may have hoped that a vigorous reaction to the manpower reduction by Germany's allies would compel the Cabinet to rescind the budget cut. The Schröder ploy had its intended effect. Washington, taken by surprise, responded forcefully. The State Department rebuked the Germans, and Ambassador McGhee returned to Washington from Bonn to confer with President Johnson. The Administration had just exerted itself to avoid big reductions in American forces, yet now the Germans cavalierly were cutting theirs. McNamara told reporters, as late as May 26: "There is no major reduction in military strength by any major NATO countries that I know of."[48] Offset seemed likely to come unstuck, as Mansfield renewed action in the Senate.

Yet Schröder's move seemed intended principally to embarrass Kiesinger. The former had counted on succeeding Erhard in the chancellorship, and relations between Schröder and Kiesinger were not cordial throughout the Grand Coalition. The dispute between the two came to involve the constitutional question of who controlled the armed forces. Kiesinger was furious at the Schröder ploy and moved quickly to neutralize it. He wrote to Johnson and announced on television that the Cabinet was "by no means decided" to pare the armed forces by 60,000. When the Chancellor visited Washington in

August he promised Johnson that any reductions made in the first round would not exceed 19,000.[49] Schröder was deterred from threatening to resign only, so far as I can tell, by the probability that his offer would be accepted.

Non-Proliferation Treaty (NPT).

As Soviet-American NPT negotiations began in earnest after the Rusk-Gromyko meeting in October 1966, it became increasingly clear that the final form of the treaty would ruffle some political feathers in Bonn. It seemed unlikely that the treaty would include specific language permitting a future NATO nuclear force with German participation, still more unlikely that it would sanction a force in which the U.S. eventually might not possess a veto over firing— the so-called "European option."[50] The issue was extremely touchy for Kiesinger. It split the Cabinet: Brandt and the socialists were inclined to look for ways the Federal Republic could support the NPT, while CDU and CSU "Gaullists" opposed the accord. With fellow Cabinet members at such loggerheads, Kiesinger kept the issue away from the Cabinet throughout the life of the Grand Coalition government.

Bonn's anxiety no doubt stemmed as much from a general feeling that the U.S. had reversed its priorities, conceding *détente* more importance than the European alliance, as from the specifics of NPT. The President's speech in October 1966 seemed to suggest such a reversal. It edged toward the view, one adopted as the rationale for *Ostpolitik* by Brandt three years later, that progress toward resolving the problem of a divided Germany would be a *product* of thaw in East-West relations.[51] By contrast, in 1966 Bonn still clung to the previous western view that progress on the German question was a *prerequisite* for lessening East-West tension.

German anxieties took concrete form in unhappiness with the state of German-American consultation. NPT was an occasion for the expression of that unhappiness. Kiesinger called Ambassador McGhee in several times during early 1967 to complain that the U.S. was not providing enough information about the negotiations with the Soviet Union. The Ambassador became something of a *persona non grata* in Bonn. Consultation was the main item on the agenda when Johnson met Kiesinger after Adenauer's funeral, in late April 1967. In all, the dispute affected the Trilaterals more in rhetoric than in substance, providing Kiesinger an opportunity to play to his

"Gaullist" sponsors. Nevertheless, it did cloud the atmosphere of the talks.

Another subject of the meeting between Johnson and Kiesinger was the size of the American redeployment of aircraft which was to accompany the troop reduction. That issue was related to, and made more difficult by, the flap over consultation. Bonn claimed it learned of the American plan to withdraw six fighter-bomber squadrons (about 144 planes) only in mid-April, several weeks before Johnson's trip to Germany. Moreover, the planes were capable of delivering nuclear weapons, and German edginess over any move which might imply a debasement of the nuclear guarantee lent special force to the issue. Kiesinger interceded with Johnson and secured a reduction in the redeployment to four squadrons (about 96 planes.)[52]

German Decisions

Bonn's key decisions en route to the Trilateral agreement can be summarized briefly. They will be played against simultaneous deliberations in Washington in chapter V. There was, of course, considerable delay in Bonn while the new ministers acquainted themselves with their ministerial machines and with each other. The first important offset decisions were not taken by the Cabinet until January 26. That session ratified what had been implicit since August, clear since the fall of Erhard: new offsets would be smaller than old and could not be composed entirely of military purchases.[53]

Once that determination was clear, and accepted by the U.S., the obvious solution was Bundesbank participation. But it was not easy to secure. The Bank resisted in February and agreed in March only after considerable arm-twisting by the government in Bonn and after the Bank's minimum desires were met through the escape clause. Washington's March 3 proposal, making public the U.S. willingness to accept financial measures in lieu of procurement, increased the pressure on the Bundesbank. Bundesbank officials could not, however, be induced to purchase British securities on terms acceptable to London.

That unwillingness meant that any offer to the British would have to come from the budget, provoking a snarly dispute in Cabinet. Strauss, acting the good finance minister, opposed any military purchases in the U.S. while the Federal Republic retained such large unspent balances there. Acting the good "Gaullist," he opposed purchases in Britain while the British continued to form common front with the Americans. The offer Dahlgrün had made to the British the previous summer apparently was withdrawn, and Strauss released a statement in mid-February announcing that there could be no offset for the British, to the consternation of Her Majesty's government.

A Cabinet meeting without civil servants was held February 22 in an effort to patch up the government. Government spokesman von Hase announced afterward that the Federal Republic would do what it could for the British, and that even without any agreement Germany would make 250 million *DM* of civilian purchases in Britain. Strauss himself retreated and issued a statement which said, "he had at no time expressed himself on the so-called Petersburg [Dahlgrün] offer."[54] Strauss apparently either did not think the British were serious about cutting the BAOR or did not think it important if they did. By contrast, Kiesinger and Brandt understood what the Erhard government had been so slow to comprehend: they worried about the effect on Washington of a British pullback. Kiesinger said that if the British withdrew in force, "President Johnson without doubt would not be able to resist the [Congressional] pressures to which he would be subject in view of the analogous retreat."[55]

Little by little the German offer grew. As late as mid-March, however, there was still disagreement between Strauss and Schröder about whether additional funds would be appropriated for military procurement in Britain. Predictably, Schröder lost and, just as predictably, did find about 100 million *DM* worth of military purchases to be made in Britain without additional appropriations. Eventually an offer of 550 million *DM* ($137.5 million) was pieced together for the British.[56] Yet the difficulty the German Cabinet had in coming to agreement on that offer prolonged the Trilaterals.

NOTES TO CHAPTER III

[1]Good studies of the processes and politics of policy-making in Bonn are starting to become available in English. For an excellent recent work, see Renate Mayntz and Fritz W. Scharpf, *Policy-Making in the German Federal Bureaucracy* (Amsterdam: Elsevier, 1975). *See* also Ralf Dahrendorf, *Society and Democracy in Germany* (Garden City: Doubleday and Co., Inc., 1967); Guido Goldman, *The German Political System* (New York: Random House, 1974); Geoffrey K. Roberts, *West German Politics* (London: The Macmillan Press, Ltd., 1972); and Karl Carstens, *Politische Führung* (Stuttgart: Deutsche Verlags-Anstalt, 1971).

[2]Roger Morgan, *The United States and West Germany, 1945–1973: A Study in Alliance Politics* (London: Oxford University Press, 1974), p. 102.

3. His study provides valuable background on more general relations between Washington and Bonn. For a summary version, *see* his "Washington and Bonn: A Case Study in Alliance Politics,"*International Affairs*, XLVII, 3 (July 1971), 489–502. (Subsequent references to Morgan are to the book, not the article.)

[3]Mayntz and Scharpf, p.171.

[4]GNP figures are expressed in constant prices. Statistisches Bundesamt, *Statistisches Jahrbuch für die Bundesrepublik Deutschland,* 1970 (Frankfurt am Main, 1970), p. 490. Unemployment rose from .7 per cent in 1965 to 2.1 per cent in 1967 (high by German standards and statistics). Deutsche Bundesbank, *Monatsberichte der Deutschen Bundesbank,* October 1971, p.63.

[5]For further discussion of these events, *see* Wolfram F. Hanrider, *The Stable Crisis: Two Decades of German Foreign Policy* (New York: Harper and Row, 1970),pp.168–72. The idea of a grand coalition was suggested both by President Lübke and by Adenauer.*New York Times,* December 28, 1965, and *Die Welt,* January 3, 1966.

[6]Some commentators have argued that the loss made Erhard's downfall certain. *See,* for example, Fritz René Allemann, "The Changing Scene in Germany," *The World Today,* XXII, 2 (February 1967), p.54.

[7]Morgan, p. 67.

[8]Franz–Josef Strauss, "An Alliance of Continents," *International Affairs* (London), XLI, 2 (April 1965), pp.191–203. To an extent, the "Gaullists" and the "Atlanticists" fought battles which had been abandoned by their putative sponsors. For example, the MLF was an issue in Germany after it had been scrapped by the Americans, and the U.S. was no less eager than France to improve relations with the Soviet Union. *See* Allemann, "The Changing Scene," p.54. On the MLF debate in Germany, *see* also Uwe Nerlich's chapter in Robert M. Lawrence and Joel Larus, eds. *Nuclear Proliferation: Phase II* (Lawrence, Kansas: University of Kansas Press, 1974).

[9]Quoted in *Le Monde,* May 21, 1966.

[10]*Le Monde,* May 17, 1966. *See* also *Neue Zürcher Zeitung,* May 15; *Die Welt,* May 16; *Washington Post,* May 18, 1966; and the *New York Times,* June 28 and July 22, 1966.

[11]Mentioned in *Die Welt,* May 23, and the *New York Times,* May 26, 1966.

[12]*New York Times,* October 13, December 10 and 22, 1966. For the texts of the letters, *see Le Monde,* December 23, 1966.

[13]*See,* for example, the comments by Defense Minister von Hassel, Federal Republic of Germany, *Deutscher Bundestag* (proceedings), 5th Period, 54th Sess.(July 1, 1966), p.2612. [Hereafter cited as *Bundestag Proceedings.*]

[14]Johnson's letter is mentioned in *Süddeutsche Zeitung,* September 5, 1966.

[15]Von Hassel did so in Washington in the latter part of June. *See* the *New York Times,* June 22, 1966. He repeated the promise to McNamara a month later in Paris. For von Hase's comment, *see* Federal Republic of Germany, Press and Information Office, *Bulletin,* June 15, 1966. [Hereafter cited as *German Press Bulletin.*] The Finance Ministry calculation appears in Federal Republic of Germany, Press and Information Office, *Aktuelle Beiträge,* June 4, 1966 (prepared by the Finance Ministry).

[16]*See* Elke Thiel, "Hinweise zur Beurteilung der Wirtschaftlichen Voraus-

setzungen für Offset-Vereinbarungen," (monograph, Stiftung Wissenschaft und Politik, May 15, 1967), p.13; and Allemann, "The Changing Scene in Germany," p.55.

[17]Mayntz and Scharpf, p. 117.

[18]For a discussion of the space proposals, *see Die Welt,* June 11 and 14, 1966. Von Hassel's remarks on the Boeing purchase appear in *Bundestag Proceedings,* 5th Period, 53rd Sess.(June 30, 1966), p.2556.

[19]For an early reference to Bundesbank assistance, *see Die Welt,* May 17, 1966; for general references to the loan proposal, *see* Hanreider, *The Stable Crisis,* p.24, and the *New York Times,* September 27 and 28, 1966.

[20]Reported by the *New York Times,* September 18, 1966.

[21]For a general discussion of the German proposal, *see* Elke Thiel, "Hinweise zur Beurteilung der wirtschaftlichen Voraussetzungen," (monograph, Stiftung Wissenschaft und Politik, 1967), p.4.

[22]Allemann, "The Changing Scene in Germany," p.55, and the *New York Times,* June 22, 1966.

[23]*See,* for example, the editorial by Heinz Barth in *Die Welt,* June 14, 1966. Adenauer referred to McNamara as a "very harsh man." *New York Times,* June 22, 1966.

[24]*Bundestag Proceedings* 5th Period, 54th Sess.(July 1, 1966), p.2613. Also reported in the *Süddeutsche Zeitung,* July 3, 1966.

[25]*Der Spiegel,* May 1, 1967.

[26]Quoted by Anatole Schub in the *Washington Post,* July 13, 1966.

[27]*See,* for example, the comments of Helmut Schmidt and Herbert Wehner of the SPD in *Bundestag Proceedings,* 5th Period, 60th Sess.(October 5, 1966), pp.2954–5, 2969.

[28]Alleman, "The Changing Scene in Germany," p.55, and the *New York Times* and *Süddeutsche Zeitung,* October 16, 1966. The events surrounding Erhard's downfall were well covered in the press on both sides of the Atlantic.

[29]The German "shortfall" is reported in the *New York Times,* September 30, 1966 and *Bundestag Proceedings,* 5th Period, 60th Sess.(October 5, 1966), p.2983. For mention of Blessing's role, *see ibid.,* pp.2969,2983. *See* also the coverage of Erhard's report to the Bundestag on his Washington visit. *New York Times* and *Süddeutsche Zeitung,* October 6, 1966.

[30] For the Mendes statement, *see Süddeutsche Zeitung,* October 26, 1966. Discussion of the platform is contained in D.C. Watt, "Manoeverings in Bonn," *The World Today,* XXII, 12 (December 1966), p.508. For the SPD platform, *see* SPD, *Mitteilung für die Presse,* November 12, 1966.

[31]For discussion of maneuverings within the CDU, *see* Allemann, p.56. The vote, on the third ballot, was Kiesinger 137, Schröder 81, and Barzel 26. Gerstenmaier had withdrawn when the CSU decided to support Kiesinger.

[32]For further discussion, *see* the *New York Times,* December 2, 1966, and Allemann, pp.57–58.

[33]Speech to the Bundestag, December 13, 1966, quoted in David Calleo, *The Atlantic Fantasy: The U.S., NATO and Europe* (Baltimore: Johns Hopkins Press, 1970), p.135.

[34]State Secretaries are more or less equivalent to British Permanent Secretaries, although they are more "political" than their British counterparts. State Secretaries rank with American Under Secretaries (now Deputy Secre-

taries). At present, both State Secretaries and their immediate subordinates are formally "political" appointees and thus serve at the pleasure of the government in power. Many of the occupants of these positions continue to be civil servants who have worked their way through the ranks, but more and more are lateral entrants from business, academia or the parties.

[35]Morgan, p.204.

[36]The dispute is discussed in general terms in *Süddeutsche Zeitung*, March 16, 1967.

[37]Actually there was an explicit interest subsidy only once, in 1971. At other times the budgetary cost of the subsidy was indirect. By law, the Bundesbank cannot make a profit and periodically returns any revenue to the central government. Thus, agreement by the Bank to accept a submarket interest rate represented a willingness by the central government to forego income.

[38]The Finance argument is mentioned in the *London Times*, June 29, 1971.

[39]Morgan, p.172.

[40]For discussion of the effects of F-4 purchases on the German arms industry and on MRCA development, *see* the article by David Binder in the *New York Times*, October 25, 1968; and the article in *Handelsblatt*, July 1, 1971.

[41]His position is discussed in *Neue Zürcher Zeitung*, February 4, 1967.

[42]Reported in the *New York Times*, March 23, 1967.

[43]Letter from Bundesbank President Karl Blessing to William McC. Martin, Chairman of the Board of Governors of the Federal Reserve System, printed in German Bundesbank, *Auszüge aus Presseartikeln*, May 12, 1967. It is interesting that Blessing came to regret having made the promise, believing that it only encouraged the U.S. to continue running deficits and thereby delayed reform of the international monetary system. *See* the interview with Blessing in *Der Spiegel*, May 3, 1971.

[44]The escape clause was made public in Bundesbank, *Monthly Report*, August 1967, cited in Horst Mendershausen, *Troop Stationing in Germany; Value and Cost*, RM-5881-PR, (Santa Monica: The Rand Corporation, 1968), p.120. For discussion of the redemption flap, *see* the *New York Times*, January 21, 1970, and John Newhouse, and others, *U.S. Troops in Europe: Issues, Costs and Choices* (Washington: The Brookings Institution, 1971), p.131.

[45]Mayntz and Scharpf, p.42.

[46]Horst Mendershausen, "Defense Policies and Developments in the Federal Republic of Germany," The Rand Corporation, P-3792, February 1968, pp.6–7.

[47]Naturally the cable and Schröder's plans leaked. *See* the *New York Times*, July 14 and 15, 1967. The doctrine officially adopted was termed "graduated presence" (*abgestufte Präsenz*). Some divisions were to be allowed to become cadres, with reservists rotating through them. For a full description of the doctrine, *see* Federal Republic of Germany, Defense Ministry, *Regierungserklärung für die Verteidigungsdebatte des Deutschen Bundestages*, December 6, 1967. As German wages rose, operating costs ate a larger and larger portion of the defense budget and procurement dropped steadily (from 5500 million *DM* in 1966 to under 4000 million in 1970). Federal Republic of Germany, Press and Information Office, *White Paper 1971–72: The Security of the Federal Republic of Germany and the Development of the*

Federal Armed Forces (Bonn: Press and Information Office, 1971), p.160.

[48]For discussion of the row, *see* the *New York Times,* July 12, 14, 15 and 31, 1967.

[49]Mendershausen, "Defense Policies and Developments in the Federal Republic," pp.6–7.

[50]What the U.S. eventually did was state during the ratification proceedings that it interpreted Articles I and II of the treaty not to preclude a European force of some sort. For the treaty, *see* Arms Control and Disarmament Agency, *Arms Control and Disarmament Agreements, 1959–72.* (Washington, 1972), pp.64–70. For the American qualification, *see* ACDA, *Documents on Disarmament, 1968* (Washington, 1969), pp.477–78.

[51]For a discussion of the speech and European reaction to it, *see The Economist,* October 15, 1966, p.257.

[52]The plane issue is mentioned in articles in the *New York Times,* April 24, 1967, and in *Die Welt,* May 4, 1967.

[53]For brief discussions of German deliberations, *see* articles in the *Süddeutsche Zeitung,* January 27, and February 20, 21, and 23 and March 16, 1967.

[54]For von Hase's comment, *see* the *Süddeutsche Zeitung,* February 23, 1967; for Strauss', Federal Republic of Germany, Press and Information Office, *Mitteilung an die Presse,* February 25, 1967.

[55]Reported by *Le Monde,* March 20, 1967.

[56]For mention of the dispute and final agreement, *see* the *Süddeutsche Zeitung,* March 3 and 16, 1967. Of the 550 million figure, however, 25 million DM was "old" money left over from previous agreements.

CHAPTER IV: WASHINGTON

Like the German government, the official creature popularly labeled "Washington" seldom was, or is, the unitary decision-maker implied by that label. In 1966 and 1967, the President who sat atop that government was the final arbiter with regard to questions of offset and force level. But for the form of the issues, information, analysis and alternatives he was dependent upon the actions of separated departments of government, each with its own perspective and procedures. Those perspectives, the first subject of this chapter, were predictable and consistent in high degree before and after 1966. They changed but little with Presidents. The President was also subject to the influence, at close range, of the cabinet officers who headed the "foreign policy" departments of government. Appointed by him, they were his men to a greater extent than Erhard's ministers were his. Yet they also represented departments with parochial missions and reported to distinct Congressional committees. On issues as contentious as those of offset and force level, that very nearly assured that the President's senior advisors would be of divergent views and that those differences would receive a full measure of play in deliberations preceding American actions.

Nor was the debate confined to the Executive Branch. The various arguments and their sponsors within the Executive were reinforced by segments of Congress and by interests within the limited public attentive to foreign policy. The degree of Congressional influence in 1966 and 1967, commonplace enough from the perspective of the mid-1970s, was far from customary at the time with regard to great matters of foreign affairs. In the mid-1960s Washington, conditioned by the postwar tradition of bipartisanship, still was accustomed to allowing the President great leeway in framing and executing foreign policy. The attentiveness of Congress before and during the Trilaterals, combined with the way arguments interlocked in the Executive Branch, served to bind offset to the question of the level of American forces in Europe.

Like counterparts in Bonn, Washingtonians understood that the deliberations in which they were engaged overlapped with what transpired in Bonn. Yet they shared with those German colleagues a preoccupation with politics internal to their own government. That was inevitable, or nearly so, given that Bonn's actions affected them only indirectly while Washington politics had direct consequences for both personal stakes and policy preferences. Washington officials were all the more likely to ignore events in Bonn because of the preconceived images of Bonn that they carried in their heads. They regarded the Federal Republic as dependent enough upon Washington so that its politics scarcely had to be considered in framing American actions. That conception, approximately true perhaps during the early tenure of Adenauer, no longer served as an adequate guide to action in 1966. But it remained in Washington.

The months surrounding the Trilaterals are divided neatly by Chancellor Erhard's fateful visit to Washington and his subsequent fall from power. That division is a convenience in describing and evaluating Washington's actions during 1966–67. In the period before the visit, offset deliberations in the U.S. government rose from the lower level channel to which decentralized operations had deputed them, and the issue came before the attention of the government's highest officials. The United States made a significant change of policy in August and another, smaller, in September. But Washington did not move beyond that position before Erhard concluded his visit with President Johnson and returned to Bonn. Posing the question why is the theme of a concluding section to the next chapter. Chapter VI is addressed to framing an answer to that question. After Erhard's downfall and the beginning of the Trilaterals, the issues of offset and troop level remained before the government's most senior officials, but those officials were deeply divided over the policy issues at hand.

This chapter will outline the politics and processes of Washington. The next sets those beside the picture presented earlier of Bonn. It raises the two central questions in the interaction of the two governments: did the two capitals misperceive one another at crucial points in 1966–67, especially in the weeks before the Erhard visit; and to what extent were the needs of the two sets of domestic politics compatible at key junctures?

I. ORGANIZATIONAL PERSPECTIVES

For officials in Washington, as for their counterparts in Bonn, the German-American alliance was more a matter of need than of sentiment. Germany, the enemy become friend, was regarded as the cornerstone of political and military arrangements for the defense of Europe, all the more so with France inactive and uncooperative by turns. But, in American eyes, the Federal Republic had grown rich in the postwar structure sustained by the United States. Responsibility seemed to lag behind capability: Germany should assume more of the burden of its own defense. When McNamara or others spoke of the "Europeans" doing more, the men in Bonn heard, as Americans probably intended them to, "German" for "European."

Offset fell naturally into that image of Germany and of the alliance. For some parts of official Washington, it was an end in itself, the least that Bonn should do. For others, it was merely a convenience. And for still others it was an instrument, perhaps even a slightly distasteful one, to achieve other goals—for example, the continuance of a large number of American forces in Europe. Yet the positions and their advocates intertwined in a way which wedded offset to the question of force level. That made offset crucial politics in 1966 and serious business thereafter.

Department of State

Within the State Department, primary operating responsibility for the issues of offset and troop level resided in the Bureau of European Affairs (EUR), the premier regional bureau in a department still dominated by its regional bureaus. In 1966–67 no operating bureau other than EUR was deeply engaged. The Under Secretary for Political Affairs, Eugene V. Rostow, took part in the later stages of

99

discussion, but his was a solo involvement; he did not draw staff from the Economics Bureau (E), whose head was an assistant secretary. After 1967 the "E" bureau assumed increasing, though not central, importance. It tended, hardly surprisingly, to be more sympathetic to Treasury Department viewpoints than were its EUR colleagues. State's Bureau of Regional Politico-Military Affairs (RPM) was at the fringes of offset deliberations.

EUR's preoccupation was politics. To it, American troops in Europe were perceived not only as a means of guaranteeing the United States a preeminent political role in the region, but also as the cement binding together the Atlantic alliance. The debate over troop level has been littered, as noted in chapter I, with references by State Department officials to the "unravelling" effect on NATO of American troop reductions. For EUR, any status quo was preferable to setting in motion any process of reduction. To be sure, State Department officials recited the military arguments against reduction, even through dual-basing troops in the U.S. and in Europe.[1] But for them those arguments were, and continued to be, as much a means as the statement of a military end.

EUR views of offset derived logically from its concentration on politics and its institutional mission as custodian of U.S.-European relations. To it, maintaining close German-American relations was both desirable in general and helpful in specific instances—for example, during the 1966 NATO crisis after the French withdrawal or during British attempts to join the Common Market then and later. For its purposes in 1966, EUR could hardly do better than Erhard, Schröder and von Hassel. Other possibilities could only be worse. An SPD government, unlikely in any event, by 1966 posed EUR little threat on substantive grounds but would have upset the expectations and close working-relationships developed during more than a decade of CDU rule. A grand coalition was certain to be messy and to play havoc with consultation between the two governments; besides, it was likely to mean that "Gaullists" would return to key Cabinet posts.

Hence, EUR—and to only a slightly lesser degree, State as a whole—were eager to make offset as painless as possible for the government in Bonn, especially Erhard's. That implied promotion of the multilateral NATO Military Payments Union in 1966 and eager support later on for offsetting through securities purchases rather than only by buying weapons. Both schemes offered promise of draining away some of the political pressure which existing offset arrangements generated on Bonn. In actual negotiations, the position of the State Department official negotiator (after 1968 the Deputy Under Secretary for Economic Affairs) resembled that of his German Foreign Office counterpart: serving as moderator of deliberations within his own government and applauding any proposal which was acceptable both to the other side and to the departments on his own side with specific interests to pursue—for the U.S., Defense and Treasury.

Of course, Congress served as a constraint for State as it did for others in the Executive Branch who opposed troop reduction. Generosity toward Bonn had to be balanced with firmness, for the benefit of Congress. Any offset bargain struck with Bonn had to be attractive enough in Washington to hold promise of serving as a means of fending off Congressional attempts to mandate troop reductions, like the Mansfield amendments. No doubt State would have been little interested in offset had not Congress periodically become exercised over the troop stationing and its financing. If State occasionally seemed less sensitive to Congressional pressures than other departments, that was not surprising. Defense, not State, bore the primary responsibility for going to Capitol Hill to defend the defense budgets to which restrictive amendments were attached.

Department of Defense

Civilians and military officers at the Pentagon differed on the troop level issue, conspicuously in 1966–67 but later as well. The official position of the Joint Chiefs of Staff barely wavered: there was (and is) no military justification for reducing the number of American troops in Europe, and dual-basing or rotation schemes were (and are) less effective for military purposes than soldiers in place.[2] Not that no one in uniform ever held a varying view—the Army, hard pressed to scrape up troops for Vietnam, in 1967 would have countenanced a reduction in Europe. But the military position for consumption in interagency discussions in Washington was consistent. For instance, the representative of the Joint Chiefs on the McCloy staff in 1966–67 was an Army general, yet he argued the position of the Chiefs and not of his own service. Military officers remained on the safe ground of military considerations, where their arguments were most forceful and their claims to expertise most credible. They shied from making calculations about the Congressional politics of the issues or from entering into the financial arguments.

101

For McNamara and his successors as Secretary, the troop level issue wore a different face. Military requirements ran against technical possibilities and political necessities. The requirements of different regions of the world and of the several services had to be balanced and satisfied, to the extent possible, within available budgets. McNamara's primary business was fighting the war in Vietnam, and doing so under sharp constraints: no call-up of reserves and no transfer of the U.S. economy to a war-time footing. The garrison in Europe must have looked like an expensive luxury, all the more so because McNamara believed the Europeans should have done more in their own defense. He made that argument often, to both Congress and the public.[3]

The concerns of the Secretary of Defense are Washington ones, and they can be consuming. Fretting about the effects of American actions on allied nations is the primary business of the Secretary's colleague across the Potomac, not his. What *is* his direct responsibility is defending military budgets and force deployments before Congress. The march to Capitol Hill was a long one for McNamara in 1966 and 1967, for Vietnam was gobbling up both budget and foreign exchange. It was difficult for the Secretary, on both intellectual and political grounds, to maintain so many troops in a Europe at peace while more forces were so desperately needed in a Vietnam at war. But Congressional pressures, if less dramatic after 1968, operated also on McNamara's successors. In 1970, for instance, Melvin Laird, pressed to limit defense spending, reportedly was prepared to trim the European force by up to 40,000 men. He sought in doing so to mollify Senatorial critics of the troops stationing.

By all accounts, McNamara took the balance of payments seriously, and his successors have been compelled to attend to it by Congress. Foreign exchange was for McNamara another technical issue, like force deployments, and another of the President's problems to "solve." On it, he had religion. He believed it would become impossible for the United States to continue to play its proper role in the world if it did not put its balance-of-payments house in order. From 1962 on, his Department gave preference to supplies produced in the U.S. It procured American goods if their cost was less than 50% *more* than foreign equivalents. The procedure produced balance-of-payments savings but added an average of 26 per cent to the budgetary cost of items shifted from foreign to domestic suppliers.[4]

At the same time and for the same balance-of-payments reasons, McNamara elected to promote the sale of American weapons to foreign countries, especially to American allies in NATO. The Office of International Logistics Negotiations, as it was labeled with some euphemism, was upgraded in fact if not in formal organization. The director of the office and the man who at the same time headed Foreign Military Sales, Henry Kuss, was in form a Deputy Assistant Secretary of Defense reporting to the Assistant Secretary for International Security Affairs (ISA), then John McNaughton. In reality, because of McNamara's interest in making sales and Kuss' single-minded determination to do so, Kuss remained independent of McNaughton and possessed direct access to the Secretary. As long as offset remained a Defense/Treasury fiefdom, not only was the State Department frozen out but so also was the Defense Department's "junior State Department," ISA.

Treasury Department

With respect to matters of offset and troop level, Treasury can be fairly treated as a unit. The two Department principals most involved in Washington deliberations have been the Secretary and his Under Secretary for Monetary Affairs (the Department's third ranking official); during 1966-67, those positions were occupied by Henry Fowler and Frederick Deming. Up through the Trilaterals, Treasury seniors were staffed by a unit in the Office of the Secretary, the Office for National Security Affairs, which originally was established to monitor the efforts of McNamara's Defense Department to reduce military foreign exchange outlays. Of the National Security office and its alliance with Foreign Military Sales at Defense, more later. After the Trilaterals, the National Security office lost influence in offset dealings to Treasury's Office of International Affairs.

The Treasury perspective, like that of its counterparts in official Washington, remained relatively constant. Treasury focused on offset — the half of the cluster of issues in which it had direct interest and claim to relevant expertise. Its objective was maximum assistance to the U.S. balance of payments. While sensitive to Bonn's argument that splitting off a "military" subaccount was artificial, Treasury countered that the only way to attack the over-all balance-of-payments deficit was to operate on various subaccounts. That was particularly true before 1971, while devaluation, the obvious general remedy, was officially unthinkable in Washington. While the Secretary of Defense had to defend military budgets before Congress, Fowler and his successors marched to the Hill to explain what the government was doing to put its foreign exchange position into balance.

Hardly surprisingly, the hierarchy of Treasury preferences with respect to offset mechanisms has been just the converse of that held by the German Finance Ministry. Direct payment by the Federal Republic of *Deutschemark* costs incurred by the American army in Germany, last on the German list, was always first for Treasury. Those payments would provide direct and unambiguous assistance to the American balance of payments, as well as reducing the budgetary cost of the troops. Treasury pressed for direct payments from the beginning of offset negotiations. Paradoxically, however, the Department opposed the first offset provision which could be advertised as "direct support" — the barracks rehabilitation program negotiated in 1971 and extended in 1974. It did so for good "finance ministry" reasons. Before the Schmidt initiative, Bonn had been willing to put up a modest sum for payments to German civilian employees, or for goods procured locally. In the Treasury view, either would have been more helpful to the balance of payments than the barracks program, since the latter replaced only future — and uncertain — American expenditures. Schmidt and his American allies — the Seventh Army in Germany and the Defense Department — in effect captured Bonn's money offer and turned it to the barracks program.

Next in order of preference for Treasury was military procurement in the United States by the Federal Republic. German military expenditures in the U.S. are comparable to American military expenditures in Germany, in both logic and custom. By contrast, Treasury questioned the utility of *civilian* procurement by German government agencies. There existed no precedent for incorporating civilian procurement under offset accords. Moreover, there was the bugbear of "additionality": the civilian purchases included might have been made in the absence of any offset agreement. Treasury agreed to civilian procurement, in 1969 and 1974, only after protracted arguments within official Washington. And the amounts of money involved were relatively small.

Treasury resistance to accepting loans — via some form of German purchases of Treasury securities — stiffened over time. In 1966-67 the purchases were reasonable enough, a way to obtain a quick infusion of foreign exchange, buying time in the hope that the U.S. position would improve or that international reforms would spare Washington the need of regressive and politically unpopular cures for its foreign exchange ills. Quite obviously, the scheme paled in later years, as the debt incurred under previous agreements had to be turned over. Treasury argued during the 1973-74 discussions that only the amount of the German *interest subsidy* ought to count under the offset agreement. At other times the Department suggested that loan principal could count as an inflow for offset purposes when it was received but that it should also count as a military outflow when the loan was repaid. In every instance, Treasury arguments against loans foundered on the desire of the Executive Branch to attach a large number to offset agreements, for the benefit of Congress.

Treasury has been timid about joining the debate over troop levels, regarding that as beyond its purview and competence. That timidity may, however, have diminished in recent years. It was, in any case, most in evidence during the Johnson Administration, and then McNamara was playing the strong "Treasury" hand. Not that Treasury had been uninterested in the troop level question; in 1966, Secretary Fowler expressed an eagerness to see the stationing in Europe reduced in the interest of economy. In addition, Treasury purposes were served by stressing the link between German offset compliance and the maintenance of a given level of U.S. forces in Europe. Secretary Anderson first drew the link explicitly during his 1961 mission; President Johnson made it official policy in a letter to Erhard in March 1964; and McNamara used it as a means of putting pressure on German Defense Minister von Hassel in the spring and summer of 1966.

Other Executive Branch "Economic" Agencies

Other agencies with economic mandates — notably the Federal Reserve, the Bureau of the Budget, and the Council of Economic Advisors—occasionally made their views on offset felt within government. Their domestic perspectives drew them into natural alliance with Treasury. In 1970, for example, Federal Reserve Chairman Burns joined Budget Bureau Director Mayo and Treasury Secretary Kennedy in expressing unhappiness with existing offset arrangements, particularly loans.[5] Yet these agencies were at best marginal participants in any given negotiation. That was the case in 1966-67, although the Federal Reserve did play a part in working out the technical details of the Bundesbank gold pledge and the Federal Republic's purchase of Treasury securities.

White House

To speak of a "White House" perspective apart from the President is to court danger. The task of White House officers presumably is to staff the President, not argue briefs. Yet arrangements for "staffing" the President vary from one administration to the next. Those differences matter. Examining *how* they matter is a topic of chapters V and VI. The essence of Francis Bator's role in 1966 and 1967 as Deputy Special Assistant was protecting the President: making sure that all arguments received fair hearing but that none prevailed before the President was ready to decide. Bator could make his own preferences clear to the President as long as it was obvious to all concerned that he was not abusing his special access to the Oval Office. By contrast, Henry Kissinger's role as Assistant to the President in the Nixon Administration varied all the way from one akin to Bator's to acting as a kind of assistant President for foreign affairs. For some issues at the end of Nixon's tenure, he might be considered the acting President for foreign affairs, with the National Security Council machinery staffing him.

Both Presidents were disinclined to make large reductions in the force in Europe — Nixon strongly and publicly so — and the actions of men in the White House reflected that preference. Yet at the White House, many issues crossed and the attendant sets of Congressional relations had to be made compatible with one another. Getting the President his way on one issue became only a partial success if the initial victory provoked retribution, from inside the Executive Branch or from Congress on another issue. With respect to offset, the art lay in assembling a package which would meet the administration's European objectives yet satisfy the domestic considerations represented in Congress, and at the same time avoid a schism within the administration over the deal struck. The practice of that art was the business of the President's White House or National Security Council staff officers.

Congress

In 1966-67, and for a decade thereafter, the Congressional interest in troop cuts in Europe was a Senate interest. Both the Johnson and Nixon Administrations, committed in opposition to large reductions, could count on the elders in the House Armed Services Committee and a pro-NATO block in the Foreign Affairs Committee. House conferees insisted in 1973 that mandatory reductions approved by the Senate be dropped from the final defense authorization bill. Yet that situation is unlikely to persist for many future administrations. More and more of the barons of both committees will be lost to retirement or defeated. One pro-Administration Congressman was reported to have told the Administration in 1973: "You are on the losing end of the age spectrum."[6] Yet exactly when, if ever, the balance of power in the House will tip against support for maintaining a large number of forces in Europe is hard to predict.

By comparison to Senatorial politics, the complicated machinations within the Executive Branch seem transparent. Explaining why a given action emerged from the upper chamber is no simple task, predicting Senatorial action still less so. On the one hand, few Senators have time and interest enough to follow European issues in any detail; probably only minorities on the Foreign Relations and Armed Services Committees, plus a few colleagues, do so. On the other hand, among America's foreign relations and traditional alliances, most Senators regard ties to western Europe, embodied in NATO, as paramount. There is a group of World War II buffs among older Senators, men who fought in the war and who look forward to the meetings of NATO parliamentarians—attractive junkets for all Congressmen — as opportunities to meet again with European counterparts. In 1967, President Johnson, aware of the special sentiment in Congress on Europe's behalf, worried that large American cuts might begin a disintegration of NATO, handing the Republicans a juicy campaign issue for 1968. Special sympathy for Europe was again evident in Senate deliberations in 1973. The reduction in U.S. forces abroad finally approved, 110,000, was calculated *not* to compel substantial reductions in the garrison in Europe.

Those Senators who have argued for force reductions in Europe seem to have been moved by varying motivations. Some, like Mansfield, felt it undesirable to maintain so many troops in Europe *regardless* of their cost. For him, the slackening of East-West tensions made it unnecessary to station 300,000 troops in Europe; after the late 1960's he appended to each of his Congressional statements a long list of events which had reduced tensions in Europe.[7] Near the end of the Trilaterals, he reacted to a published report that offset difficulties would force a one-division reduction by calling for the separation of offset from the question of force level. Offset, for him, was "the one consideration which ought not to govern in a situation which involves vital defense needs." If the troops were needed, they should stay, but he found the U.S. deployment "swollen

107

beyond present need."[8] Much of Mansfield's support in the Senate was drawn from Senators who shared his view simply that the United States had too many commitments and too many troops as the earnest of those commitments in too many foreign countries. Some of his supporters, Harold Hughes for instance, pointed to deteriorating race relations among the troops in Germany, low morale and drug use as other reasons for bringing troops back to the United States. For these men, cost was a consideration but not an overriding one.

While the first group of senators used financial issues, if at all, primarily as levers on the troop issue, a second identifiable group appeared to care deeply about the cost of the troops, both budgetary and foreign exchange. Stuart Symington is the most obvious representative of that group, Senator Jackson perhaps another.[9] In 1966 and 1967 the issue for these men was gold; by the 1970s it was simply whether or not the United States could afford its existing role in the world.

Other sources of anti-European feelings entered into play, especially in the late 1960s, and other linkages were struck. Some Senators were angered at Europe's less than enthusiastic attitude toward American involvement in Vietnam, and that made them readier to contemplate force reductions in Europe. Other of Mansfield's supporters were farm-state Senators miffed at the EEC's restrictions on American grain exports to Europe; for them the balance-of-payments link was not arms sales, but grain exports.

Since the mid-1960s members of Congress have not felt powerful constituent pressure to withdraw troops from Europe,[10] although from time to time the American people have registered opposition to the size of the existing contingent. For instance, in a Gallup poll taken in September 1973, 57 per cent of those sampled favored unilateral force reductions in Europe.[11] No doubt many Americans also regard the U.S. presence in Europe as too expensive and feel that the Europeans shoulder too little of the burden. Yet what sentiment is apparent takes the form of a general desire to "bring the boys home," vague and seldom pressed on legislators. When members of Congress have heard from the districts about troops, what they have heard is the feeling that there are too many American GIs abroad in general, not complaints about specific regions. Most Americans probably have agreed with the balance of Congressional opinion that if the United States is to station forces outside its borders at all, those forces should be in Europe first.

If there has been no strong constituency lobbying for troop reduction, neither has there been broad support for the stationing. American troops abroad are a tempting target for those in Congress who would brake the rise in defense budgets and are frustrated at Congress' inability to do so. They remain a target even though merely bringing troops back to the United States does not save budget money. Congressional efforts to intervene in the process of weapons development and procurement have met with little success,[12] and eliminating bases in the United States gores oxen which reside in a particular Congressman's district. Foreign bases and stationings are exposed. They are no one's constituents.

The searing experience of the war in Vietnam surely contributed to the feeling that the United States had too many commitments and troops in too many places, and that sentiment affected perceptions of the forces in Europe. In 1973 some of the Senate's elders, internationalist in temperament and liberal by persuasion — Humphrey, Pastore, Pell and Muskie — took second thought about the wisdom of the European station. In the wake of Vietnam, specific grievances reinforced general unease: frustration at having lost control of American foreign policy to the Executive Branch and anger at having been deceived. Those emotions no doubt played a role in the passage of troop cuts through the Senate in 1973. Their connection to the troop level issue did not persist into 1975 and 1976.

The fact and form of Mansfield's leadership of Senatorial troop-cutters affected the Senate's actions. As majority leader he seldom had time to take the lead on a specific issue, so his personal involvement in efforts at force reduction underscored his interest in them. Yet the field of vision of Senators, and especially of the leadership, is as wide as the President's. Hence Mansfield could concentrate on the troop levels question only sporadically, a tendency reinforced by personal style. His early proposals took the form of sense-of-the-Senate resolutions, not binding on the President. Mansfield probably cared little whether they passed or not; making the signal sufficed. Once the proposals became binding amendments, the reductions they demanded were large, more than most Senators were willing to accept. But Mansfield had marked the issue as his and that dissuaded other Senators from placing proposals for more modest reduction before the Senate, at least until 1973. To poach on another Senator's issue is to breach the ethics of the "club," risky business, all the more so if the colleague whose domain is breached is the majority leader.

109

Groups outside Government

It is no longer easy, if it ever was, to draw sharp lines around the institutions comprising the American government. "Private" groups are conceded "public" responsibilities, and people move easily from one sector to the other. John McCloy, who had held senior government posts as early as 1940 and who had served as U.S. High Commissioner for Germany during postwar occupation, came from his New York law practice to be the American negotiator during the Trilaterals. Earlier in 1966, Dean Acheson, former Secretary of State and another Europeanist of McCloy's stature and generation, served in form as a consultant to Secretary of State Rusk but acted in fact as Assistant Secretary for Europe during the convalescence of John Leddy, the man who formally held the position.

McCloy and Acheson were both members of a loose group, centered in New York and Washington, of bankers and lawyers, government "in and outers," Atlanticists in vision, men who had constructed the postwar alliance structures: the "Eastern Establishment" by popular label. The impact of the group is as hard to calibrate as it is to indicate precisely who was "inside" and who "outside" at any given time. Yet its influence was obvious at several points in government deliberations with respect to offset and troop level. In 1966 and 1967, the group, fiscally conservative, joined the chorus urging the President to take harsh measures to "solve" the balance-of-payments problem, reinforcing the entreaties of the "gold bugs" in Congress. McNamara may have been especially susceptible to the arguments of that group, with whose representatives he met often, for he calculated that he needed its support for Vietnam policy. In 1971, the Nixon Administration called upon many government officials who had served previous administrations to lobby against the Mansfield amendment then before the Senate.[13]

II. THE 1966 "CRISIS"

The policy preferences of various parts of the United States government were not disconnected from the process of governance in 1966 and 1967, but at the heart of it. There may have been "agency" positions, but they were seldom merely that. Disagreements were substantive, the arguments and their governmental representatives linked implicitly or explicitly to domestic interests and constituencies. Nor were the deliberations mere bureaucratic games, although "games" occasionally were played. I use the language of games sparingly, as convenient metaphor, for want of better terms. The language is meant neither to imply frivolousness nor suggest precise analogy to the economic literature on games.

The outcomes of the processes were decisions and actions by the United States government. Responsible people disagreed on the course of action to be followed, sometimes differed deeply. The consequences of their choices mattered, not only to personal careers and bureaucratic influence but to the substantive interests of America and its allies.

How did the various positions combine to produce governmental decisions which most often, though not always, were Presidential? That question is the subject of this section and the next. This one looks at American decision-making in the period leading up to Chancellor Erhard's visit to Washington in September 1966; the next examines the period from then until the conclusion of the Trilaterals in May 1967.

Context

In Washington as in Bonn, offset decisions were not made in isolation. Other issues crowded in, competing for attention. Deadlines were imposed or relaxed, and the matters of offset and force level were altered in form by the other major issues the American government confronted at the same time. The influence of particular officials was enhanced or undercut by debates or outcomes with regard to other issues. Of the many interlocking pieces in the mosaic of policy-making, four had direct effect on the character of deliberations concerning offset and force level: most important, the balance of payments; and then the French withdrawal from NATO, the war in Vietnam and the Nonproliferation Treaty (NPT) negotiations.

Balance of Payments. Offset was primarily a balance-of-payments matter to the United States, hence its handling fell into the context of American balance-of-payments policy, to critical effect. American balance-of-payments deficits were a subject of continuous concern in Washington. The President was counseled by many — by his Treasury Secretary, by the Federal Reserve and by many in Congress and the banking community — to adopt a set of hoary measures to erase the deficit, including restrictions on tourism, capital flows, and imports. Gold was a powerful symbol; deficits meant not merely bloodless statistics but compelled the sale of what many took to be the national patrimony.

111

At each stage, however, the President resisted the harsh proposals and opted instead for measures which were, in essence, cosmetic. He was supported only by the advice of the responsible White House official, with occasional assistance from the Council of Economic Advisors. But the President probably was neither clear about nor comfortable with the policy, nor, to be sure, could it be articulated publicly. The result was that Fowler, McNamara and other Cabinet officers were at once pressed by the President to be good soldiers on the balance of payments, especially before Congress, yet prevented from taking measures which actually might have "solved" the problem.

Throughout the 1960s, the United States was constantly subjected to lectures by Europeans on its balance-of-payments sins, on "exporting inflation." Both the German Bundesbank and Finance Ministry eagerly chimed in, and the U.S. position in the international monetary (SDR) negotiations was weakened. While the United States was lectured about balance-of-payment deficits by one part of the German government, another part of the Bonn machine appealed to it to increase those deficits by granting the Federal Republic relief from part of its offset burden. The lectures almost certainly made American officials, including the President, less willing to be generous with their German allies on offset, especially since generosity with foreign exchange was politically unpopular at home.

The balance of payments had a specific bite during the August and September deliberations in Washington. Projections of the U.S. payments position for the first quarter of 1967 were bleak, and officials worried that forgiving the Germans part of their offset commitment might, when added to an already severe deficit, cause a run on gold early in 1967. After all, the $900 million or so from which Bonn desired to be unencumbered was much more than half the total U.S. liquidity deficit in 1966.[14] A run on gold might have pushed the U.S. to press in 1967 for the kind of two-tier gold market adopted in March 1968. Doing so, "shutting the gold window," surely would not have been the end of the world in itself, although there were those in official Washington who argued that it would. But it would in all probability have wrecked the international monetary negotiations and the Kennedy Round trade negotiations, both of which came to crucial stages in the spring of 1967.

The French Withdrawal from the NATO Military Command. The French pullout was a profound shock to the American government, especially to the generation of State Department officials who had invested their careers in the task of constructing a unified Europe. "Europeanists" at State — Ball, Acheson, McCloy and others — pressed for retaliation on France and searched for levers the U.S. possessed. In the end, they felt their chief — Rusk — bowed too easily to Presidential instructions to seek accommodation with Paris. The dispute was replayed in discussions over the status of French forces in Germany, with the "Europeanists" initially urging the Germans to take a hard line with France. The episodes diminished the credibility and force of the "Europeanists" in the offset deliberations which followed, and caused relations between White House and State Department officials to grow frosty. The damage done to State's position was magnified because the French withdrawal closely followed the President's decision to scuttle the multilateral force (MLF): the President had twice rejected the eager pleading of State's Europeanist "theologians."

Vietnam. The war in Vietnam affected policy-making with regard to offset in two respects: it preoccupied nearly everyone, and it lent McNamara a strong position in the Administration. Rusk devoted most of his attentions to the war; George Ball was left to carry the European brief. Francis Bator, M.I.T. professor and former A.I.D. official who had been brought into the White House by McGeorge Bundy, minded the European beat at the White House, while Bundy's successor as Special Assistant to the President for National Security Affairs, Walt W. Rostow, tended to the war. In 1966 the Defense Secretary's position in the Administration was extremely strong; the President would not overrule him lightly. Ball could not easily confront McNamara over European issues from the Under Secretary's chair, at least he could not do so successfully often, all the less so because the two men had engaged in a running debate about Vietnam policy, in which Ball's dovish positions consistently had been overruled.

NPT. As mentioned in the preceding chapter, Bonn worried that the U.S. would agree to NPT terms which precluded future formation of an allied nuclear force involving German participation (especially one, the so-called "European option," in which the United States might not possess veto power over firing). That concern was expressed in a series of letters over the spring and summer (including the July 5th letter), mingled with requests for offset relief. For Washington, however, it was not yet clear in August and September that the Soviets were serious about NPT. Reassuring the Federal Republic that the "European option" was still open was sure to leak

113

and be read in Moscow as a signal that the United States was itself not serious about NPT. On the other hand, it was clear that explicitly closing the European option would cause Erhard problems with his Gaullists, so it was better to avoid responding to his queries. But it was difficult to hedge on NPT and at the same time reply in detail to the Chancellor's comments on offset. Maintaining the ambiguous status quo on both issues was tempting.

American Policy-Making

Washington's actions with respect to offset and force level were the combined outputs of two levels of decision processes. The manner by which offset was handled routinely in the U.S. government — the American offset "channel" — framed the issue and conferred momentum on certain kinds of policy interests. Deliberations could be lifted from that track in July and August 1966 and elevated to Presidential attention. From then on, the President made major decisions after full consultation with his Cabinet-level advisors. Yet in August and September, the character of the debate among those senior officials, and of the considerations represented in it, made it extremely unlikely that Washington would change its course of action enough — or fast enough — to suit Bonn's purposes.

The Washington Offset "Channel." The lower-level offset track in Bonn found its counterpart in Washington. The American government's perspective on offset was the obverse of that held by Bonn: what wore a military procurement face to Germans was, for Americans, a matter of military sales and balance-of-payments accounting.

The two offices with direct concern were Foreign Military Sales in the Office of International Security Affairs (ISA) at the Department of Defense and the Treasury Office for National Security Affairs. Their outlooks were perfectly compatible; several officials moved from one to the other. Their approach to the Germans was simple and direct: Defense secured weapons orders from the Germans, Treasury extracted payment in advance of delivery. Bonn was required to place orders totaling the amount agreed to in each two-year agreement by the end of the second calendar year. They were then to deposit the total amount in blocked accounts with the U.S. Treasury by the end of the U.S. fiscal year, six months later, in most cases well before delivery of any of the weapons ordered had even begun. American officials naturally were more dogged in securing payments than orders, and, as German procurement slowed, payments ran well ahead of orders. By the beginning of 1968, the Germans had almost a billion uncommitted dollars in two offset accounts with the U.S. Treasury.

Officials along the offset track resisted the encroachment of other agencies, especially the State Department. At working levels, there was a good deal of antagonism between the Defense/Treasury group and members of the State European bureau. The former believed the latter were merely jealous of the "good deal" which had been worked out and were more attentive to German than American problems. For their part, State officials regarded their colleagues across town as zealots willing to endanger Washington's relations with the Federal Republic for the interests of American arms manufacturers and a few dollars of foreign exchange.

So long as offset responsibility rested with Defense and Treasury, the two were free to press their preferences on the Germans with little attention to the effect of their actions on German politics or German-American relations in general. McNamara met with German Defense Minister von Hassel in Washington on May 13, 1966, and explicitly linked the level of German offset with the future level of American forces in Europe. In a press conference on his return to Germany, von Hassel indicated that the threat had been made, provoking a storm of criticism in the German press and eliciting a formal German request for explanation.

Throughout 1965 and 1966, Defense and Treasury opposed all of the various schemes put forward for alterations in the offset system under a successor agreement (to begin in July 1967). To them the *status quo* was not to be tampered with; any deviation from it was sure to lead to a British-style offset composed mostly of civilian procurement, ridiculed by Defense and Treasury. The history of German compliance created the presumption that it would continue. At least, in the view of those officials, the U.S. should not take the lead in scrapping its favorable arrangement. In the early summer of 1966, the Germans again proposed shifting some offset to the procurement of space hardware, but that proposal was opposed vigorously by Defense and quickly withered.

The plan for a NATO Military Payments Union represented a more serious attempt to restructure offset.[15] The scheme — devised in State's Economic bureau and pressed on McNamara and Fowler by Ball as early as July 1965 — was multilateral, not bilateral. Under it, NATO allies with military balance-of-payments deficits would have received foreign exchange IOUs from countries in surplus. Those

115

IOUs could have been canceled by the surplus nations in a variety of ways, not merely through military procurement in the deficit countries. In 1966 the plan was fed into the newly created National Security Council machinery, where it moved through the Interdepartmental Regional Group (IRG) for Europe, an Assistant Secretary-level body, and eventually came before the Senior Interdepartmental Group (SIG), a committee of Under Secretaries.

Deputy Secretary of Defense Vance approved the Payments Union on behalf of Defense at a SIG meeting on June 7. The SIG decision should have gone as a recommendation to the President for final approval. But McNamara objected, disavowing Vance's approval. "What's SIG?" he said, in effect if not in fact. He argued, against all efforts to persuade him otherwise, that it was better to sell weapons than IOUs, that the Payments Union would diminish American leverage on the troop level question and that, in any case, it would only postpone the foreign exchange problem. In fairness to McNamara, there were objections to the Payments Union less parochial than his. It was complicated and technical, hence hard to explain to principals and to negotiate. At the same time, the European bureau at State feared it might be rejected out of hand by the Germans because it would have increased their total liability. To have made the SIG result operational, Secretary Rusk would have had to set it before the President. Given McNamara's firm opposition, he declined to do so.

The Debate Among Principals. The offset channel defined the issue, but during 1966 offset moved upward to the attention of the highest officials in the American government. Erhard's letter to Johnson insured that would be the case; from then on, Cabinet-level deliberations determined U.S. actions.

The views of offset held by the Secretaries of Treasury and Defense concurred with those of their operating offices. For Fowler, the existing offset scheme neatly complemented the Treasury role as guardian of American foreign exchange. But McNamara was the primary figure, and his position is harder to describe. He regarded offset as an important issue and played it close to him. Foreign exchange was serious business to him. Witness, for example, his repudiation of the SIG agreement on the Payments Union.

For McNamara, defense was a technical problem, not a political one. His intellectual predilection was for flexible forces; if mobile forces based in the U.S. equaled forces in Europe for the purposes of conventional defense—as studies done by his Systems Analysis unit showed that they did—then forces in the U.S. were as good also as a link to the nuclear deterrent.[16] The Europeans, sensible people, would eventually accept that. At the same time, McNamara's primary task was fighting a war. Vietnam was consuming men, budget and foreign exchange. Whether or not he sought to pull troops from Europe for use in Vietnam (or had made a treaty with Congressional leaders to that effect, as some State Department officials believed), the garrison in Europe must have looked not only like an expensive luxury but also a source of ready manpower.

In the months before and after Erhard's visit, McNamara lobbied for either a large financial offer from the Germans *or* a sizable troop cut. He planted hints of a reduction of two divisions (about 75,000 men) throughout the summer of 1966.[17] No doubt he regarded firmness on offset as a means of inducing the Germans to "ask" the United States to make troop cuts in order to reduce foreign exchange outlays (although I do not believe that the McNamara threat to von Hassel was merely a "pretext" for the transfer of troops to Vietnam, as many Germans charged). With respect to the effect of American action on German domestic politics, McNamara either had a deaf ear or regarded *that* concern as an improper basis for American policy.

State Department officials, especially Ball, did fret about the political effects of American action. The Embassy in Bonn expressed concern on that score even before McNamara's warning to von Hassel in May. The Europeanists at State, however, had declined in influence; Ball (and Dean Acheson, acting for Assistant Secretary Leddy) championed the multilateral Payments Union, with some support at the Pentagon, but to no avail. By August, Ball—dispirited at the course of American policy in both Europe and Asia, and due to leave government in the fall for investment banking in New York—was a lame duck. He could not prevail over McNamara's firm opposition. Not, at least, without his Secretary's support, and Rusk did not make his weight felt strongly or early with respect to offset. No Europeanist, Rusk was absorbed by Vietnam and regarded offset as McNamara's terrain. Generally timid about engaging the Defense Secretary, Rusk did not do so on this issue, which McNamara was driving aggressively. Rusk became more active after Erhard's downfall. In any case, his inactivity mattered less later, with McCloy engaged and the questions at issue out on the table in several arenas of discussion. But in August and September the Secretary's reticence made considerable difference.

At the White House, Francis Bator shared the State Department's concern. From his perspective, many issues crossed one another, and

117

he felt that American rigidity on offset, in the context of other decisions already taken or soon to be, courted political danger. He made his own attempt to persuade McNamara of the merits of the Payments Union. Bator's role, however, was delicate. He was a staff officer, not a Cabinet official. By the summer of 1966 he had the confidence of the President and his relations with Cabinet officers were collegial. That meant he could express opinions forcefully to the President, especially in advance of meetings of the principals. Yet the balance of payments hung over proceedings, especially so from his perspective. As the principal official, often the only one, encouraging the President *not* to take harsh foreign exchange measures, he could hardly ask the President to forgive the Germans their commitment. Doing so would have added more millions to the U.S. deficit. While McNamara regarded that as bad per se and threatening to his Congressional relations besides, Bator feared it because it incurred the risk of a run on gold in early 1967. That in turn would have threatened several of Bator's principal missions: the monetary (SDR) and Kennedy Round trade negotiations he was orchestrating for the White House.

The August Decision. The debate in Washington over the summer dealt only with the upcoming offset agreement (to begin July 1, 1967). That fact was important to subsequent events. When McNamara threatened troop cut to von Hassel in May, he had been discussing a follow-on agreement; similarly, the Payments Union had been intended to provide Bonn some relief, but only the next time around.

McNamara secured Rusk's signature to a firm response to Erhard's July 5th letter. The draft reaffirmed the link between the level of American forces and the size of German offset. Bator, the responsible White House staff officer, however, held up the letter for over a month (and thereby skated to the edge of the implicit rules under which he operated). He argued that Rusk had not yet provided the President with a position on NPT and, in any case, that it would be unwise for the President to commit himself to such firm language until the Chancellor's political and economic problems became clearer. Bator satisfied the requirements of form by notifying the President, the State Department Secretariat and ISA at the Pentagon that he was holding the letter.

A cable from the American Embassy in Bonn about August 10th forced the government to act. It reported that the German Cabinet would soon reach decisions on the 1967 defense budget and suggested that Washington should act quickly if offset were not to be threatened by the Chancellor's economic stabilization program. McNamara, of course, had wanted his draft response sent several weeks earlier. The issue could be postponed no longer.

McNamara continued to favor sending a firm reply and doing so immediately; he believed that waiting diminished the chances of securing favorable action from Erhard. Ball, Bator and George McGhee, the U.S. Ambassador in Bonn, did not, however, think that the Chancellor would pull apart his stabilization program in any case, and they opposed sending a tough letter. To base a troop cut on money was to play into the hands of the French, who had argued that the Americans were unreliable partners. The President, about to leave for the ranch, took a serious look at the issue for the first time and made his first important choice. He decided to wait on a reply, risking adverse German budget actions, and did not convene his principal advisors. Instead, he authorized a creation of a joint State/Defense/Treasury/White House exercise to prepare strategy for discussions with the Germans. Given the travel schedules of senior officials, it would be several weeks before offset could receive a full-dress review.

The principals were brought together on the 24th of August. At that point, with the British problem pressing, the issue of whether or not to join the Anglo-German Mixed Commission was explicitly on the table. The idea of making those talks trilateral apparently occurred simultaneously to those in the White House and Departments of State and Defense who feared that a British withdrawal would trigger a larger American reduction. The other, and related, issue was whether or not to accept a wider offset—including, perhaps, civilian goods and securities purchases—under a *new* agreement. McNamara and Fowler continued to argue for holding firm on the new agreement (although the latter was willing to relent provided the U.S. eventually thinned its force to a more economical size). Rusk, who had not expressed himself since agreeing to the McNamara draft, expressed the State case for leniency but did not force the issue to a point.

In the end, the President, while not expressing a clear position, indicated his unwillingness to press Bonn too hard. He then left the room, leaving his aides at the Cabinet table, Bator drafting. Language implying Washington's readiness to consider nonprocurement offset under the upcoming agreement was drafted and reluctantly agreed to by McNamara.

At the same time, the U.S. expectation that Germany would fulfill

119

its *existing* commitment was included in the letter. There had been no discussion of that issue; the language seemed of little consequence. In the same meeting, it was decided to join the Anglo-German offset commission and to throw American offset and force level into the agenda. That proposal was conveyed in letters to Erhard and Wilson. McCloy was agreed upon as Washington's negotiator, although that decision was not then formally shared with the allies, for McCloy had not been approached nor had the allies agreed to the discussions.

The existing agreement had been ignored in the meeting. Participants, surprisingly, did not regard it as an issue. To be sure, Erhard's letter had described his offset problem only in general terms, but cables from the embassy in Bonn had implied, as early as August 12, that Erhard might come up $300 million short under the *existing* agreement. Bator, and perhaps Ball, regarded the package of American decisions as a generous offer, the beginning of a process which surely would break the back of the German offset problem. Hard language on the existing agreement was a small enough price to pay in order to neutralize McNamara and set the process in motion. If the Germans still had problems, they had been given abundant avenues through which to seek solutions—a month to begin a dialogue, the possibility of convening the trilaterals immediately, and, above all, the Germanophile McCloy as negotiator.

By contrast, McNamara no doubt saw the outcome of the August deliberations in a different light. He regarded, or seemed to regard, the President's indications as ambiguous, certainly not as a clear defeat for his position. After all, there was the language on the existing agreement. And, at his insistence, the President included in the reply to Erhard a reference to German budget discussions, a phrase which to other presidential advisors smacked of lecturing the Chancellor. The trilateral scheme meant that the issue would slip from McNamara's sole control, but it also ensured that there would be many more rounds of discussion, both within Washington and with Bonn.

In the month between the reply to Erhard and his visit to Washington, evidence mounted that compliance with the existing agreement *was* the Chancellor's problem. On September 9, Erhard finally admitted to McGhee that the current agreement was in danger, and by the 15th the embassy in Bonn was reporting that Germany would be able to find only $350 million for offset in the 1967 budget and so would want to stretch out a similar amount of its existing commitment. The embassy also correctly anticipated Bonn's desire to cut its obligation under the subsequent agreement in half. The Chancellor was expected to make a personal appeal to Johnson; if that appeal were to fail and Erhard were required to raise German taxes, the embassy apparently reported, his days might be numbered. Intelligence reporting also correctly predicted the scenario of the Erhard visit, though apparently not until the eve of the visit. During the course of the month, Walt Rostow and Bator made several attempts to induce official Bonn to clarify its position and continue the dialogue on offset which they, at least, had intended to start. Those efforts came to naught.

The principals and their senior aides convened again on September 21 and 23 to prepare for the visit. By that time it was clear that Erhard would ask for relief from his existing commitment. The President was informed of that in summary documents prepared by Bator, and in a report prepared by Bator; Ball; Frederick Deming, the Under Secretary of the Treasury for Monetary Affairs; and John McNaughton, the Assistant Secretary of Defense for International Security Affairs (ISA).

The American position had evolved since August: the President's senior advisors were willing to separate the German *payment* commitment (which carried a June 30, 1967 deadline) from their *orders* commitment (which came due December 31, 1966). All opposed reducing the level of payments, since it registered immediately in the U.S. balance of payments, but were willing to permit it to be fulfilled with purchases of Treasury securities. It was by then obvious that the Germans could not meet their orders commitment. McNamara, who expressed his view in a separate memorandum to the President, was prepared only to extend the orders deadline by six to twelve months, while Bator and Ball recommended letting the Germans fill the shortfall with purchases of bonds (and Fowler was willing to agree, provided the duration of the bonds was long, 12–15 years). Bator, who indicated clearly to the President that the price for the U.S. of a good visit was softening on the current agreement, suggested a procedural solution: in Washington the President and Chancellor could appoint representatives who would meet in the following weeks to work out a scheme for German compliance.

In the event, however, the President chose not to take that way out. In their private meeting on the first day of the visit, September 26, the Chancellor asked Johnson to permit the Germans to carry over into the subsequent agreement whatever portion of the existing agreement could not be fulfilled. The President expressed disappointment that the Germans were not meeting their commitment; he did raise the possibility of meeting the commitment through purchases of space or other civilian goods, but Erhard did not respond. The issue was then passed to working sessions of American and German senior officials, with the two heads of state not present. In those meetings, German Defense Minister von Hassel asked that the orders commitment be stretched to June 30. He proposed various means of fulfilling the existing payments commitment, including delaying $250 million in payments to 1968 and 1969 and purchasing medium-term Treasury bonds. He argued, moreover, that Germany could meet the payments requirement under the current agreement only if future commitments, for the five years between 1967 and 1971, could be cut in half, to $350 million per year.

McNamara objected strongly to deferring payments, and Fowler spoke against the proposal to purchase medium-term bonds; both worried about the American balance of payments in early 1967. Washington did, however, agree to count a $215 million German prepayment of post-war debt against the offset commitment. Yet the package which was negotiated forced the Chancellor both to secure action by the Bundesbank and, more important, draw more budgetary appropriations from the Bundestag.

The United States insisted that the current and the subsequent agreements be kept separate, with discussion of the latter deferred until the Trilateral Negotiations. In effect the link between offset and troop level was maintained. No offset deal could be put together apart from a decision on troops. The German setback was made clear in the published communiqué of the meeting, which stipulated that Germany would meet its existing obligation "insofar as financial arrangements affecting the balance of payments are involved"—a clear reference to payments. All the Germans could do was record in the communiqué their unwillingness to agree to future offsets of the existing kind and magnitude.

III. TRILATERAL NEGOTIATIONS

Despite the change of government in Bonn, there was no sharp break in the character of American deliberations between the August-September period and the central decisions of the Trilateral Negotiations in February and March 1967. Issues addressed, positions of principals and mechanisms through which the issues were handled: all stayed more or less constant. Divisions among departments and their chiefs remained no less deep than before, but the Trilateral format and the change of government in Bonn gave the government time to play out its internal divisions. McCloy had become a participant by September, and his involvement served to strengthen the force of State Department arguments.

Washington confronted three issues: what kind of redeployment of American forces in Europe could be worked out; how could the U.S. secure adequate protection for its balance of payments; and how tightly would the first issue be bound to the second—to what extent would Washington link its force level to the size of German offset. And throughout the discussions, the American government had to decide what role to play in bringing Bonn and London to a solution acceptable to Her Majesty's government. The Trilateral format was at once coordinating and complicating. American officials had to discuss at one table issues which formerly had been delegated to several forums and to deal simultaneously with the needs of two sets of foreign domestic politics.

The British Problem

The British problem seemed likely to undo the Trilaterals before they had begun. Prime Minister Wilson had assented to the Trilaterals because they offered him the chance to ride on the American coattails and, perhaps, to switch some German offset from the U.S. to the U.K. But the British had set an October deadline for the conclusion of the Trilaterals. The British problem became pressing when German negotiator Carstens made it clear, at the second Trilateral meeting, November 9–10, that the change in government in Bonn would delay the negotiations. British Foreign Minister George Brown approached the Americans for help. Walt Rostow reported to the President on those approaches and on McCloy's impressions of the first Trilateral meetings, and the three Secretaries (Rusk, McNamara and Fowler) jointly recommended that Washington agree to make $35 million more purchases in Britain (which equaled half the 38 million pound yearly foreign exchange savings Wilson had hoped to achieve from the BAOR) in order to prevent British force reductions for six months after April 11, 1967. Their recommendation was based on work done by the sub-Cabinet working group which had come together in August and September, composed of Bator, Bowie, Deming and McNaughton.

The President accepted the recommendation of his advisors and

123

made the offer to Wilson on November 15. Eugene Rostow, who had recently left his law professorship at Yale to become Under Secretary of State for Political Affairs, met with Callaghan and Wilson in London November 22 and concluded a general agreement. Wilson announced the agreement to Commons on December 12.[18]

The McCloy Report

John J. McCloy had been given a dual charter: to serve as the U.S. negotiator in the Trilaterals and to prepare an independent report to the President. He put together a staff which included officials from State, Treasury, the Central Intelligence Agency, Defense's Office of International Security Affairs (ISA), and at McCloy's special request, an officer from the Joint Staff. Officials attached to McCloy's staff participated in the tripartite working groups established as part of the Trilaterals and worked on McCloy's report to the President.

The establishment of the McCloy task force and the commencement of the Trilaterals altered the balance of opinion within official Washington. McCloy argued a strong "State Department" hand in high-level deliberations. With the onset of international negotiations, the State Department, and its operating agent, EUR, acquired legitimate right to preeminence in Washington's deliberations. In addition, when the Trilateral exercise began, operating responsibility for offset and force level within several departments passed from one office to another, invoking new procedures and bringing new perspectives to bear. The shift was most notable in the Pentagon. Control was withdrawn from Kuss and Foreign Military Sales and moved to ISA, Defense's political operation. John McNaughton's deputy for Europe, Frederick Wyle, worked on McCloy's staff. He and his subordinates opposed a substantial withdrawal of American forces from Europe and injected that preference into discussions. They also were able to demonstrate that the United States could make arms purchases in Britain with no great discomfort, thus enabling Washington to compensate for any shortfall in the German offset for London.

Through participation in the Trilateral exercise, the Joint Chiefs of Staff came to see both offset and force level in a different light. Previously they had taken the view that the German Army needed a large number of new weapons and so they had supported the American arm-twisting. It was not clear to them then, but became so during the fall and winter, that too much pressure might backlash on the troop stationing.

More important, the Chiefs developed a new perspective on the relationship between estimates of the military balance in Europe and decisions about the level of American forces. Their official position had it that the conventional forces of the Warsaw Pact overwhelmed those of NATO. In any attack the threshold to tactical nuclear weapons would be crossed by NATO in a matter of a few days. Yet at the same time, the Chiefs argued, inconsistently, that any reduction in American forces would tip the military scales dangerously. Of course, if NATO actually were hopelessly inferior, American reductions, even large ones, would have made little military difference.

McCloy insisted on developing a government-wide consensus on the military balance in Europe, to be presented to the allies. He argued that the agreed position would serve either as a basis for justifying American withdrawals or as a brief against reduction. Working with men like McCloy and Bowie, who were sympathetic to military arguments and were trusted more than Pentagon civilians by military officers, members of the Joint Staff came to see the utility of a realistic assessment of the balance in Europe. Exaggerating the Soviet advantage only encouraged rash reductions born of hopelessness. By contrast, if the forces of the two sides were roughly equal, holding the line on American troop strength became more crucial.

McCloy made his report to the President on November 21, framed as a personal assessment.[19] It expressed his desire to dissociate troop level from offset, first reaching a decision on troops and then putting together an offset. He opposed any reduction in American forces in Europe. Not only would the cut itself diminish NATO conventional strength, but in addition American allies would follow suit, he judged, and the over-all reduction in NATO strength would be three to four divisions. If domestic political or foreign exchange considerations compelled a cut, then he suggested a "rotation" plan involving one division, like the scheme eventually adopted. The entire division's equipment would be left in Germany and the division's three brigades would rotate through Germany in turn, with provisions for the rapid mobilization of the entire division in Germany if need be. McCloy's report calculated that the rotation would save $28 million per year in foreign exchange after a one-time budgetary cost of $150 million for a second set of equipment.

McCloy's basic argument against troop reduction recited a familiar litany of objections to the Systems Analysis study on which McNamara's position ostensibly was based: redeploying U.S. troops to Europe in a crisis with C-5A's was likely to take weeks, not days, even if the force's equipment had been left behind in Germany; reductions might produce balance-of-payments savings but at budgetary cost; the several weeks of "political" warning time before an attack, on which McNamara counted, was uncertain,[20] or whatever warning there was might not be heeded, or redeploying in the midst of a crisis might itself be provocative; airfields in Europe might be destroyed; and so on.

The President, however, set aside the McCloy report since the Trilaterals were in suspense until a new government was formed in Bonn. The three international working groups which had been established continued to work in the interim, and there was one formal Trilateral meeting, November 28–30 in Bonn, but the serious business of the negotiations did not begin again until February.

Both the British on one side of the Atlantic and American "troop-cutters" on the other grew restive as the Trilaterals dragged on. Senator Mansfield had introduced a sense-of-the-Senate resolution September 1 calling for a "substantial reduction" in the U.S. force in Europe. In mid-October he had shelved it pending completion of the Trilaterals, but he reintroduced it January 19, labeling the Trilaterals "a prolonged exercise for deferring decisions and action." He was supported by all but one member of the Democratic Policy Committee in the Senate and garnered forty-one co-sponsors the day the resolution was reintroduced. Senator Javits and eleven co-sponsors introduced a counter-amendment which had the tacit support of the Administration.[21]

The February Decision

The informal sub-Cabinet group which had formed in August and September continued, with only a slight modification in membership, to serve as the senior staff operation for offset and force level. Chaired by Eugene Rostow, it included Bator, who set the agenda and controlled the timing of discussions; Deming; McNaughton; Robert Bowie, the State Department Counselor (on McCloy's behalf); and John Leddy, the Assistant Secretary of State for European Affairs (EUR), back at work again by fall. To the President, people mattered more than departments, and he took decisions after meetings in which the three Secretaries—McNamara, Rusk and Fowler—had a chance to make their cases face to face. McCloy was an occasional participant in those meetings. Bator convened them, oversaw the preparation of background documents and staffed the President.

The involvement of McCloy provided a counterweight to McNamara, since the latter continued to take an active role and Rusk remained slow to become engaged. McCloy's presence, however, also raised complications because officially he was the President's aide and hence formally could be given instructions only by the President. Yet he was at the same time a State Department partisan, especially in the eyes of McNamara. To an extent, the "Rostow group," as the *ad hoc* working group came to be called, served as a means of keeping McCloy at arm's length and maintaining White House control of the process.

The Rostow Group, which overlapped with a group chaired by Deming dealing with international monetary matters, provided for unobtrusive but effective centralization.[22] No agency could feel that its views were not being given representation, yet none could ride roughshod over deliberations, as had Defense in the spring and early summer of 1966. The group could function only so long as its members understood that "solos" were against the rules. Deputies often argued the briefs of their superiors, with McNaughton criticizing the McCloy position which in turn was defended by Bowie. Yet the participants were senior enough so that they did not merely represent agency viewpoints, pat and predictable, but could speak for their chiefs and carry argument back to them. At the same time, the White House could keep all the threads in its hands since Bator controlled the agenda and since only he had easy access to discussions at all levels. Issues could be kept fluid until the President was ready to decide on a package.

The reopening of negotiations in February 1967 meant that McCloy needed new instructions, if indeed he were to be the negotiator (his October 7 instructions had reserved him the right to depart if he could not live with the eventual Presidential decision). The President and his senior advisors met again February 25. In preparation for that meeting, the [Eugene] Rostow group produced and cleared with superiors a long memorandum expressing the views of the three Secretaries. Fowler expressed no opinion on the troop issue, for it lay outside his Department's domain, on terrain where Treasury could claim no competence. The memorandum contrasted

Rusk's preferred alternative—a reduction of one division and three air wings—with McNamara's—two divisions and six air wings. It also presented a summary case for the McCloy no-cut position.

The Rusk alternative implied an annual foreign exchange saving of $100 million and annual budget savings of $25–40 million, after one-time budgetary costs of $50–160 million. For McNamara's position, the numbers were, respectively, 200, 50–80, and 80–240, although the Joint Chiefs attached a dissent, believing that those figures understated budgetary costs and overestimated savings. The Chiefs opposed any reductions in troop strength, on the argument that McNamara's analysis (which predicated the ability to return the troops and planes within thirty days) overestimated the speed of reinforcement and underestimated the rapidity of a Soviet attack.[23] Rusk's argument against a reduction of as many as two divisions was primarily political: a cut of that size would diminish Washington's influence in Europe and encourage centrifugal tendencies in the alliance.

McCloy submitted a written comment on the Rostow group memorandum. It reiterated his opposition to any cut but indicated his willingness to accept a one-division/three-wing "rotation," provided it was coupled with a commitment not to reduce further in the absence of allied agreement and Soviet reciprocity. Bator summarized the various positions for the President and expressed his own preference for no reduction, siding with McNamara's judgment on military grounds but arguing that political considerations made any reduction risky.

For Washington, the troop issue boiled down to a choice between the quick surgery of a cut to a credible "plateau"—a level which Europeans could be confident would be maintained—and the attempt to avoid putting pressure on the Atlantic alliance during NPT and international monetary negotiations. All the principals in the Executive recognized the force of Congressional sentiments. But those opposed to reduction argued that there were domestic dangers involved in cutting. For them, a no-cut position might be defended as a means of urging the Soviet Union toward mutual reductions. That defense might stick if Bonn's money deal were attractive. There was by then no chance of getting a full offset, nor one composed primarily of military procurement, but Bator and others argued that a combination of securities purchases and the gold pledge would serve just as well.

The President decided, tentatively, to have McCloy seek an agreement based on a reduction of one division and three wings. That left "plateau" issues, both tactical and strategic. In the negotiations, should the U.S. condition the one-division cut on an attractive offset? Rusk wanted to give no such signal, but McNamara argued for indicating that additional cuts would follow if Bonn were not forthcoming financially or if London made substantial cuts of its own. Would the United States force level reached *after* the Trilaterals be advertised as a "floor" for the several years ahead? The two Secretaries disagreed over that as well: Rusk thought so, McNamara not.

Offset and the Trilaterals were the subjects of a Presidential breakfast with Congressional leaders on the 27th of February. The meeting was carefully orchestrated to let Mansfield have his say but to surround his view with opposing positions. At the same time, the President used the breakfast and a subsequent meeting with McCloy to impress McCloy with the problem faced by the Oval Office. White House officials, not least the President, worried that McCloy was inclined to be too gentle with the Germans and not sympathetic enough to the British. The President's discourse was, according to second-hand accounts, vintage Johnson, laced with graphic hill-country metaphors. He explained, in no uncertain terms, how difficult it would be to hold the line on troops with Congress if Bonn's offset offer were skimpy or if London were driven to make wholesale reductions.

The President's March 1 instructions to McCloy formed the basis for an American proposal laid before the Trilaterals March 3rd.[24] It was based on three premises, innocent-sounding enough, but principles which had been warmly debated for a year in Washington and about whose application senior officials in the American government continued to differ: force levels would be determined by the allies on the basis of security considerations, broadly construed; German military purchases in the U.S. and the U.K. should be based on the military requirement of getting German military forces to appropriate strength; and any remaining financial problems should be dealt with through cooperation in the management of monetary reserves. At the same time, the President expressed his desire to prevent reductions in the BAOR and directed McCloy to review the Anglo-German deadlock.

Offset for Washington

Discussion of alternate offset formulas for the United States had taken place throughout the fall, and it intensified in February.

Issues became better understood on both sides of the Atlantic, and both governments made concessions. The U.S. moved gradually to acceptance, as offset, of German purchases of Treasury securities on terms the Bundesbank would accept. McNamara and others who had argued that selling bonds only postponed the U.S. deficit came to accept that buying time was, after all, the name of the balance-of-payments game. In 1967, there was no way to do more, short of devaluing or implementing nastily protective measures, the first then unthinkable and the second a remedy worse than the disease. Fowler and his colleagues came to decide that the terms the Germans would accept would suffice for American purposes. It was not, however, that easy to assemble a package for the British.

Tripartite working group three, dealing with finance, could not reach agreement because the three nations approached the analysis with very different assumptions. Of that, more will be said in chapter V. Washington and Bonn both recognized, however, that the net German "gain" was somewhat less than the gross American "drain" because of feedbacks of the American expenditures on U.S. exports. That provided a rationale for American acceptance of an incomplete offset.

Still, there remained the problem of how to fill the gap between what military procurement Bonn was prepared to make and whatever offset target Washington accepted. Bundesbank purchases of Treasury securities were the obvious candidate for gap-filler; the idea had been in the air since before the Erhard visit to Washington. What remained was to agree on amounts and on terms which would be both palatable to the Bundesbank and useful to the Americans.

Under Secretary Deming met with Bundesbank officials early in February, and the Germans offered to purchase $400–500 million in securities. What was important to the U.S. was that the securities be nonconvertible and of more than a year's duration, so that they might be counted in the liquidity balance as a *capital* inflow (ultimately they were credited only as a means of *financing* the deficit). For their part, the Germans wanted an "escape clause" which would permit them to convert the securities to a more liquid form in case Bundesbank reserves dropped sharply. The Bank also was edgy about committing itself to make further securities purchases as part of any future offset agreement. Deming and Bator drafted a letter to the Bundesbank February 24, asking for clarification of the German offer and suggesting that the "escape clause" was not a problem, provided there was informal agreement that inconvertibility would be sustained for 13–15 months. The Bundesbank intention to purchase $500 million in securities was expressed in the Blessing letter to Federal Reserve Chairman Martin on March 30 (later made public). At the same time, the German reservation was set forth in a cable from a senior Bundesbank official to Deming.

Exactly how the idea of a gold pledge arose is not completely clear to me, but it was the logical extension of informal "gentlemen's agreements" previously concluded with several developed countries. Those stipulated that the countries would not exchange their dollar holdings for gold. In fact, the Federal Republic had not been making large claims on the U.S. gold stock, but a public commitment was attractive to the U.S. as a means of solidifying the practice, hence issuing a signal to international financial managers, and as an example to the French. Bundesbank President Blessing apparently mentioned in a conversation with McCloy that he would not object to putting the promise in writing.[25] The Deming-Bator letter of February 24 asked for confirmation of the German willingness, and the [Eugene] Rostow group drafted language which was suggested to the Bundesbank in another Deming letter, March 5. Acceptable language was worked out and included in the March 30 letter from Blessing to Martin.

Assistance to Offset for London

By early March, the offset package for the United States was virtually complete, but London and Bonn were far apart. Wilson still was publicly committed to a full offset (as much as $250 million) but the existing German government offer—thrown into doubt by February's events in Bonn—was only $88 million. Wilson needed at least $154 million to meet his BAOR foreign-exchange saving target. However, German negotiator Duckwitz hinted to McCloy that the Germans might be able to raise their offer to $114 million, despite the resistance of Finance Minister Strauss. That left a gap of $40 million.

The principals in Washington convened again to decide what to do about the gap. The financial issue again touched the question of American force levels, for what the Federal Republic could be induced to do for Her Majesty's government hinged partly on what signal Washington gave about its intentions with respect to force level. Bator suggested a package: McCloy would press the Germans to increase their offer to $114 million, and the British would be urged to make only a small cut (theoretically 5000 but actually only 1500 from existing BAOR strength); as a last resort, the United States would itself fill some portion of the gap. The President met with the three Secretaries, plus McCloy, Bator and Walt Rostow, on March 8. McCloy pressed the President, urging him to intercede with Bonn and London to induce each to give halfway on the $40 million gap. But the President, not ready to commit himself, instead called a meeting for the next day, requesting that the [Eugene] Rostow group prepare a list of ways the U.S. could fill the gap.

The Rostow group offered four possibilities: the British could credit increased American military spending in Britain (occasioned by the redeployments from France) against the gap; U.S. procurements in the U.K. related to the F-111 fighter plane could be accelerated; a new American procurement bundle might be prepared; or the United States could release $40 million of the German obligation under the previous American offset for use in Britain. Bator recommended to the President that McCloy be authorized to try any of the possibilities except the speedup in F-111 procurement. In the meeting on the 9th, Rusk, who had been urged on by Assistant Secretary Leddy and other members of the Rostow group, argued strongly for filling the gap. Treasury Secretary Fowler, however, was reluctant, having concurred in the earlier "bail-out" of London only because the U.S. was in bilateral balance-of-payments surplus with the U.K. The President apparently countered the Fowler argument in colorful terms, calling the $40 million a "medium-sized poverty grant in New York City" and noting that the intervention in the Dominican Republic ate up that much money in one day!

London heard of the discussions in Washington, and the same day, March 9, Foreign Secretary George Brown conveyed to Rusk his government's interest in the package under discussion. Washington's decision to help fill the gap facilitated the piecing together of an adequate offset for the U.K., although there was considerably more discussion of details. In the end, Bonn found more money than anticipated for procurement and raised their offer to $137.5 million, and the United States needed only to commit itself to $19 million more in procurements in Britain.

With offset for London falling into place, there remained but one final object of friction before the conclusion of the Trilateral Negotiations. Bonn objected to the U.S. Air Force portion of the one-division/three-air-wing redeployment Washington had proposed. Washington had planned to withdraw 144 planes from the three wings, but German officials, anxious because the planes possessed a nuclear capability, felt that number was excessive. Officials in Bonn asked McCloy to trim the reduction in half, to 72 planes, and Kiesinger raised the issue with Johnson when the two met in Bonn, in April.[26]

McCloy recommended that the President compromise and reduce the number to 96, but McNamara and McNaughton used the eleventh-hour debate to reopen the question of the force reduction. McNamara declared himself willing to whittle the plane redeployment down to 96, *provided* the Army withdrawals were increased to 45,000. Bator sided with McCloy in a memorandum to the President on April 27, the day before the Trilaterals were scheduled to end. The U.S. could withdraw only 96 planes, as a personal favor to Kiesinger, perhaps prompting him to be more cooperative on NPT, international money, trade and other outstanding issues. Costs to the U.S. would be minimal, as the Army portion might be increased slightly in order to keep the total number of men withdrawn at 35,000. The President decided in favor of McCloy and Bator.

Enough of separate looks at Bonn and Washington. I turn now to their interactions during 1966 and 1967.

NOTES TO CHAPTER IV

[1]An example is McCloy's position in 1966–67. *See* also the 1970 comments by Assistant Secretary Hillenbrand on the difficulties inherent in the kind of redeployments made after the Trilaterals. *United States Security Agreements and Commitments Abroad, Pt. 10: United States Forces in Europe,* Hearings before the Subcommittee on United States Security Agreements and Commitments Abroad of the Senate Committee on Foreign Relations, 91 Cong., 2 sess. (1970), p.2250. [Hereafter cited as *United States Forces in Europe (Senate, 1970).*]

[2]No doubt considerations other than those of a strictly military nature have played a role in determining military positions. For example, questioners in the hearings cited above displayed considerable concern over the disproportionate number of senior American officers stationed in Europe compared to the number of troops there. The official military response was that the presence of the officers was necessary to enable the force to be rapidly beefed up by troops transported from the United States. However, the desire for attractive billets in Europe may also influence the pattern of deployment. *See* Timothy W. Stanley, "Mutual Force Reductions," *Survival,* XII, 5 (May 1970), p.152.

[3]*See,* for example, his remarks to the press as reported in the *New York*

Times, May 19, 1966, or his comment to Congress the next year, in *United States Troops in Europe,* Hearings before the combined Subcommittee of the Senate Committees on Foreign Relations and Armed Services, 90 Cong., 1 sess.(1967), p.19. [Hereafter cited as *United States Troops in Europe (Senate, 1967).*]

[4]*See* the testimony of Charles Hitch, cited in Richard Cooper,*The Economics of Interdependence: Economic Policy in the Atlantic Community* (New York: McGraw-Hill, 1968), p.162.

[5]Their comments appear in *United States Forces in Europe (Senate, 1970),* p.2230.

[6]Reported in an article by John Finney in the *New York Times,* September 29, 1973.

[7]*See,* for example, *U.S. Forces in Europe,* Hearings before the Subcommittee on Arms Control, International Law and Organization of the Senate Committee on Foreign Relations, 93 Cong., 1 sess. (1973), pp.8–9.

[8]Quoted in the *Washington Post,* February 25, 1967.

[9]As a crude check on the anecdotal evidence presented in this paragraph and the preceding, I examined the 1967 hearings conducted jointly by the Foreign Relations and Armed Services Committees, *United States Troops in Europe (Senate, 1967).* I looked at the questions each Senator asked—not at prepared statements or insertions, for those may represent the interests of legislative aides more than Senators—and classified each question according to the concern it indicated. I used four categories, two political and military, the other two economic: (1) American troops and the East-West balance, (2) American troops and NATO, (3) the balance-of-payments cost of the troops, and (4) their budgetary cost.

Of those who asked more than two questions, several were interested only in the political and security considerations attached to the troop presence: Fulbright [2 questions in (1), 1 in (2)]; Hickenlooper (same as Fulbright); Stennis (same); Miller [6 in (1)]; and Pearson [2 in (2)]. One Senator, Sparkman, asked one question in each of the four categories. Several others seemed predominantly interested in cost: Symington [three questions in each of (1), (3) and (4)]; Jackson [3 in (1) and (3), 2 in (4)]; and Church [1 in (1) and 2 in (3)].

[10]For a similar assessment, *see* Annette Baker Fox, "Domestic Pressures in North America to Withdraw Forces from Europe," in William T.R. Fox and Warner R. Schilling, eds., *European Security and the Atlantic System* (New York: Columbia University Press, 1973), p.222.

[11]*See* the *Washington Post,* October 8, 1973.

[12]A packet of case studies prepared in 1974 for the federal Commission on the Organization of Government for the Conduct of Foreign Policy surveys the process of weapons acquisition. It makes the point of this sentence in a compelling way, and it suggests some of the reasons why. Those cases appear in Appendix K to the Report of the Commission (Washington, 1975).

[13]For examples of the arguments of the ex-officials, *see* the articles by George Ball and John McCloy in the *Washington Post,* May 19, 1971.

[14]The figure for 1966 (liquidity basis) was − 1.357 billion dollars; for 1967 it was −3.544 billion. *Economic Report of the President 1970* (Washington, 1970), pp.276–277.

[15]For a brief description of the debate inside the U.S. government over the space proposals, *see* the article by Benjamin Welles in the *New York Times,* June 10, 1966. For comment on discussions of the Payments Union, *see* the article by Max Frankel, same paper, June 12, 1966.

[16]*See,* for example, McNamara's speech in Montreal in early June 1966. In it he said, "Advancing technology will reduce the requirement for bases and staging rights at particular locations abroad." *London Times,* June 6, 1966.

[17]Many commentators, on both sides of the Atlantic, cited roundabout activities which seemed to presage a reduction. *See,* for example, an article by Anatole Schub in the *Washington Post,* July 23, 1966.

[18]The agreement was announced by the State Department on December 9. *See* the *New York Times,* December 10, 1966.

[19]McCloy described his views in 1967 to a later Congressional hearing. *See The American Commitment to NATO,* Hearings before the special Subcommittee on NATO Commitments of the House Committee on Armed Services, 91 Cong., 1 Sess.(1971–72), p.13564.

[20]For a discussion of the political warning time issue and especially of differences among allies with respect to it, *see* the column by C. L. Sulzberger in the *New York Times,* August 12, 1966.

[21]For newspaper reports on Mansfield's actions, *see* the *Washington Post,* September 1 and October 19, 1966, and an article by John Finney in the *New York Times,* January 20, 1967. The texts of the Mansfield and Javits amendments appear in *United States Troops in Europe,* Hearings before the combined Subcommittee of the Senate Committees on Foreign Relations and Armed Services, 90 Cong., 1 sess.(1967), pp.1–4.

[22]Francis Bator has referred to the [Eugene] Rostow group and others like it during the Johnson Administration as "clubs." For a description of their character and operation, *see* his testimony in *U.S. Foreign Economic Policy: Implications for the Organization of the Executive Branch,* Hearings before the House Committee on Foreign Affairs and its Subcommittee on Foreign Economic Policy, 92 Cong., 2 sess.(1972), pp.107–21. The Deming group was similar, although Bator obtained a formal charter for it from the President. That charter is reprinted at the end of Lyndon Johnson's book, *The Vantage Point: Perspectives on the Presidency, 1963–69,* (New York: Holt, Rinehart and Winston, 1971).

[23]For a description of the competing analyses of troop reduction and dual-basing, see the *Washington Post,* March 13, 1967.

[24]That proposal was made public in a State Department press release on the 3rd. *See* the article by John Finney in the *New York Times,* March 4, 1967.

[25]For Blessing's account of that conversation, and for his later regret at having made the pledge, *see* "Interview mit Karl Blessing," *Der Spiegel,* May 3, 1971, p.82.

[26]The disagreement over the Air Force redeployment was mentioned by both Secretary Rusk and Under Secretary Katzenbach, in *United States Troops in Europe,* Hearings before the combined Subcommittee of the Senate Committees on Foreign Relations and Armed Services, 90 Cong., 1 sess.(1967), pp.62 and 50, respectively. It is also discussed in an article in the *New York Times,* April 24, 1967.

CHAPTER V: BETWEEN WASHINGTON AND BONN

The foregoing two chapters have treated the politics of governing in Bonn and Washington as largely self-contained. External events might require action, or hasten it, but the shape those actions took was treated as the result of the politics and processes internal to each capital. That focus was more than merely a device for presentation, for concerns within their own deliberations were what most moved both Germans and Americans. Yet officials in both capitals sought to influence events in the other; sometimes they did so explicitly and with calculation. Whether or not they sought influence, decisions by one capital affected actions in the other. Those actions in turn bore on deliberations in the first capital. Describing the interactions of Bonn and Washington during 1966–67 is the immediate subject of this chapter. It lays the portrayals of deliberations in the two capitals on top of one another. My reconstructions include not only how actions by one actually affected the other but also what officials in one expected of the other, or what they hoped for from their counterparts abroad. These latter reconstructions are hazardous endeavors but necessary ones in assessing American policy-making.

To the two sets of politics must be added a third—that of the United Kingdom. While the crucial interaction in the offset case was that involving Bonn and Washington, British politics affected both the timing and the substance of that relation. Washingtonians saw the actions of the American government as crucially affected by decisions in London. Men in Bonn occasionally were blind to that link, or could only see it as a menace, while at other times they regarded it as an inconvenience. In 1967 during the Trilaterals, participants in all three capitals had not only to consider at one time a range of issues which by custom were dealt with separately, they were compelled to attend simultaneously to the requirements of three sets of domestic politics.

The second half of this chapter turns to the performance of the American government. It asks how well Washington did in handling both the substance of the issues and its relations with its allies. Its intent is to determine what part the form the issues took in Washington, and the structures and procedures through which they were treated, played in producing American decisions and actions. It is an inquiry into the effect of process, construed broadly, on policy. In what particulars did the structures and procedures of 1966 and 1967 differ from those of later episodes in the handling of offset and force level? And to what effect?

This chapter closes with the puzzle which forms the point of departure for the next. In retrospect, there seems to have been no way for Washington to have met the German Chancellor's needs in September 1966 at an acceptable cost to itself. The difficulty lay beyond the nature of the policy process or of the personalities of the men who sat atop it. Rather it derived from a confluence of governmental process and domestic politics, one which over time had become rigid, given expression in the offset instance by senior American officials yet at the same time constraining their actions. That combination, its nature, source and implications for the future conduct of American relations with nations regarded as allies: these are the subjects of chapter VI.

The questions I ask of American politics and process are, of course, matched on the German side. I have alluded to many puzzling aspects of German action in the course of previous chapters. Issues associated with the making of policy in Bonn are no less interesting than those regarding Washington, quite the contrary. Discussion of them would make for a fascinating book, but they are not my subject. That book I leave for someone on the other side of the Atlantic.

I. ALLIED INTERACTIONS OVER OFFSET AND FORCE LEVEL: WASHINGTON BETWEEN BONN AND LONDON

The offset affair of 1966 and 1967 must be understood in the context of "business as usual" in alliance relations. "Business as usual" means decentralized operations, on both sides of the Atlantic, constrained by routine coordination among the units of each nation's governmental machine. Procedures for clearing cables, preparing for visits by foreign leaders and the like assure some awareness by the departments of each other's intentions. But most of the decisions and actions, most of the time, are taken by individual departments and agencies, each dealing bilaterally with its foreign counterpart. In the American government, each department operates its own "buttons" within the broad guidelines of Presidential policy, subject only to routine clearances from its sister agencies. American officials, from many departments of government and at various levels, communicate, day-to-day, on literally hundreds of issues with their counterparts in the government of the Federal Republic. So it must be in relationships as close and complex as those which link Americans and Germans, Britons or Japanese. The alternative to decentralized operations is paralysis.

For example, at the same time McNamara was pressing von Hassel over German offset compliance, the Defense Department was urging the Federal Republic to increase its contribution to NATO. The Department of State was endeavoring to enlist the German Foreign Office in common front during the NATO crisis which followed the withdrawal of the French. State also was seeking German support for U.S. policy in Vietnam and beginning to fret about the effect of Soviet-American nonproliferation treaty negotiations on German politics. Treasury was looking for German help with the French in international monetary affairs. Kennedy Round trade negotiations were coming to a critical stage, so Commerce and Agriculture had their own issues to take up with Bonn. And so on. It was within this context that deliberations with respect to offset and force level took place.

Spring and Early Summer, 1966

The form of the existing offset agreements suited the purposes of the men on both sides of the Atlantic who managed the accords. Their stake in that form went deeper than proprietary interest or bureaucratic pride. For the American Departments of Defense and Treasury, the stake was obvious. Selling arms to the Germans both served the narrow interests of the Defense Department and aided the American balance of payments. The issue of what weapons Germany needed obviously was a contended one, in Bonn as in Washington. McNamara argued that the Bundeswehr lacked many items, particularly if it were to grow to the size projected for it, and many German officers agreed. Nevertheless, McNamara's lectures came to be deeply resented, and the efforts of his indefatigable aide for Foreign Military Sales, Henry Kuss, are now remembered in Bonn only with mutters. Even a Treasury official who worked on offset admitted to me later that there had been "too many trips, too many meetings and too much pressure."

Selling arms was better than selling IOUs, and for that reason McNamara wanted no part of the NATO Military Payments Union scheme. And he had another reason: severing the link between offset and force level would have reduced the leverage on the force level issue which the United States possessed and which the Defense Secretary wanted so badly to maintain. Moreover, the Payments Union was the creation of the technicians, acceptable—apparently— to the Treasury on technical grounds but complicated, and hard to explain or defend to the government's political leaders.

Officials astride the offset "channel" in Bonn had little more reason to scrap the existing arrangements. Not only were the arrangements cozy and symbolic of close defense cooperation with the Americans, but they gave Defense Ministry officials leverage on defense budget and procurement decisions within their own government. The Foreign Office shied away from anything so difficult to negotiate as the Payments Union. And such a scheme would have increased the total amount Germany had to pay, never mind that it might have made payment easier. Acquiring additional liabilities in a time of economic downturn and budget stringency was political poison. So, at least, many in official Bonn believed.

Some senior German officials were interested in switching some of their offset commitment—if, in fact, it was a commitment—to the purchase of space hardware or other civilian goods. These proposals, however, met with the same obstacles on the American side as did the Payments Union. The Pentagon was opposed. Whatever their balance-of-payments effect, sales of civilian goods neither conferred advantage with respect to force level nor helped to amortize military research and development costs. Treasury was lukewarm,

139

willing to go along provided it could be convinced that the purchases were truly "additional." But "additional" civilian purchases cost Bonn budget money just as did military hardware, and budget money was precisely what was hard to come by in 1966. The Germans were willing, in the words of an American negotiator I talked with later, to do everything they could "so long as it didn't cost them any money." By summer it was obvious, if it had not been all along, that any civilian purchases which the Federal Republic would be willing to make, and the United States to accept, would not total up to a large number.

So long as no official decision in Washington withdrew offset from the sole control of Defense and Treasury—and none did so explicitly until August 24—McNamara was free to run the issue in line with *his* primary mission. He could, and did, insist on the link between German offset compliance and the maintenance of the existing level of American forces in Europe. In May, he vigorously reasserted that link in meetings with German Defense Minister von Hassel.

The link became a major political issue in Germany. Germans already were edgy about the transfer of U.S. troops from Europe to Vietnam—fifteen thousand were transferred in early 1966—and McNamara's tenacity seemed to presage substantial reductions. In fact, of course, the Defense Secretary desired cuts, and so the atmospherics served his purposes, at least to a point. But the reaction in Bonn became quite bitter. McNamara was portrayed as a hard man, an arms salesman driving a bargain. Von Hassel was subjected to thorough questioning in the Bundestag about his visit to Washington, and government spokesman von Hase pointed to any shred of evidence from Washington which indicated that the link was not official policy. Yet it was just that.

Chancellor Erhard's July 5th letter to President Johnson gave offset only secondary emphasis. The letter dealt first with possible Soviet-American discussion of a non-proliferation treaty (NPT). That issue was potential dynamite for Erhard's government, one sure to split his party, and offset deadlines were still months off. Time enough to fix offset with the Americans later if the budgetary situation did not improve. Erhard apparently thought a general warning to the United States would suffice.

The letter put Washington in an awkward position. McNamara, of course, seized the Chancellor's comment on offset and drafted a stern reply, one which reiterated that the U.S. could not divorce force level from offset. The issue was still McNamara's, and Rusk apparently signed off on the strong language as a matter of routine. The government, however, was not ready to respond to the German request for assurances on NPT. Bonn wanted to be told, at a minimum, that the United States would not agree to NPT terms which foreclosed the possibility of a NATO nuclear force in which the Germans might participate. The "Gaullists" in Erhard's government would have liked more. They preferred that the so-called European option—a European force in which the United States eventually might not possess veto power over firing—not be ruled out. But Washington did not know in July whether the Soviets were serious about NPT negotiations, and did not find out until October. From the perspective of American officials, any assurances given to Bonn were sure to leak and be read in Moscow as evidence that the United States was shooting down its own trial balloon. On that argument Bator cut off the reply to Erhard. A full reply on offset coupled with a dodge on NPT would, he argued, only bring another Erhard letter in short order. Besides, a delay served his purposes by buying time to see how desperate the Chancellor's budgetary plight was.

The British Problem

While McNamara's draft reply to Erhard was being held in the White House, trouble appeared in another quarter. Her Majesty's government long had fretted over the foreign exchange cost of the BAOR, estimated at about $250 million per year.[1] Prime Minister Wilson had in fact renegotiated the existing Anglo-German offset agreement after taking office, but the British still did not receive a total offset and much of what they got took the form of German purchases of civilian goods. In the May 1966 budget statement, Chancellor of the Exchequer James Callaghan had expressed the British intention to seek a full offset from the Germans.[2] An Anglo-German working party was formed.

London's intention became urgent action in July, after another run on the pound sterling. Wilson announced a package of measures designed to save foreign exchange. Overseas expenditures would be slashed by $280 million dollars (100 million pounds), with Germany the obvious target. The package was hammered out in a Cabinet meeting on July 19, and the government locked itself into a mid-October deadline.

Callaghan flew to Bonn on the 20th. He tabled his government's

141

demand for a full offset, and, at an airport press conference, made public Britain's threat to draw down the BAOR to a level whose foreign exchange cost equaled whatever offset the Germans were willing to provide.[3] The British had forged a "link" of their own. In making that link public, Callaghan may have acted somewhat rashly, but he acted against a clear background of Cabinet support. After July, offset had become, for the British, purely a matter of foreign exchange. "Saving the pound" was a cry to which even Labour back-benchers rallied; in mid-summer 1966, only George Brown among senior party leaders spoke openly of devaluation. The Anglo-German Mixed Commission of defense and finance experts began work under the threat of British withdrawals and against a September 30th reporting deadline.

Bonn regarded the British threat as a nuisance. The British and American offsets previously had occupied different "channels," the former in the Finance Ministry and the latter at Defense. That low-level separation was mirrored at high levels. Senior German officials did not regard the two offsets as related to one another. For them, arrangements with the Americans were serious business, the British offset secondary. They cared most about U.S. troops; if the British wanted to withdraw some of their expensive garrison, the Germans were willing to let them. Von Hase announced July 24th that the Cabinet saw no way to reconcile the German and British positions.[4] Bonn did not appear to realize that if the British made substantial reductions, it would be hard for the United States not to follow suit. To Americans, the German defense effort, while important, was a thing of necessity. By contrast, conventional forces stationed on the continent by insular Britain were tangible evidence that the Europeans were willing to do their share. The Federal Republic's leaders remained blind to the potency in Washington of the British symbol until well into the fall of 1966.

August and September

The British threat provided one stimulus to American action, the timing of the German budget process another, more direct still. When the German government resumed work after the August holiday, the first item on the agenda was the Chancellor's economic stabilization program. Critical decisions were to be taken in the last days of August, and the American embassy in Bonn warned Washington August 12th that a lack of reply to Erhard's letter risked having offset possibilities foreclosed by German budget decisions. The President took his first serious look at offset, and he made his first important decision, albeit one taken somewhat casually. By not sending the McNamara draft reply immediately, he discarded the option of putting much pressure on the Germans in time to influence their budget decisions.

When the Washington principals met August 24th, the salient issues were tactical. Would the United States use pressure on offset to induce the Germans to accede to a United States force reduction? What would the United States do for the British? The trilateral scheme offered a means of providing some help to the Germans, but, more important, it was a way to forestall immediate British reductions. Even those who wanted to be lenient with Erhard—Ball and Bator—accepted the necessity of sustaining the link between offset and troop level. Congressional considerations seemed to compel it. That meant that Washington could contemplate no offset proposals apart from decisions on force level. The best that could be done was to begin a process. And that was difficult enough to accomplish against McNamara's continued firmness.

The focus on process made them inattentive to the specifics of Bonn's problem, contributing to the inattention to the *existing* agreement. McNamara had no reason to raise the old agreement; Ball and Bator felt they had no need to do so, if in fact they noticed it might be in doubt. Besides, budget statistics were always uncertain, all the more so in a time of difficulty, and who could be sure what kind of game the Germans were playing. They had lagged behind their offset payments schedules before, but they always had made a large payment at the end of the calendar year from unexpended Defense Ministry funds.

The idea of separating the old agreement from the new emerged only in drafting a response to Erhard. The President had given only general guidance, and once he left the room McNamara continued to argue for including hard language in the letter. Including firm language on the old agreement was a way to satisfy him. At the same time, for those who had argued the soft line, the letter seemed to contain sufficient signals to the Germans that the United States had altered course: the intention to join the Anglo-German Mixed Commission, plus the willingness to throw American offset and force levels into the agenda, plus the appointment of McCloy, which was sure to leak.

But the Erhard government focused on the requirement, not the opportunity, and it froze. Sorting out the measures of confusion, intrigue and calculation in German action is no mean feat. It is clear, however, that the American proposal for tripartite discussions looked, to Schröder and probably to Erhard, like an Anglo-American scheme for ganging up on Bonn. It flew in the face of the German tendency to separate the two sets of dealings and to give precedence to the United States. Bonn's suspicion of the trilateral idea was not diminished by its dealings with the U.S. embassy in the first days of September. The proposal was packaged as a means of solving the *British* problem, one to which the Federal Republic was inattentive anyway, not of aiding the Germans with *their* problem, at least not soon. The word of McCloy's appointment must have been reassuring, but it does not appear to have been decisive. Exactly when Bonn heard of the decision to appoint McCloy, I do not know. But McCloy's appointment was linked to the trilateral idea. And Bonn must have realized that he would not be a strong participant immediately, for there was some delay in Washington in working out the terms of his position as negotiator.

It would be hard to overstate the degree of confusion in Bonn. Erhard's government never had been a decisive one, and by late summer it had come unglued. Critical budget legislation was slow to reach the Bundestag, and the Chancellor could not seem to make up his mind about reorganizing his Cabinet. It is possible that he and his senior advisors were slow to understand just how serious their budgetary situation was. It had become clear to many in the CDU that Erhard had to go, that it was only a matter of time. Worse for Erhard, some, including CDU Bundestag leader Barzel, sought to hasten the Chancellor's departure. What Barzel did quite openly, others did covertly. Whether or not anyone used offset as an instrument to provoke Erhard's demise is impossible to determine. Opportunities to do so abounded.

The Chancellor apparently believed he needed a resounding victory for his political survival, and he thought, against the counsel of Westrick and Knappstein, that President Johnson would give it to him. Both Walt Rostow and Bator made attempts to establish communication with Erhard in the month before the visit. The White House, however, had no easy, informal links to the Chancellor's Office comparable to those it traditionally nurtured with 10 Downing Street. One attempt, through Erhard's nephew, did get to the Chancellor, but Erhard, imprisoned in a simplistic map of Washington, apparently saw no virtue in interchange below the level of heads of state. He sought victory at the summit.

Washington, however, could not give him his victory. Its leaders were willing to move beyond their August position, but the link between offset and force level still obtained. Even the "soft-liners" did not think an offset deal attractive to Erhard, arranged without some interallied agreement on force level, could be sold to Congress. Giving in further on offset but at the same time proposing a force reduction would only have compounded the Chancellor's problems. Besides, most American officials thought the United States was already being generous; McNamara and Fowler no doubt thought it was being too forthcoming.

European harpings on American balance-of-payments sins, to which the German Finance Ministry and the Bundesbank eagerly contributed, made it all the more difficult for the United States to grant Bonn relief from its existing offset commitment. Those concerned in Washington, including the President, were hardly eager to be so generous with their "lecturers" when doing so would have unleashed storms of domestic criticism. That effect was apparently lost on Bonn, where issues proceeded down tracks more rigidly separated than those in Washington. During the Erhard visit, Francis Bator mentioned to German Foreign Minister Schröder the consequences for offset of the German lectures on the U.S. balance of payments. Schröder responded with surprise, saying "but that's another issue and another part of the government, one that I don't know anything about."

In Washington, President Johnson did not use the procedural solution which had been suggested to him: appointing someone to negotiate a package with Erhard's agent, instead of hastily arranging for German compliance in Washington during the visit. Johnson may have been looking over his shoulder at Congress, or he may have been piqued with Erhard. The Chancellor had given a press "backgrounder" September 8, full of tough language. He called McNamara "arbitrary" and told a reporter "you can bet" he would raise the issue with Johnson in Washington. The President heard of the briefing and it cannot have served to make him gentler with the Chancellor. Or Johnson may have sensed when he saw Erhard that the Chancellor was a goner and decided that any concessions made to the Germans then would be dead losses when a new government reopened the issue.

Erhard's Downfall and Trilateral Delay: Once More the British

The chain of events which led to Erhard's political end was compli-cated enough, and reached back far enough in time, so that the United States escaped public responsibility for his fall. Yet there were many in both Bonn and Washington who believed that the U.S. had undercut the Chancellor, if craftily or even somewhat in-advertently. Many more thought the U.S. had nudged Erhard over the brink he previously had only tottered beside. My own view is that, *by August and September,* what Erhard believed he needed was greater than those in Washington could grant. His politics were incompatible, then, with theirs.

It was clear once Erhard resigned that the successor government would contain more "Gaullist" overtones than had his government. So it did. Kiesinger, after all, owed his election to the efforts of the Gaullist Strauss. The former had at least to make the proper oratori-cal flourishes. In the end, German-American relations probably were affected more in rhetoric than in substance, but bilateral delibera-tions in the next months, including those with respect to offset, were hindered.

The interesting question about the weeks following Erhard's re-turn from Washington is why a better face was not put on the visit. The United States had not caved in, but it had given much since July. Erhard did attempt to claim success, but the visit was generally deemed a failure. In part, the German press had soured on Erhard. And the Chancellor got little help from American officials in billing the visit as a victory. More important, however, the Chancellor had walled himself into a corner. Having sought a striking personal victory and having let it be known that he sought it, he could not credibly claim success for a negotiated settlement. Having over-looked the August change of policy in Washington, he could not in October claim it as a success for German diplomacy. Even so, the Germans might have done better. That they did not is additional indication of the sorry state of the Erhard government.

The trilateral scheme was from the start a mixed blessing for Prime Minister Wilson. He had agreed to it in the first week of September, but not without misgivings. On the one hand, the Trilat-erals offered Britain the opportunity to do just what Germany feared it would—ride on the American coattails or even to switch some German offset from the United States to itself. On the other hand, however, Wilson was locked into a tight Cabinet bargain over timing. The government had told the Permanent Council of NATO in August that it would draw down the BAOR if that became necessary to meet the foreign-exchange saving target.[5] Her Majesty's ministers counted on working out a reduction by the time the Anglo-German Mixed Commission was to report in mid-October. The reductions would have been announced at the December meeting of NATO foreign and defense ministers, and redeployments could have started before the beginning of the next British budget year, in April 1967.[6]

At the Anglo-German ministerial meeting on October 13, the Germans made an offer of 350 million *DM* per year (about $88 million) and held out the promise of sweetening that offer later, during the Trilaterals. That was acceptable to London, but only if the Trilaterals could be brought rapidly to a conclusion. The negotiations were for the British purely a means of arranging a money deal (and of securing allied agreement to reductions in the BAOR); the thorough studies of NATO capabilities and the Warsaw Pact threat, exercises on which Washington placed so much emphasis, only portended delay to London. The American government, while insisting that the talks be broadened beyond finance, compromised in October by agreeing that the tripartite working groups should present interim reports at the end of November.[7]

That agreement was rendered insufficient when it became clear, early in November, that the Trilaterals would be delayed considerably by the change of government in Bonn. The United States commitment to purchase $35 million more in military equipment in the United Kingdom provided the stopgap, forestalling British reductions for six months after the beginning of the next British budget year, April 11, 1967.[8] But it was an interim measure which pleased no one. Many in the American Congress were upset because the only result of three months of negotiation was the expenditure of more American money. And when Wilson took the arrangement to Commons, December 12, it was roughly received on both sides of the aisle. Tories taunted the Prime Minister for needing to be bailed out by the United States, and Labourites, particularly those on the left, were unhappy because the deal would delay cuts in the BAOR.[9] Throughout the offset deliberations, London's actions were colored by the vague anti-Germanism which permeated postwar British politics. Neither party was immune, but the sentiment was most obvious among Labour adherents, both those of the working class and those of intellectual stripe.

At the start of the Trilaterals, three tripartite working groups of officials were established: one, an intelligence group, examined the threat posed by Warsaw Pact forces; the second, a military group, studied NATO capabilities; while a third, the finance group mentioned before, endeavored to trace net foreign exchange gains and losses. The working of the groups was less obvious than the high-level bargaining which followed it, but the studies undertaken left their mark on the Trilateral outcome. More important, their influence on the thinking of the three governments persisted after the negotiations had ended.

The third group began, on the initiative of Washington and Bonn, a thorough economic analysis of the foreign exchange flows and "feedbacks" touched off by the American stationing in Germany. Officials attempted to calculate "net" effects — net German "gain" and net American dollar "drain." By all accounts, Bonn's participants in the exercise were tightly instructed, more so than their American or British counterparts, unwilling to accept assumptions or techniques which, while perhaps good economics, promised to produce big numbers for "gain" and "drain." As a result, the elaborate exercise was never brought to an agreed conclusion, but it did lay the basis for United States acceptance of a less than full offset.[10]

The exercise also provided graphic illustration of the fact that the foreign exchange flows were valued differently by the various governments. The losses were serious for the United States and especially for the United Kingdom, both countries running balance-of-payments deficits. On the other hand, the gains were not as valuable to the Federal Republic as the losses were damaging to its negotiating partners. Germany maintained substantial foreign exchange surpluses, and its economy operated at full employment with the exception of 1966-67. Additional foreign exchange inflows, in the view of officials in Bonn, only raised the specter of inflation, playing to an ever present German phobia. At one point in the deliberations of tripartite working group three, an official from the German Economics Ministry said he would prefer it if all the foreign troops left the Federal Republic, for any foreign exchange inflow their presence occasioned only increased the inflationary pressures in the German economy. The stationing of NATO troops on German soil could also be seen as requiring the presence of more foreign laborers in the Federal Republic, a social issue to which Germans became increasingly sensitive in the late 1960s and the 1970s.

The deliberations of working groups one and two made it clear that the allies held quite varying assumptions about both the threat from the East and the capability of NATO. The discrepancy was most marked between American and German estimates, although the British tended to make calculations which more closely concurred with Bonn than with Washington.[11] Germans tended to judge Warsaw Pact capabilities as much greater than did Americans; similarly, the former were more pessimistic about NATO prospects for withstanding a conventional attack than were the latter. The Trilaterals coincided with the sweeping reevaluation of the military balance between East and West which was proceeding within the United States government. That review was alluded to in chapter I. It had important effects within the United States government, especially within the military, as noted in the last chapter. The activities of the Trilateral working groups provided the opportunity to press that reevaluation on the major American allies in Europe. "Flexible response," the official United States doctrine for several years, was formally accepted by NATO in June 1967. More important, the allies began the process of coming to agreement on military calculations, a beginning which was useful as NATO entered MBFR (mutual and balanced force reduction) negotiations with the Warsaw Pact in the 1970s.

John McCloy's November report to President Johnson produced no action on the American side. There was then no government of the Federal Republic with which to negotiate. Nor was the President ready in November to force the issues to a head. The activities of the McCloy task force did widen the circle of people in official Washington who were familiar with the peculiar mix of international economics and military strategy which was the subject of the Trilaterals. McCloy's report assured the Joint Chiefs that their position had been well represented before the President. By shelving the report, however, the President tacitly rejected McCloy's desire to dissociate force level and offset, first deciding on a force level and then worrying about an offset. From then on it was clear that the two issues would remain linked. To American participants, the link was necessary in order to secure an attractive financial offer from the Federal Republic. They calculated, moreover, that Congress would insist upon it.

The February Decision

By January the government in Bonn was ready to reopen the negotiations. For Washington, that meant that McCloy had to be

149

given fresh instructions. Or, if he wished to step down after seeing the new guidelines, another negotiator had to be selected. In either case, decisions had to be made.

The important decisions were Washington's, but they were cast against events in Bonn. German Cabinet decisions in late January turned the opportunities afforded Bonn the previous August into clear constraints on American policy: new offsets would be smaller than old, and could not be composed entirely of purchases of military equipment. The Federal Republic told the United States that it would meet its old payments commitment by June 30, 1967, as Erhard had agreed, but that there would be no money for military procurement in the U.S. during the last half of calendar year 1967 and little money for 1968. The Germans would place orders totaling $300-400 million per year, but those orders would in effect be paid for with funds previously deposited with the United States under past offset accords.

German decision-making, and the Federal Republic's dealings with its allies, were complicated by several sets of politics. There was, first, the bureaucratic politics of the offset issue, broadened by the onset of international negotiations and reshaped by the Finance Ministry's acquisition of a dominant role. At the top of that process lay the politics of coalition government, made more strident because the bedfellows were so strange. The government seldom spoke with a single, clear voice, as various ministers sought to make their policy preferences prevail within — or sometimes, without — official government policy. Finally, Kiesinger had simultaneously to keep the government together *and* to sound a bit "Gaullist." The combination made for neither order within the government nor serenity in dealings with the allies.

The choices pondered in Washington were really the strategic counterparts of the tactical questions considered in August and September: how many troops, how much offset and how strong the negotiating link between the two. The President decided in February on the basis of a much richer "map" of the issues than he had received in the fall. The report prepared by the (Eugene) Rostow group in February contained concrete estimates of the cost savings entailed in various reductions, gave full airing to the military arguments for and against reduction — an issue on which the Defense Secretary differed with his military commanders — and made explicit predictions of the effect of American reductions on the defense efforts of allies.

The President's decision — while it bore superficial resemblance to the classic bureaucratic compromise between two extreme positions no reduction and a two-division cut — represented a serious attempt to balance the considerations before the President. Choice continued to be constrained by the existing form of the issue and by the perceived need to sustain the link between money and force level. That link was obvious in the decision to aim at a result based on a one-division/three-wing reduction: Bonn was told, in effect, that the reduction might be larger if the Federal Republic were not forthcoming financially. How much difference that condition made in inducing the men in Bonn to put pressure on the Bundesbank to join in, or to accept the eventual American reduction is, in the nature of the case, hard to know. It certainly made some difference. Officials in Washington thought it counted for a great deal.

Final Obstacles

By March, the pieces of a German-American package were coming together. The United States would make, and Germany would accept, a one-division reduction. At the same time, the U.S. would accept less than a full offset—80 per cent was the figure which emerged from Trilateral working group three — and would agree to count Bundesbank purchases of Treasury securities as offset. For its part, Germany would make the purchases in a way useful to the Americans and would give the pledge on gold, the Bundesbank implementing and the central government endorsing both actions.

Yet there was still the Anglo-German deadlock to contend with. Wilson was farther and more publicly out on a limb with Parliament than was Johnson with Congress. The Federal Republic continued to accord priority to the United States and was slow to respond to British entreaties. It was slower still because of intra-Cabinet politics. Strauss, now Finance Minister, was not eager to spend money for any purpose, all the less eager to spend it for an "Atlanticist" scheme in a forum entered by Erhard. Schröder, as Defense Minister, opposed Kiesinger at every turn and did not relish appropriating *his* defense budget to serve the Chancellor's purposes.

The U.K. and the Federal Republic were far apart. Wilson still was publicly committed to a full offset, but the Bundesbank was unwilling to purchase securities denominated in sterling, and the existing German government offer — cast into doubt by events of February — was only $88 million. Wilson needed at least $154 million to meet his BAOR foreign-exchange saving target (and even $154 million was at

151

least $80 million less than a full offset). On February 28, British negotiator George Thomson threatened "massive withdrawals" from the BAOR if there were no "substantial" German commitment by April 11, the British budget deadline. He and the German negotiator, Georg Ferdinand Duckwitz (who had replaced Carstens after the formation of the Grand Coalition), clashed over whether or not the British had rejected the German offer of the previous October.[12] Later, however, Duckwitz hinted to McCloy that the Germans might be able to raise their offer to $114 million, despite the resistance of Finance Minister Strauss. That left a gap of $40 million.

Again the United States intervened, this time with both stick and carrot. The threat was implicit in the link between the American reduction and the British: if the BAOR were drawn down drastically, the United States might feel compelled to increase the size of its redeployment. At the same time, the U.S. offered to fill part of the gap itself between the existing German offer and the British goal. Chancellor Kiesinger understood better than his predecessor the extent to which British decisions impinged on American actions. He said in late March that if the British withdrew massively, "President Johnson without doubt would not be able to resist the pressures to which he would be subject in view of the analogous retreat."[13] Schröder was pressed to find more money for procurement in Britain, and in the end the German offer exceeded the amount Duckwitz had hinted. The United States had to contribute only $19 million more.

The final flap about the size of the United States Air Force redeployment was, on the German side, part serious business and part "Gaullist" theatrics. The planes to be withdrawn did possess nuclear capabilities, and any reduction in the nuclear protection offered Germany was not a trifling matter in Bonn. Yet the dispute merged with Bonn's grumbling about German-American communication, an unhappiness which had punctuated the Trilateral negotiations. In part, Soviet-American NPT negotiations did cause the Chancellor political problems, but the series of disputes offered Kiesinger the chance to play to his "Gaullist" audience, proving that he was less acquiescent to Washington than Erhard had been. The plane issue gave him the chance to earn a "victory" in dealings with Washington. United States officials conceded him that success for purely political reasons. They reasoned that if the U.S. compromised on the plane question, which cost little, Kiesinger might be more helpful in other international negotiations then underway, matters in which American stakes were greater.

Effects of the Trilateral Form

A lesson of alliance relations, perhaps *the* lesson, is that form matters at least as much as substance, perhaps more. The Trilateral Negotiations reinforce that lesson. Of course the trilateral format was complicating, and many of its complications have been mentioned, but a purpose was served. For the first time, civil servants and military officers sat down to discussions of force levels in Europe and the financial and political questions associated with those troop stationings. The discussions took place in a framework more conducive to frankness than the formal NATO structures. Many effects of that process have been noted: disagreements over foreign exchange flows aired, agreed estimates of NATO capabilities and the Warsaw Pact threat hammered out, and the Joint Chiefs of Staff and their allied colleagues exposed to a new line of argument about the relationship between force reductions and evaluations of the military balance in Europe. Several other effects should be highlighted:

The offset negotiations often have been drawn out, and occasionally they have been acrimonious.[14] Yet in 1966-67 the protracted nature of the deliberations worked to advantage. What had been the occasion for polemics and political crisis became the subject of long, often tedious debate. Both Washington and Bonn moved gradually away from inflexible stands and toward acceptance of positions that each formerly had opposed. In particular, Germany had heard rumors of large American reductions for so long that when the moderate cut was made, it was accepted, greeted almost with relief. To that extent, McNamara's hard hand of the previous summer turned out, paradoxically, to be beneficial. The American reductions could even be claimed as a (relative) success of Grand Coalition statecraft. In any event, while the Germans could mutter about some aspects of interallied political consultation, they could have few complaints about the adequacy of the deliberations which preceded the American and British force reductions resulting from the Trilaterals.

Paradoxically, the Trilateral format, the creation of those who opposed American troop withdrawals, ended by providing a deadline for Presidential decision on the force level question. The result was reduction. Prior to the formation of the Trilaterals, McNamara, as has been mentioned, pressed often for a cut of several divisions. But Secretary Rusk refused to join him in those requests, and McNamara's memoranda to the President were disregarded by Johnson, or were stopped short of him. The Trilateral process hooked force level decisions on offset deadlines, both British and American. The President could not postpone a decision. Nor, with Congress looking over his shoulder, did he feel he could avoid making a reduction. McNamara got less than he wanted but more than he had achieved before.

What the Trilateral exercise did *not* do was alter the basic form of the offset issue. It did not advance public education, on either side of the Atlantic, about the troop stationing in Europe, international money, or relations between the two. The Trilateral outcome ratified the link between offset and troop level. To be sure, the notion of a dollar-for-dollar offset through military procurement was abandoned, and the Germans made the gold pledge. But the practice of separating out a "military" foreign exchange account and then "offsetting" deficits in it was maintained. More important, the United States again left the impression that whether it sustained the existing level of forces in Germany depended in large measure on how generous the Germans were financially. The link remained. It was easy for members of the American Congress or for ordinary citizens to fall into the belief that by stationing troops in Europe the United States primarily was providing a service to the Europeans, for which they should gladly pay. By the same token, it is not surprising that Germans often felt they were in fact paying for the troops, that the U.S. was twisting German arms in negotiations instead of acting to cement an alliance rooted in common interest.

II. AMERICAN POLICY-MAKING

This section evaluates the performance of the United States government in the offset cases. In particular, I seek to be explicit about the effect of policy-making *process* on policy outcome (that is, governmental action) in the cases. What role did the form the offset issue took in the American government and the structures through which it was handled play in producing the decisions and actions which emerged? I concentrate on the events of 1966 and 1967, with only side-glances at later episodes. Those glances, however, permit limited comparisons between policy-making structures — especially the contrast of informal coordination during 1966-67 with the more formal National Security Council process into which offset was fed in 1969.

I will treat the events of 1966-67 in reverse order, first discussing government performance during the Trilaterals and then returning to the puzzles which inhere in the actions of the American government in the period preceding Chancellor Erhard's visit to

Washington. It is, of course, slightly artificial to break down the process into discrete intervals. Not every phase produced an important governmental action or intergovernmental outcome; some stages could be construed as way stations *en route* to an eventual outcome. The central question is whether the decision-making process at one stage facilitated or hindered reasoned action in the next phase. And to answer that question there is no alternative to examining events period-by-period.

Policy-Making during the Trilaterals

Considerations and Alternatives. In the deliberations which led up to the conclusion of the Trilateral Negotiations, the American government evaluated a wide range of considerations and examined a spectrum of alternatives. Five main considerations were important, and each received attention: the U.S. balance of payments, American force deployments, NATO capabilities for conventional defense, German politics and European politics/NATO alliance. The set of alternatives considered ranged from no troop reduction to a cut of two divisions, and included an array of financial mechanisms and forms of aid to London. Those alternatives were evaluated, for instance in the Rostow group's February memorandum, against the major considerations: effects on NATO's capability for flexible response, given likely Soviet reactions; implications for European politics and defense efforts; foreign exchange and budget effects; and, not least, likely responses within domestic American politics. However, two constraints on deliberations lingered on: the form of the offset issue — offsets to military deficits — and the perceived necessity of sustaining the link between offset and force level.

The length of negotiations provided the opportunity to consider and reconsider a broad range of factors; the form of deliberations inside the U.S. government insured that would be the case. The onset of international negotiations gave the State Department claim to central participation; no longer was the issue McNamara's. McCloy's presence as negotiator strengthened the State Department hand. He drew much of his staff from the Department, from the Joint Staff and from ISA, and generally saw to it that advocates of the no-cut position would be well represented on his task force.

At the same time, the informal (Eugene) Rostow group provided a means of keeping McCloy at arm's length and making sure that he did not back the President into a corner before Johnson was ready to

155

decide. Group members were senior enough to speak for their departments, yet not so senior as to be too busy to master the detail of the issue. They both staffed their respective Cabinet officers and communicated laterally across department lines. The process was kept fluid. Deliberations of the group depended on collegiality; members might argue the briefs of their superiors, but end runs were known to be against the rules.

Bator served as master of ceremonies and filled the gaps. He was, for instance, able to revive the no-cut option and present it to the President after it had all but disappeared. Only he had access to deliberations at every level, giving the White House effective control of the process.

By accounts, the more formal National Security Council process in 1969 produced as good a "map" of the issue as was drawn during the Trilaterals. During the study (NSSM) phase, departments presented a wide range of options. Departments were enjoined from compromising their differences early in the process; each was to present its favorite alternatives. Severing the link between offset and force level not only was considered—as it had not been in 1967—it was the option chosen. There was even a "no offset" alternative, although it was recognized as a Treasury ploy, an attempt to use a "Treasury" issue—offset—to force action on a matter which lay beyond Treasury competence—force level.

Information-Gathering and Assessment. Information was not a problem during the Trilaterals as it had been during the period leading up to Erhard's visit to Washington. The protracted negotiations provided both time and abundant channels, both "front" and "back," to Bonn. Hunches could be tested and estimates refined, often through direct conversations: witness the communications between members of the Rostow group and Bundesbank officials over the gold pledge and the terms of the German purchase of Treasury securities.

Implementation. Nor was implementation a difficulty during the Trilaterals. While McCloy obviously did not completely share the President's preferences, the terms of his charter bound him to Presidential instruction. The Rostow group lengthened the reach of the White House into the various departments, helping to insure that no actions would be taken by McCloy or others which might foreclose possibilities the President would want to retain. No one was left free to press parochial concerns on the Germans, as McNamara had in the spring and early summer of 1966.

The faithfulness of implementation to Presidential intent turns, I believe, on whether or not follow-up can be deputed to some group or individual at once responsive to the President's intent and a force to be reckoned with for the bureaucracy, especially for careerists in the State Department. The informal coordination of the Johnson Administration built groups by handpicking individuals, as in the Rostow group, but a formal system like the 1969 NSC structure may find it harder to construct them. Formal systems may assume that most of the problem is getting good decisions. The Under Secretaries Committee in the Nixon Administration, a fixed committee, sometimes adequately supervised implementation, at least when chaired by Elliot Richardson; the Interdepartmental Groups, chaired by Assistant Secretaries of State, seldom could. And it may be difficult for the National Security Advisor to tailor special groups for many issues, given that he is only one man and given that he spends much of his time overseeing the pre-decision process.

The comparison of 1969 with 1966–67 is instructive. To the extent that implementation diverged from Presidential intent in 1969, the problem seems to have been that no official was identified as the one who would—and could—see that the process produced a final result faithful to the President's decision. Nathaniel Samuels, Deputy Under Secretary of State and the American negotiator, was not so identified, nor did he regard himself as that man. By contrast, McCloy was singled out as the President's agent in 1966 and 1967, and the President was careful to make sure that McCloy understood the White House perspective. In 1969, President Nixon appears to have taken little interest in offset once he had made the decision; Kissinger was attentive but not active (and since offset came at the beginning of the Administration, he would, in any case, have been disadvantaged because no one could be sure initially that he always spoke for the President). Richardson, who had close ties to Kissinger, played only a small role after the Presidential decision.

Impact of Congress. Congress remained at the fringes of discussion of United States policy during 1966 and 1967. That portrayal is probably accurate as a description of Congress' role; it is not correct as an evaluation of Congressional impact. Calls for action by the "gold bugs" in Congress strengthened the force of the balance-of-payments context within which offset/force level deliberations took place. The Mansfield resolutions (of September 1966 and January 1967) strengthened the hand of McNamara and Fowler. They gave McNamara another argument for withdrawing troops or, if not that, at least for holding firm in negotiations with the Germans, for reforging the link between German offset compliance and the maintenance of the existing level of American forces in Europe.

While the arguments of Mansfield and his supporters were and continued to be most visible and probably most important, other Congressional considerations affected President Johnson and his successor. In February, he worried about the possibility that American reductions might initiate the disintegration of NATO, handing the Republicans a tempting campaign issue for 1968. In 1969, the Nixon Administration managed to de-couple offset from force level and commit itself firmly not to withdraw troops from Europe for two years without provoking storms of Congressional criticism. Of course much had changed by then—the balance of payments had improved temporarily, and the Administration was committed to winding down the war in Vietnam.

Policy-Making Preceding the Erhard Visit

Viewed in the context of 1966, the sequence of American actions prior to the Erhard visit is easily explained. Indeed, in retrospect events are more likely to seem overdetermined than underexplained. By the light of context, the decisions of August and September represented a nimble redirection of policy in a situation where one was difficult to accomplish. If the United States had persisted in the McNamara line, Erhard would have fallen with a bang which would have reverberated in Washington, not merely with a whimper little heard outside Bonn. That Washington's decisions in August and September were, for Bonn, too little and too late owed principally to the state of confusion in Bonn. That was a problem Washington could not be expected to solve.

Yet the force of context should not obscure the fundamental puzzle in the offset case: if the outcome of the Trilaterals was a reasonable one for all concerned, why could it not have been assembled *sooner*, so that offset would have played no role in any flap in Bonn? I will return to that puzzle. To raise and address it makes clear the importance of the form of the policy process and of the interests at play within it in shaping the issues of offset and force level. Certain kinds of opportunities were foreclosed, and the range of American choice in August and September was sharply constrained.

Prior to the Erhard Letter: the Offset "Channel." Offset began as a balance-of-payments issue with a military sales face. That fact was crucial in shaping American policy during the period prior to the

Erhard letter, when the issue was consigned to the Defense/Treasury channel by decentralized operations in the Executive Branch, but it colored later deliberations as well. Despite the fact that there was sporadic attention being paid to offset elsewhere in the government, its handling was dominated by Defense and Treasury interests: selling arms and protecting the American balance of payments. Neither department had any incentive to produce alternatives beyond a new procurement-only offset. Why serve up alternatives which threaten a *status quo* one prefers? Jurisdiction, coupled with the active intervention of McNamara, meant that Defense and Treasury successfully could restrict the menu for Presidential consideration. Notice the apparent ease with which McNamara rejected the SIG decision on the Payments Union or, somewhat later, induced Rusk to sign on to firm language in response to Erhard's July 5th letter.

The formal SIG/IRG structure, implanted early in 1966, centered on the State Department.[15] Its fatal weakness no doubt was that none of the principals it was designed to serve was enthusiastic about the system, not even the senior State Department officials—Rusk and Ball—whom it was supposed to advantage, while the President was distracted by the war in Vietnam. But the system was organizationally deficient as well. It made its recommendations to the Secretary of State, not to the President, and the Secretary had to carry the proposal to the President. There was no way to bring *alternatives* to Presidential attention; he merely accepted or rejected a *proposal*. In the offset case in the summer of 1966, for Rusk to set the SIG decision before Johnson (or for any White House official to reach out and gather it to the President's desk) was to ask the President to overrule McNamara. That Rusk plainly was unwilling to do.

Because the views of the Secretaries of Defense and Treasury concorded so neatly with those of their operating offices, it was difficult for the State Department to secure attention to other considerations, those *it* represented. Nothing in the structure of the process compelled McNamara, for example, to devote nearly as much attention to the effect of American offset actions on German or European politics as he paid to relations between offset and *his* primary business: fighting a war in Asia, and doing so under the Presidential constraints of no call-up of reserves and no transfer of the economy to a war-time footing. He was left free to threaten von Hassel in May, with little concern for the political cost to the United States of doing so.

July through September: Achieving Coordinated Management.

When Erhard's July 5th letter arrived and the McNamara response was held up by Bator at the White House, offset moved out of its "channel." It began to move toward a forum in which the several departments with an interest in the issue (actual or potential), and the considerations they represented, all could be brought to bear on the process leading to a decision. Had the management of offset remained entirely decentralized, McNamara's letter would have been sent. Bator's intervention was the first stage in a series of phases of coordination: before the July 5th letter, offset was handled in a thoroughly decentralized manner, though with the responsible White House officer exercising a "watching" brief; in July, that officer—Bator—intervened in the process; in the first round of Presidential attention in August, the departments were not engaged in any systematic way, but the White House officer "mapped" the issue for the President; and in late August and early September a fully coordinated procedure developed, licensed by the President, with the informal sub-Cabinet-level working group staffing the principals.

The analysis of the issue done for the President by his White House staff officer in mid-August suggested that for the United States to proceed with the McNamara line risked serious political costs and, besides, was unlikely to induce the Chancellor to undo his economic stabilization program. Johnson's decision in effect foreclosed one option—putting pressure on Erhard *in time to influence early German budget decisions*. The President also authorized the joint State/Defense/Treasury/White House exercise to begin preparing positions for the Erhard visit. The basis was laid for considering offset and force level in a fashion which did not necessarily concede preeminence to considerations represented by Defense and Treasury.

In preparation for the meeting of the President and his senior advisors, called for August 24, a broader conception of American objectives was developed. Bator and Ball were able to make a successful case for relenting on the *successor* agreement, based on the U.S. interest in not administering a shock to NATO by quickly drawing down its forces in Europe. Still, the previous handling of the issue framed the debate. Rusk's general reluctance to do battle with McNamara no doubt was strengthened by the feeling that the issue still lay within Defense jurisdiction. Ball, as a lame-duck Under Secretary and protagonist in the French pullout debate, was hampered both organizationally and personally in making a strong case for political interests, and Bator was somewhat constrained by his role at the White House.

The range of alternatives considered was limited to the tactics associated with negotiating a *successor* agreement: withdraw troops whatever offset offer the Germans made; press hard for a new offset agreement of the customary type, perhaps withdrawing troops if the pressures failed; or agree to *consider* additional forms of offset under the next agreement. McNamara, Fowler and their deputies had little incentive to broaden the agenda; the State Department continued to find it difficult to marshal compelling rationales for doing so.

Deliberations may have been constrained by Washington's failure to notice that German compliance with the existing agreement also might be in doubt. Not that American officials lacked completely for information about events in Bonn; they did not, *especially when they asked the right questions.* For example, the cable sent by the Deputy Chief of Mission in Bonn, Martin Hillenbrand, in response to Under Secretary Ball's request of August 12th was a clear statement of the German budgetary problem. Its analysis cast shadows directly on the existing agreement. In the absence of well-formulated questions from Washington, however, State Department reporting on the budgetary situation was vague and that on the Cabinet and Bundestag politics surrounding offset amounted to little more than journalism.

Several organizational and quasi-organizational features may have played a role in inhibiting the information flow. There was a Treasury man in Bonn, one with considerable tenure there, but if he knew more than his State Department colleagues, he had little incentive to share information which, after all, periled *his* Department's preferred position. Some intelligence reporting was useful, as mentioned in chapter IV, but much of it was "froth," composed mainly of comments on personalities. Nor, by accounts, were officials aided by reports prepared by State's Bureau of Intelligence and Research (INR); INR does not by custom provide the kind of short-term analysis which would have been necessary. Finally, as previously noted, the White House had no informal links to the German Chancellor's Office. White House officials could not pick up the telephone and find out what was happening in Bonn.

Yet adequate hints of German difficulties lay within easy reach of Washington officials. Those hints were not grasped, and the August deliberations contained no trace of concern that the existing agreement might be an issue. Perhaps the information was disregarded in the rush of events. Or the importance of it might have been lost in a nuance of difference between American and German budgeting procedures. The Federal Republic budgeted on *calendar* years while

161

offset payments came due at the end of U.S. *fiscal* years; the 1967 German budget thus affected *both* the existing and the successor agreements. More likely, Americans seized on convenient analogies with previous years ("the Germans always have paid before"), reinforced by images of chicanery ("who knows what games they are playing with the numbers").

Would the course of American decision in August 1966 have been decisively altered by the addition of that important bit of information—the likelihood of German problems with the existing agreement? It is far from certain that the answer is "yes." At least, had Washingtonians grasped the dimensions of Bonn's problem, they should have seen more clearly the trade-off between their offset wishes and their interest in not putting too much pressure on German politics. On the other hand, McNamara might have become still more reluctant to relent even on the successor agreement. And to predictions that Erhard would fall from power if pressed too hard on offset, McNamara still could have countered that those predictions were unprovable. He did so in the actual event.

The force of the balance-of-payments context would have remained; it might have become stronger with the magnitude of the German problem and hence of the donation the U.S. might be called upon to make. By August, the form of the issue—offsets to military deficits—and the link of offset to force level were both so firm that it was difficult, perhaps impossible, for the United States to move much farther, much faster than it did. The U.S. could not contemplate the one possibility which might have given Erhard the "victory" he wanted at no cost to the U.S.: joining the old and new agreements in a financial package like that which emerged from the Trilaterals. Even those who did not want to lean on German politics accepted the imperative of sustaining the link between offset and force level, for reasons of negotiating tactics and Congressional politics. With that link taken for granted they calculated, probably correctly, that an offset deal, even a generous one from Washington's point of view, if coupled with a "made-in-America" proposal for troop reduction, would have done Erhard more harm than the American policy actually pursued.

The link, as well as the balance-of-payments context, continued to obtain in September. Information was less of a problem than it had been in August, as the Chancellor himself admitted his difficulty with the existing agreement (although White House officials continued to lack the ties to the Chancellor's Office which might have enabled them to orchestrate the Erhard visit with their German opposites). Bonn's motivations, however, continued to puzzle Washington. Officials were quick to credit Erhard's reluctance to endorse the Trilaterals to incompetence. They believed—or many of them at any rate believed—that Washington had made a generous concession in August. They professed surprise that Bonn did not perceive and act on that concession. Yet on the evidence of my conversations it was not obvious, even in retrospect and even to American embassy officials closest to the Germans, that Washington was being so forthcoming. Perhaps the opportunity for the Federal Republic was there, and perhaps the Germans only refused, stubbornly, to recognize it. But by my account of deliberations in Bonn that is yet an open question.

By September it did become obvious to all concerned in Washington that the Germans would ask for relief from some portion of their commitment under the existing agreement. The President was clearly informed that the price Washington had to pay for a successful visit was some softening of the American position with respect to the existing agreement. Later he was told that even the package agreed to by the Cabinet principals (and prepared by the sub-Cabinet working group) might not suffice for Erhard. In Bator's words, the Chancellor was by the time of the visit a man with one foot hanging over a precipice, tottering in a high wind.

The President knew the risks and chose to run them. He did so, apparently, counseled by his sense of the domestic politics of the balance of payments, an instinct reinforced perhaps by his politician's reluctance to do a favor for a counterpart he judged unlikely to persist in office long enough to be able to reciprocate. In Johnson's White House, responsibility for international monetary affairs and the balance of payments crossed with European politics, organizationally, in one White House officer—Bator. By contrast, American politics and international money seldom intersected at all in Bonn. Offset was a balance-of-payments issue in Washington and retained that "face" right into the White House. In all probability it would have been a foreign exchange issue whatever organizational arrangements existed in the White House. But suppose the beat of the staff officer responsible for offset had included the war in Vietnam, as Bator's did not. McNamara's use of offset as a tactic for securing a force reduction might then have seemed more reasonable. Or suppose the opposite, that offset had been the responsibility of a senior official whose business did not include international finance, or for whom those considerations were less pressing. Offset might then have become the occasion for an act of pure statecraft, not for balancing international relations and Congressional politics, however artfully.

In context, American policy in August and September seems reasonable enough. Washington made concessions. That it did not make more owed partly to Bonn's obtuseness but principally to the demands of American balance-of-payments accounting as reflective of domestic politics. By August, Washington's politics seemed incompatible with Erhard's. There was no time to redefine the offset issue, to consider general solutions to the military foreign exchange problem or even to work out a modest troop reduction. The United States government was frozen into a situation in which a particular—and not altogether reasonable—form of German offset was of serious moment to the balance of payments. There was no time to switch to arrangements which might have met Washington's legitimate foreign exchange objectives with less spillover on European politics.

The NATO Military Payments Union, approved some months before by SIG and then demolished by McNamara, might have served in that regard. It was not an ideal arrangement, but neither was it pure fiction. While it was complicated, hence difficult to explain to political leaders of government and to negotiate, and while it was open to German rejection because it would have increased Bonn's total liabilities, it carried both long-term and tactical benefits. It at last would have severed the link between foreign exchange and force level, and done so in a way which might have satisfied the American Congress. In the meantime its complexity provided political advantage: neither Erhard nor Johnson could have felt political heat from a creature as complicated as the Payments Union. But the Payments Union had been pronounced dead in Washington. In August there was no way to revive it, at least not in time to do Erhard any good.

NOTES TO CHAPTER V

[1]That concern had been expressed in the February Defence White Paper. *See* Ministry of Defence, *The Defence Review, Part I of Statement on the Defence Estimates 1966* (London, 1966), p.6.

[2]For his statement, *see House of Commons Official Report,* May 3, 1966, p.1449.

[3]Wilson's July announcement can be found in *House of Commons Official Report,* July 20, 1966, p.633. For a background to the Cabinet deliberations,

see Harold Wilson, *The Labour Government, 1964–70* (London: Weidenfeld and Nicholson, and Michael Joseph, 1971), pp.257–59. The Callaghan threat was well reported in the press. *See,* for example, articles in the *Christian Science Monitor,* July 23, 1966; in the *Süddeutsche Zeitung,* July 24; and in *The Economist,* July 30, 1966.

[4]Reported in the *Süddeutsche Zeitung,* July 24, 1966.

[5]For an account of that meeting, *see* the *New York Times,* August 20, 1966.

[6]British intentions are described, in general terms, in articles in the *Washington Post* and the *London Times,* October 15 and October 19, 1966, respectively.

[7]For discussion of the compromise, *see* the *Süddeutsche Zeitung,* October 19, 1966.

[8]The agreement was announced by the State Department on December 9. *See* the *New York Times,* December 10, 1966.

[9]The reaction of the *New Statesman* was representative of left-wing Labour opinion. *See* December 16, 1966, p.896.

[10]For discussion of the exercise, *see* Georg Ferdinand Duckwitz, "Truppenstationierung und Devisenausgleich," *Aussenpolitik* (August 1967), p.473.

[11]For a discussion of British defense policy, and the low value it ascribed to conventional forces, *see* John Garnet, "BAOR and NATO," *International Affairs,* XLVI, 4 (October 1970), pp.671–79.

[12]For a newspaper account of Thomson's threat and the subsequent row, *see* the *New York Times,* February 28, 1967.

[13]Reported in *Le Monde,* March 20, 1967.

[14]After the 1971 negotiations, negotiators on both sides wanted that round to be the last. *See* Timothy W. Stanley, "NATO and the Balance of Payments" (revision of a proposal made to the London Assembly of the Atlantic Treaty Association, September 1971), p.8.

[15]The system was proposed originally by General Maxwell Taylor. It was established by NSAM (National Security Action Memorandum) 341. While that document is yet classified, most of the structure's particulars were made public in Foreign Affairs Manual Circular Number 385.

CHAPTER VI: MANAGING THE POLITICS OF ALLIANCE

I. MISPERCEPTION AND MISUNDERSTANDING BETWEEN ALLIES

... the conscious exercise of influence by players in one game on actions in another is hard to do effectively. It is hard, at least, for those who have to do it. It is hard because it calls at first for an unnatural diversion of attention from necessitous concerns in their own game. Yet such perception may belie counsels of caution in one's own game, whence one's stakes are made.

In the instance of Great Britain as an ally, at least during the course of our two crises, Washingtonians may well have lacked for nothing save an adequate conception of the overlapping games in which they were engaged. While in practice they had insufficient information on the British game, and on its structural detail, and on details of motivation, they did not lack for information *sources;* appropriately used—that is, to answer the right questions—these sources almost surely could have met most information needs ... We have no other ally of which so much can be said. Indeed, for some of our allies I probably should say the opposite ... Consider, for example, the German Federal Republic.[1]

The quoted sentences are Richard E. Neustadt's reflections on two crises in Anglo-American relations, the Suez affair of 1956 and the Skybolt misadventure six years later. They evoke a central problem in the management of alliance relations: officials in one capital may become trapped in images borne of their own deliberations. Framing their own actions to account for the politics of the other capital is at least a bother, and risky to boot. They may be sorely tempted to conceptualize their allies by resort to comfortable analogies from their own processes. That may be so, perhaps especially so, when the allies are "friends" and the analogies can be buttressed by images of friendship. Yet the phrases imply that the difficulties most certainly will be magnified when the allied capital is not as familiar to those in Washington as is London. In those instances, Washington officials may lack for the wherewithal in information about structure and detail necessary to take account of the ally's politics, even in the unlikely event that they should be moved to make the attempt.

The offset cases serve as tests of Neustadt's propositions, extended to the enemy-become-friend-but-still-a-stranger, the German Federal Republic. Consider first the question of information.

American officials in offset during 1966–67 resembled Neustadt's Washingtonians during the Suez and Skybolt episodes in that they did, as a routine matter, lack information. They had neither solid estimates of the German budgetary situation nor analyses which shed light on the intricacies of Cabinet and Bundestag politics surrounding offset, let alone suggestions of what moved Erhard or immobilized Schröder. Did they lack for information sources? The evidence suggests a mixed answer, but one closer to "no" than to "yes." By 1966 Bonn may have been mostly unknown but it was not unknowable. When Washington asked the right questions, as it did several times in the late summer of 1966, State Department officials in Bonn charged with reporting on Germany responded with budget estimates which turned out to be pretty much on target. Their colleagues astride the intelligence channels produced similarly useful descriptions. Neither group produced evaluations to match their estimates, and the estimates themselves became fuzzy in the absence of prods in the form of questions from senior officials in Washington.

Other sources of information on the details of German deliberations were available to Washington officials, though scarcely in abundance. Several businessmen, journalists or academics, German and American, were close enough to the German machine and to the men in Washington to have been of some help. One or two were in fact called upon. That there were not more such people is a comment on

167

the strangeness of Bonn and Washington to each other. The situation is different a decade later, but the need of the two capitals for people who can help them understand each other still far outstrips the supply.

What was true outside government was mirrored within official Washington. Not since the time of Dulles and Adenauer had senior American and German officials been linked by the ties of familiarity and friendship which were customary in Anglo-American relations through the 1960s. There were no easy, informal means of resolving doubts about what German leaders expected, or hoped, or feared. That was true throughout the upper echelons of the White House and the State Department. Especially after the Skybolt debacle, White House officials picked up the telephone to communicate with their counterparts at 10 Downing Street and did so often; they barely knew whom to call in Bonn.

Yet the relative paucity of sources of detailed information about Bonn cannot obscure the more obvious fact of the case at hand: the information senior United States officials possessed, while less than they needed, was more than they used. When the principal Washingtonians convened in the latter half of August, there lay before them hints that only a major change in American policy would suffice to avert an unhappy outcome in September. Those hints could have been sharpened. In retrospect, they seem like obvious goads to ask more questions and seek more information. It would have required prodding from Washington, more telegrams from the Under Secretary of State to his subordinates in the field, an effort and a diversion of attention. The results could scarcely have been conclusive—such is the nature of the enterprise—but what failure there was in offset in September 1966 cannot be laid to the lack of information *sources*.

Information aside, did those in official Washington misperceive and misunderstand their German allies? Evidently. In 1966, the German government was little more than a decade old. Few in Washington understood how the governmental establishment of the Federal Republic operated, even in general outline, let alone comprehended the intricacies of politics in and around the Cabinet and Bundestag or sensed what moved the officials who comprised that strange machine.

Worse, most Washingtonians held images of Bonn which seemed to make it unnecessary to seek for the details of deliberations there and to tune American actions accordingly. They believed German politics hardly mattered to American decision. They had heard Bonn say "yes" so often that when it said "no", it was easy for those in Washington to assume that the refusal was shallow—rhetoric for bargaining advantage or playacting for domestic political purposes. Washingtonians' implicit frames of reference were years out of date, appropriate, if at all, to the Adenauer years, dangerous anachronisms during the incumbency of Erhard. The defect appears most pronounced with McNamara, reinforced in his case by aspects of personality, but the other principals do not seem immune. For McNamara, if Erhard could not control his government sufficiently to keep his promise to the U.S., he scarcely was worth saving. A successor government would do better. It is hard to imagine senior U.S. officials dealing so cavalierly with a Macmillan, or even a Wilson.

Washingtonians' picture of the German governmental machine was dominated by the twin images of dependency and central authority—the first in relations with the U.S., the second in internal governance. Bonn, they assumed, eventually would meet most American demands, for it had little choice. Intentions would be converted into actions; all the Chancellor had to do was decide. That attitude ran to the top of government, strengthened in Johnson's case, no doubt, by his general urge to personify institutional relations, to seek for solutions to problems in those relations through bilateral negotiations, face to face. Erhard, however, was no Adenauer, never had been. Perhaps the machinations surrounding Erhard would have seemed less strange had Germany been Italy, or even Britain. The difficulty faced by American officials was thus thrice compounded: the beast was unfamiliar, information was not easy to come by and the character of German deliberations had altered in ways for which they had no precedents. It is hardly surprising that these Americans were tempted to fall back on comfortable images and easy assumptions.

When events began to call those assumptions into question, the men in Washington were prone to leap to their opposites, from dependence and authority to hostility and incompetence. When Schröder opposed the Trilaterals, it was easy for those in the United States government to assume that he was being obtuse or that he saw the chance to do in Erhard and fulfill his long ambition to the Chancellorship. To be sure, neither possibility was remote, but both went untested. The issues before Washington officials were dominated by their economic face. On the evidence as I have it, no one asked the key political question: how could the United States give Erhard the political "victory" he sought without incurring a "defeat" for itself? With that question unasked, no one searched for the keys to the behavior of Erhard and his ministers, and strategies which might have met both German desires and American requirements, like the scheme mentioned in the last chapter, went unconceived.

So far offset seems to run parallel to Neustadt's conclusion on the Anglo-American episodes. Washingtonians found it hard to comprehend the politics of an allied capital and realize their relation to their own concerns, and to frame actions accordingly. They relied instead on images borne of their own deliberations and on comfortable assumptions about the behavior of their allies. Those tendencies may have been reinforced in the instance of offset by ignorance and by difficulties in obtaining information. At lower levels in official Washington, the attempt to frame strategies based on calculations of foreign politics was too risky to lure officials to action, its product too "iffy" to persuade. The Europeanists at State remained interlopers in economic and military issues. Their dire predictions were dismissed as ritual. Those officials did not, in any case, turn those assessments into strategies which sounded like anything other than "give Erhard what he thinks he needs." At higher levels, the risks to personal position of making the attempt or of being wrong were less, but the inconvenience remained. More important, the images senior officials carried in their heads of deliberations in Bonn and of relations between the two countries spared them the necessity of venturing too far into the unknown and confusing terrain of German politics. Those who worried at all about what was happening in Bonn in late August and September confined themselves to asking why the Germans were not doing what it was clear to Washington that they should do.

Yet the message of the offset case is of a different order than Neustadt's conclusions about the Suez and Skybolt instances. The apparent parallels between the German and the British cases are more misleading than illuminating. For Neustadt suggests that misperceptions and misunderstanding are causes of unhappy outcomes in dealings between the United States and its allies *independent* of the issues and their merits. Put another way—before the fact, ignorance, uncertainty and native caution may make it unlikely that Washingtonians will adjust their actions to the other nation's politics, but after the fact, all (or nearly all) will agree that doing so would have been both possible and fruitful. So it was with Suez and Skybolt. In each case the responsible American officials would have agreed that there was a set of adjustments in the execution of government policy, steps which depended for their conception on knowledge of nuances in the governance of the United Kingdom, which would have done less damage to American interests, broadly conceived.

The offset case, however, belies that conclusion. On balance, my judgment is that hinted at in the previous chapter: by August, German and American politics had become incompatible. Their differences went to the heart of the politics of each. Those differences almost surely could not have been compromised even had U.S. officials possessed more information and understanding of Bonn, or sought it, or made better use of what they had. While Washington needed time to restructure the offset/force level issue and heal its divisions, Erhard needed immediate concessions. He needed money which Washington believed it could not give. Both sides were constrained by external events translated into parliamentary sentiments. Alliance relations had become a zero-sum game, with Erhard's gain in his politics registering as a loss for Johnson in his, and the prestige of both was on the line by September. It is not clear that symbols alone would have sufficed for Erhard, however inept he was at making use of those offered him. And there were strict limits to the symbols Washington was willing to offer. When it came to avoiding the signals which might have touched off a run on Fort Knox gold, symbols were what mattered. It is to Washingtonians' credit that they made what limited tactical adjustments they could. Otherwise Erhard would have fallen with a bang, and the United States would have been directly implicated.

My might-have-been from the last chapter was, at best, a bare possibility. For Johnson to have made, in August or September, the offer the U.S. made at the end of the Trilaterals, and to have done so while holding out to his Congress only the *possibility* of a troop cut, was to run large risks on behalf of a dubious enterprise. Even had Washington made the offer, Erhard might not have been able to swing it with his Bundesbank. And even had he been able, the two capitals would have retained contrary interests in the kind of signals about future U.S. troop levels to be emitted simultaneously. For its purposes, Washington needed to indicate more than the possibility that reductions would follow, and soon. Bonn's "victory", of course, would have depended on the appearance of continuity in the level of American forces. Perhaps it would have been possible to surround any deal struck with atmospherics which suited the purposes of both governments. But I doubt it, and so do several of the participants in the case, men who in the event desired not to lean on the Germans.

In any event, arranging it would have required an extraordinarily precise orchestration of actions by Washington and Bonn. That, I believe, was beyond the capabilities of the two governments, perhaps especially of the Erhard government.

II. THE OVERLAP OF POLITICS AND ECONOMICS

The message seems painfully clear. On the American side, better information about German politics, or better use of what information existed, or better understanding—none of these alone, or even all together, would have sufficed to avoid the September row in German-American relations. The difficulty lay not in Washingtonians' understanding of German deliberations but in the demands of their own politics. Yet the question remains: why? Whence derived the special order of difficulty?

Most obviously, the overlap of politics and economics added to the difficulty of noting the effects of American actions on allied politics. It was necessary not only to comprehend exactly *how* a particular United States decision or action would register on the games of governance played routinely in allied capitals; first Washington had to understand *what* it was doing, or might do, which would affect its ally, and of *what sort* those effects would be. "Economic" or "military" actions had effects on German politics, perceived or not in Washington, hence touched bilateral relations and became political issues. So it was with offset, especially while the issues resided in the Defense/Treasury channel. There was a bit of difficulty of this sort in the Skybolt affair. McNamara canceled the Skybolt missile for reasons of budget and technical failure, domestic reasons unconnected to Anglo-American relations. But in the Skybolt case it was easily noted that cancellation would have an effect on those relations, given the earlier U.S. promise to develop Skybolt and given Britain's reliance on the missile as a means of preserving its symbolic nuclear independence through the 1960s. And the departure from current practice was American, not British, for the latter sought to sustain the *status quo,* so the U.S. could not escape minimal responsibility for assisting the British with *their* problem. Washington officials stumbled over difficulties involved in perceiving and comprehending nuances of the effect of their action on the summit of British politics.

In the offset affair, however, the political impact—on the Federal Republic and on its relations with the United States—of actions taken in pursuit of economic purposes went unattended. For some time it went unnoticed. Then, those who noticed and worried about the effects had no means of altering American actions. Actions of the Defense/Treasury alliance were based on a definition of the offset issue which, while illogical in retrospect, was regarded as legitimate at the time. Legitimate, also, was their claim to sole responsibility for American action. In context, and in combination with other actions of the United States government, their actions risked putting more pressure on German politics than Bonn could bear.[2] Yet taking action within the domain of issues deputed to them was their prerogative; the task of totting up American actions across domains and calibrating effects on German politics was not their primary business.

Yet so far offset would seem to have compounded the problem of alliance management by adding the difficulty associated with "early warning" when politics and economics cross. The officials in Skybolt found it hard to calculate the precise impact of their actions on British politics, even though none of them doubted that there would be an impact. What they lacked was an adequate sense of the connections between their deliberations and those in London. Washingtonians during offset lacked for something more. They had first to understand that their actions had an effect in Bonn and that the effect was serious. That awareness had to be brought home to them with enough force to cause them to alter their own actions. They had to understand that United States actions which they regarded as business-as-usual in the decentralized operations of their government were doing serious damage at the political center of their ally. That realization was hard to make, in time, its implications for American action harder still to make persuasive. The difficulty was compounded because Erhard believed his politics prevented him from crying "help," and Washington was thus denied one customary stimulus in alliance relations to raising issues to high-level attention.

But the difficulty of offset ran deeper still. The issues of offset and force level went to the heart of fundamental concerns of various parts of the "inner" government: State, the military, Defense and Treasury. Those agencies of government and the officials who constituted them divided along two lines of argument, two perspectives which over time had become articles of faith and matters of ritual. For State Department Europeanists and for the military, maintaining a larger number of American troops in Europe had become, long before 1966, a point of orthodoxy. The two could agree on a policy preference, although paths of reasoning by which they reached that preference differed. What was a military estimate, prudentially hedged and professionally conservative, for the Joint Chiefs of Staff was primarily a political judgment for State.

Civilians in Defense and the Treasury viewed the issues from a perspective dominated by economy and efficiency, budget and balance of payments, technical matters bound up with money. Concern with foreign exchange was a newer element of this orthodoxy, but by 1966 it was ingrained. The Treasury of 1966 was not the powerful machine which Washington has seen on occasion before and since, but it was still a power to be reckoned with across its range of issues, and offset fell neatly into that range. If the hand of Treasury-as-treasury was weaker than it might have been in 1966 and 1967, McNamara's role more than compensated for that weakness. He played the strong "Treasury" hand, partly because doing so suited Defense purposes and partly, I think, for reasons which were deeply personal.

All the protagonists within the Executive Branch were linked to and reinforced by constituencies without—in Congress and among the restricted public attentive to such matters: Treasury to the "gold bugs" and "dollar drain-ers"; Defense to the troop cutters and to those on Capitol Hill who conceded priority to Vietnam; the military to its Congressional committees; and the Europeanists at State to Europeanists in Congress and in the press. State's claim on Congressional opinion and the interests behind it may have appeared to be weaker than the claims of its counterparts in 1966, but on its side State had the history and sentiment of America's commitment to Europe. The troop level debate of 1971 made clear that latent Atlanticist emotions still could be translated, in short order, into public advocacy of State's cause.

The opposition of the two perspectives was not merely a disagreement on the merits of the issues. It was that—witness the dispute between McNamara and his Chiefs on terrain which purportedly was strictly military, hence technical—but it was more. The difference was one of perspective, of view of the world; the two sides attached different weights to the considerations at issue, assigned different priorities to those concerns. The perspectives conflicted but scarcely intersected. They were articulated in different tongues. For Defense and Treasury, the offset/troop level link was essential, for the purposes both of negotiating with the Germans and dealing with the American Congress. It was to be assumed, not analyzed. By contrast, Europeanists and the Chiefs ranked the issue of troop level above money. They wanted the government first to decide on a force level—preferably to sustain a number not far from the existing one—then fiddle with offset. The technical and foreign exchange considerations which moved McNamara were, for State Department diplomats and military professionals, of a lower order. Troops were the imperative, finance but an unavoidable nuisance. For the Defense Secretary, however, that "imperative" was quickly reduced to an interest, primarily political, one among several, perhaps to be sacrificed to the urgencies of economics or Congressional relations.

The collision of the two perspectives precluded fresh thought and fresh looks at alternatives in time to make a difference. The time to rescue the situation was months before September, not in August when the summit loomed and the need for haste put inordinate pressure on the capability of the two governments to orchestrate their actions. But the Payments Union episode is illustrative of the difficulties. State Department arguments on behalf of the Union, based on European politics, rang in McNamara's ears as the ritual pleading of the other perspective in which arguments always reduced to the importance of being nice to Europeans. Offset was, for him, business of another sort. One did not scrap a favorable arrangement without even being asked.

When Washington confronted Bonn over offset in the fall of 1966, it found itself with little room to maneuver. Not only was it difficult to see the need for considering the impact on Bonn of Washington's policy on offset; not only was framing strategies based on predictions of German politics a bother, and risky to boot, "iffy" and unprofessional; in addition, the form of the issue and the clash of competing perspectives on it left little room to fashion a course of action which might have avoided the unhappy outcome in September. Bonn was similarly constrained, and for reasons which were not too different. Offset had become enmeshed in the process of budget-setting during a time of fiscal stringency, while the Chancellor's authority waned. Erhard had little room in which to accommodate his Atlanticist inclinations with the constraints of Bundestag and Cabinet politics.

Return again to my might-have-been. It was conceivable, barely, that Washington might have severed, provisionally and temporarily at least, the link between offset and force level. That might have been done in a way which satisfied both Erhard's sense of his Bundestag and Cabinet and Johnson's reading of Congress. The pieces of such a deal can easily be imagined in retrospect: measures permitting the Germans to comply with the existing agreement—vital to Washington's purposes—without drawing more money from the budget, coupled with provisions which granted Erhard the kind of relief under the upcoming agreement which Bonn was given at the end of the Trilaterals. The troop level question could have been blurred purposefully, with Erhard free to claim victory over the few weeks which were crucial to his political future, and Washington left to continue making the dark hints of reduction which McNamara had planted for months.

But who was to conceive such a policy in Washington? Hardly McNamara or Fowler or one of their staffers in action on offset. Not Rusk. Then the Europeanists at State or their allies in the White House? Yet for any of them to do so was not only to frame strategies based on predictions of the German situation which McNamara would say they could not prove; it was to move, directly and immediately, against an entrenched habit of thought, appearing to seek to displace it with another. It would have been to move against a strong team, against the interests of major departments backed by important Congressional constituencies. And, moreover, the team had controlled policy, set the face on the issue. Offset was, in substance, economic and, in form, negotiation, not the occasion for statecraft or for the exercise of alliance comity. Negotiators did not concede their negotiating partners gains before the negotiations had even started, nor did they throw away bargaining counters in advance. The American government could be moved, eventually, to arrive at the Trilateral outcome, a kind of reconciliation of the two perspectives. It could not be moved fast, not fast enough to save Erhard.

How do the constraints at play in the offset affair square with other instances in U.S. relations with its major allies in which politics and economics have overlapped? The Skybolt affair of 1962 scarcely involved the overlap of politics and economics in a fashion comparable to offset. When McNamara decided to cancel the Skybolt missile, he did so for reasons of cost and technical feasibility, arguments with which his Air Force did not concur but ones it could hardly brand illegitimate. The decision to cancel taken, action shifted to diplomatic ground. The question, for all the government save a fragment, was not *whether or not* to give the British something as a substitute for Skybolt, another symbol on which the British could hang their nuclear independence, but *what* to give. State's Europeanists, for whom Britain-into-Europe had priority, first longed for the restoration of the Skybolt *status quo,* then opposed with all their might giving Polaris submarines to the British. They preferred leaving the British with nothing rather than to concede them Polaris. In the event their opposition was troublesome, but they were hardly a machine to match Defense and Treasury in offset, especially so since their chief, Rusk, merely acquiesced in their activities.

To be sure there were competing considerations, one economic, one political. Terminating Skybolt meant saving budget money, always welcome. On the other hand, living up to the spirit of Eisenhower's Camp David agreement with the British meant offering London something in lieu of Skybolt. Kennedy was inclined to be forthcoming with the British anyway, all the more so when he met Prime Minister Macmillan; influential eastern papers had chided him for pulling the rug from under London by canceling Skybolt, thereby threatening bipartisanship in foreign affairs. Yet unlike offset, the conflicting considerations intersected within the heads of all the principals—Kennedy, McNamara, Rusk. Both concerns seem to have weighed on each in roughly equal measure. And between saving money and satisfying the spirit of Camp David there remained considerable terrain. That ground was not acted upon, for the reasons of misperception and misunderstanding Neustadt describes, but it existed.

Or consider the sequence of events which led to the 1969 American decision to return Okinawa to Japanese administration. In outline, American actions with respect to Okinawa paralleled the early handling of offset: in both cases decentralized management had conceded "buttons" to a department, authority which the department then exercised in accord with *its* sense of primary mission, largely ignoring other important considerations.[3] The American military controlled Okinawa and regarded it as an island base, not as an island with bases on it; the side effects of military hegemony on Japanese politics and the U.S.-Japan alliance were not the military's primary business.

Yet maintaining complete operational freedom in the use of Okinawan bases, which implied retaining sovereignty over the island, was not of crucial importance even to the military. It was a convenience, of course, one which preferred operating practice indicated should be retained. It may have been a matter of faith, but it was not a subject which excited military passions as did troops in Europe. Nor was American action constrained by short deadlines, although there were spurs to action in the form of biennial Japanese-American summits at which Okinawa was sure to come up. Through a decade-long series of study processes, the military came to see that the political effects of continued American administration of

Okinawa were substantial. However, the military became willing to agree to reversion only, I judge, when they perceived that to perpetuate the *status quo* was to risk serious *military* interests. Had the Okinawa issue been left to fester, renewal of the mutual security treaty, due to expire in 1970, might have been jeopardized. That, in turn, might have meant that the military would have been denied the use of bases throughout Japan. *That* was a danger serious enough to dislodge men from the comfort of ritual opposition to change.

One final instance, again offset/force level, this time 1969. Evidently, the American government was less constrained in dealing with the cluster of issues in 1969 than it had been in 1966. Circumstances, both externally and within the U.S. government, were less limiting than in 1966. There was a false spring in American balance-of-payments accounting early in 1969, so Congress was less attentive to offset. The issues had been depoliticized to some considerable extent by conscious choice on both sides of the Atlantic, a fact reflected in the deputation of negotiating responsibility to lower levels of both State Department and Foreign Office, and in Willy Brandt's determination to keep the political thorns of offset at a safe distance from the Palais Schaumburg. Both sides acted under a general deadline, but it was the rhythm of offset expiration rather than the short fuse of Erhard's political life or death in 1966.

Within the American government, also, there was more leeway. Much of it was *created,* by the President's decision to sever offset and force level, never mind Congress. The money and foreign exchange perspective remained, but it lacked for champions. David Kennedy was an inactive Treasury Secretary, and Melvin Laird was no McNamara.

By contrast to these other examples, the aspects which made offset and force level such an intractable cluster of issues in 1966 can be pieced together. It was the combination of external constraints with internal rigidities. Washington's actions in the later summer of 1966 were subject to the constraints of economic stringency and eroding Erhard authority in Bonn and to the demands of balance-of-payments accounting at home. The first two demanded immediate generosity on the American part; but the last forbade it.

Those external constraints played upon the internal rigidities of the American government, made the orthodoxies more evident and brought them into stark opposition. External constraints meant that there was little leeway to frame policies which might have satisfied Bonn at an acceptable cost to Washington. The internal rigidities made it harder still to do so. Moreover, the conceiving of such policies became hard, perhaps impossibly so. To frame strategies which gave Bonn what it needed was to appear "soft" on a matter of negotiation, to move directly against the face the issue had acquired. McNamara might be willing to see the government take a less rigid line with Bonn; he resisted allowing the issue to be cast in the mold of troops-first-and-politics. By light of his perspective, to make the entreaties of State Europeanists was to be not merely soft but soft-headed and sentimental in a game played by other rules. Those rules might be altered, but incompletely—and slowly. The link between offset and force level was sustained through the Trilaterals.

In the instance of offset, the problem seems imbedded in the overlap of economics and politics. However, that overlap was more the immediate occasion for trouble than its cause. Rigid positions, the internal orthodoxies, grew up around the central concerns of major departments, reinforced by Congressional and public constituencies. With an American government organized by function, those orthodoxies tended to take functional form: economy and efficiency, international politics, and military strategy. Through the 1960s, the priority concerns of the four "inner" departments coalesced into two broad perspectives: economy and efficiency, troops and politics— "economics" versus "politics" in shorthand. The alliances derived from shared preferences under the pressure of events—the U.S. balance-of-payments drain, the war in Vietnam and the loosening of NATO.

In ordinary times, decentralized operations kept the perspectives apart, allowed each play within its own domain. Only external circumstances made it impossible to ignore cross effects of those operations and made the implicit overlap of politics and economics manifest. Only then did the perspectives come to loggerheads. For serious trouble to ensue required *both* the existence of perspectives linked directly to the central concerns of major departments *and* circumstances which brought those incompatible perspectives into collision. As my other examples suggest, if the overlap of politics and economics forces together only secondary concerns of several departments, not deep-rooted interests, the policy problem is more manageable. That, alas, was not the case in 1966.

III. MANAGING DECENTRALIZED OPERATIONS

Remedies for the ills encountered in the offset case are not easily conceived. Decentralization is a fact of life in the American government and is likely to remain so, granted the plethora of issues which the government will be called upon to address. In relations with allies, American departments carry on their business with counterpart bureaucracies abroad, through a variety of formal as well as informal channels. In the small, with respect to individual cases, the problem pointed up by offset is one of management: noticing and correcting inappropriate decentralization. It is identifying and managing situations in which continued handling of an issue by separate departments in accord with parochial considerations would either end in unhappy outcomes or forfeit major opportunities.[4] The case also raises a larger question, one of organization, not with respect to particular issues but in general. It goes not to the management of decentralized operations but to the nature and extent of the decentralization. That issue is the subject of the next section.

Identifying specific situations of danger will be hard enough. Managing them may be harder still. The instance of offset in 1966 makes that painfully plain. When divisions in the government run as deep as those in 1966, and when the positions of the opposing partisans are so firm, the framing of sensible policies will be neither easy, nor painless, nor swift. Doing so seems certain to require the creation of special mechanisms and procedures. The issues at hand must be withdrawn from their current handling and subjected to a centralized process of analysis and decision, with implementation monitored and any new deputation of authority supervised. Two mechanisms for those purposes were important in the offset cases—the informal working group (the Rostow group) in 1966–67 and the formal National Security Council procedure in 1969—and another formal structure, the SIG/IRG system of the Johnson Administration, handled the issue briefly in 1966. The three by no means exhaust the range of possibilities. Nor are they exactly commensurable, for the policy problems to which they were responses differed, at least in degree, for reasons I mentioned before. Nonetheless, they suggest the different advantages and disadvantages inherent in different styles of operation in response to broadly similar policy problems.

(1) *Informal Working Groups.*[5] Informal groups of sub-Cabinet officials were formed, most often at the behest of the responsible White House staff officer, to review issues (or clusters of issues) and make recommendations to the principals. The White House officer—one of several coequals—orchestrated the group *and* staffed the President, thus attending meetings of the principals.

Group members were Under Secretaries or senior Assistant

Secretaries—McNaughton for example—officials of sufficient rank to speak for and carry their Secretaries, not merely represent their departments. Secrecy of deliberations encouraged frank discussion, not merely playing to departmental galleries. Group members were handpicked, most often by the White House, chosen because they knew the issue up for decision and because they carried authority in their departments. No agency was given to feel it had a right to participate; meetings were not cluttered with bystanders. Groups died and reformed for different issues. Several coexisted, with overlapping memberships. The chief advantages were serious discussion of alternatives and flexibility for the President, since the White House staffer controlled the timing and agenda of the group's activities and he alone had access to deliberations at all levels. The system also facilitated implementation by building centers of power throughout the bureaucracy which were responsive to Presidential intent, and by extending the reach of the White House staff officer.

Several disadvantages inhered in the secrecy and "clubbiness" of the group's operation. The groups depended on secrecy; many people and departments would notice an issue, then see it disappear. Officials and departments excluded from the *ad hoc* process might resent it, risking their retribution during implementation or on subsequent issues. For example, the Joint Chiefs of Staff apparently felt that their opinions often were not heard at the top of government during the Johnson Administration. Since crucial discussions were closeted, it might be hard for Congress to supervise or even know about what happened. We have learned in recent years, all too painfully, that the outcomes of confidential processes may not reflect national interests.

Other disadvantages of the arrangement were its *ad hoc* character and the demands it made on the White House staffer. Groups might be convened only when external deadlines loomed, since officials are busy and distracted, and by then opportunities might have been lost or errors made in a last-minute rush. Time pressure may account for the failure to attend to the old agreement in the August 1966 deliberations. And the structure made severe demands on the White House staffer, suggesting that the number of groups which could be managed simultaneously, and thus the number of issues treated, was quite small. Nor would it have been easy to increase the number of senior staffers beyond several, since the mechanism depended on each having independent access to the President.

(2) *A Formal System: National Security Council in 1969.*[6] Several layers of fixed committees existed to study issues and frame options.

Issues entered the system with the issuance of a NSSM (National Security Study Memorandum), calling for a study of the issue. The study was then done by one of a number of regional fixed interagency committees (IG's) at the Assistant Secretary level (or done by a special group and approved by the committee), passed to a Review Group chaired by the President's National Security Assistant, eventually discussed by the National Security Council and options presented for Presidential choice. Decisions were then announced to the government with the issuance of NSDM's (National Security Decision Memoranda).

The 1969 NSC structure bore superficial resemblance to the SIG/IRG system of the Johnson Administration. IRG's became IG's and SIG the Undersecretaries Committee, the last given responsibility in the NSC for dealing with sub-Presidential issues and often—as in offset during 1969—for overseeing implementation. The SIG/IRG structure, however, centered on the State Department, a defect mentioned before and a fatal one to the minds of President Nixon and Henry Kissinger. Under Johnson, State had been required to become the advocate of a particular *recommendation*. It could not merely pass an issue and alternatives to the President for decision. In the end, SIG/IRG probably failed because none of the principals cared enough to make it succeed, but it was internally defective as well.

The advantage of the 1969 NSC was form: all agencies with stakes in an issue could feel that they had been heard and at high levels, and decisions were clearly communicated to the bureaucracy via NSDM's. Many alternatives could be formulated and considered by the President before the various agency positions coalesced around a single option. Papers which contained but one serious alternative surrounded by nonstarters (the famous "option B") were, in theory, rejected by the Review Group. The system gave the President the flexibility either to reach out and pull an issue to him before the departments would serve it up or to delay an issue they were pressing by feeding it into the study procedure. It may also have eased the President's problem of choice: a decision between conflicting advice was not necessarily also a direct choice between differing senior advisors, as was most often the case during the Johnson Administration. Finally, the orderliness of the formal process may have facilitated Congressional oversight.

What effect, if any, the system had on the quality of analysis done is uncertain. On the one hand, departments were given incentives to see their preferred alternatives stated fairly and buttressed adequately; on the other hand, the process was large and "leaky," so department officials may have been tied to simple "agency" positions because they had to play to their departmental audiences. Options may have been presented laundry-list fashion, with no serious comparisons among them. Or serious debate may have receded to the fringes of the formal processes.

The other question mark in the NSC system was implementation. On the record, while most decisions were communicated clearly, monitoring subsequent actions was difficult. The President and NSC staffers—and there is no inherent reason why there could not be, contrary to early Nixon Administration practice, several with access to the President—were easily preoccupied with the *decision* process. At most, the Presidential deputies could follow only a few issues. The Under Secretaries Committee sometimes served as monitor, as it did in 1969 when chaired by Elliot Richardson, who was close to Kissinger. But since its members were marginal to the decision process, the Committee was as a routine matter neither able to act in the President's name nor sensitive to his intent. The will of the President may have been more attenuated still by the time assignments reached the operating bureaus of the implementing departments, most often the State Department.

The definitions of the various structures are themselves imprecise. What I labeled an informal working group, for instance, may be more the description of a collegial style of operation than of a system. It is not clear that such groups could be created at will; the Rostow group in offset relied on preexisting personal relationships among the men who became members. By the same token, while essential parts of the definition of informal group used in this chapter are White House control and responsiveness to Presidential desire, the collegial style of operation surely might characterize other groups with other purposes. "Working groups"—"cabals" to those who dislike their purposes—of officials opposed to American policy in Vietnam apparently formed at several levels of government during the Johnson Administration. The collegial style may be neither easy to call forth when it does not already exist nor simple to destroy when it does.

Distinctions between the structures obviously are not absolute. For example, the Deming group which handled international monetary affairs in the Johnson Administration—and which was considered an informal working group by participants—was not very different from any of several of the fixed committees which comprised the 1969 NSC apparatus. Both possessed the bureaucratic legitimacy conferred by explicit Presidential charter; both had fairly fixed memberships. Both dealt with a cluster of issues which evolved over time.

The choice between the two mechanisms, or among them and kindred structures, for responding to the kind of problems in managing the U.S. government which are displayed in the offset case may depend mostly on the personalities and preferences of the President and his senior advisors, and to a lesser extent on the issues they choose or are compelled by events to confront. I doubt, however, that it should be purely a matter of personal preference and circumstance. The two approaches, embodying varying styles of operations, do confer different advantages and imply different risks.

In 1966 and 1967, with the advisors closest to the President deeply engaged and sharply divided, deliberations preceding critical decisions were bound to be reserved to a small circle in which each man could make his case to the President, directly and frankly. In that context, the Rostow group performed staffing functions. It expanded the information available to principals and extended their analytic grasp without altering the character of final deliberations. Had the context of 1966–67 been played through the structures of 1969, the results would have been similar. With a settled administration, it seems likely that the issues quickly would have passed out of the formal study mechanism into more private circles around the President. By my reading of events, it was obvious to disgruntled officials engaged in the offset study process even in 1973 that any issues touching force levels in Europe would be decided with little regard for the results of formal studies. Nevertheless, the Administration was well served by the formal process in 1969. Senior officials could be given a fresh look at a recurrent issue, at once coming to understand the merits of the issue and the actions of the machines over which they presided.

The two styles of operation do not seem easily compatible. Both make subtle demands on the White House officials charged with tending them. Both play on the White House officer's role as custodian of internal debate, filler of gaps in analysis, and preserver of Presidential options, but the two do so in somewhat different ways. Tending the informal working groups is a direct extension of the White House officer's role as staff assistant to the President. The essence of the role is unobtrusiveness. Advocacy is acceptable; becoming an advocate is not. On the other hand, the formal structures enshrine the White House official's role as immediate advisor to the President and add other functions: maintainer of White House institutions and official arbiter. They bring the official out of the White House basement, make his several tasks obvious, and in doing so lay him open to the charge that in advising and staffing the President he undercuts the institutional apparatus he is charged with maintaining. At a minimum, the problem is one of time, for if the White House official spends most of his time staffing the President on the few most pressing issues, second-order matters are likely to go untended and study procedures may decay.

Adding to the roster of White House officials with access to the President, and charging each with tending to one of the roles, may be a solution, but it is likely to be a partial and probably unstable one, even apart from the increased demands it would make on Presidential time. The officials would have to have quite fixed beats, which hazards disputes over "turf" and more important, risks that issues will fall between cracks or be handled in contexts which are no longer appropriate. Carving out foreign economics and European politics as a White House beat, and doing so on a semipermanent basis, seemed appropriate in 1965–67. I doubt that it would be so judged today. Yet it is not easy to conceive divisions which would be deemed acceptable for periods of more than several months. Even the customary division of the White House staff into domestic and national security functions, with limited overlap, now seems suspect.

IV. LIMITS ON REORGANIZATION

The several foregoing paragraphs pertain to but a piece of a large problem. Their topic is techniques for managing particular sorts of policy problems, once identified. Not that the problem is simple; in the 1966 offset affair it was very nearly intractable. But the problem is limited. It presumes that deficiencies in the previous handling of the matters at issue have been noted, and it takes as given an existing general structure of the American government. It is more a problem of management improvement than of basic structural reform. It assumes a given distribution of responsibilities and interests among the great departments of government. The art is adjusting procedures by which those interests are combined in order to alter the policies which result, not once-and-for-all but case by case.

Yet the offset story also suggests conclusions of a larger order. They pertain to the general structure of government for the making of foreign policy—what considerations are represented and how strongly—and how issues fit into that structure. The seeds of trouble in offset were sown years before 1966. The problem went back to the initial form of the issue and to its delegation to Defense and Treasury. And the sources of difficulty may run back further still; they may be symptomatic of a general bias in the vesting and weighting of interests in the making of postwar American foreign policy.

The obvious problem is that the offset issue was given to departments which over time developed rigid perspectives on it. And not much time was needed for positions to harden. Defense and Treasury controlled offset until the late summer of 1966 and treated it in accord with their sense of primary mission, predictably narrow. Despite the clear implications of offset for German politics and German-American relations, those concerns, represented by the State Department, could scarcely gain entry into deliberations preceding American actions. The set of interests which bore on processes of decision was too narrow. Offset was, in form, strictly foreign economic, and military. It acquired that form initially when a matter of general concern to the government, one represented by Treasury and taken seriously by McNamara—the balance of payments—coincided with a specific interest of the Defense Department—selling weapons abroad. That convergence of purpose soon became fixed in procedure and attitude.

The case raises a more general question. Military sales to major allies were treated as strictly military matters despite their clear political importance. Contrast sales with the provision of military *assistance:* the political interests involved in military aid may generally have been underrepresented (or even wrongly conceived), but at least it was acknowledged that such interests existed. The handling of Okinawa was similar to military sales: the maintenance and operation of foreign military bases were regarded as the military's business, again despite obvious political reverberations. In both cases, the State Department was left to tend to the political spillover from military actions yet at the same time denied a serious part in framing those actions. Both issues were framed in a way dominated by a conception of military security, narrowly defined. That conception derived largely from the American experience of the Cold War, one enshrined in structures—both Executive and Congressional—little changed in more than two decades.

Historically, departments of the American government have been divided from one another by function. When a large set of problems has straddled the functions of several departments or fallen outside them all, the customary response has been to reshuffle functions, creating new departments, merging old ones or expanding their domains. By the functional criterion, general organizational arrangements are effective when problems fit neatly into the purviews of organizations, when there is a neat one-to-one correspondence between issues and departmental domain, when the organization represents (or appears to represent) the full range of considerations which ought to receive attention in taking decisions on given issues.

By that criterion the lesson of offset would be to expand the domain of the State Department and upgrade its capability for dealing with "military" matters; or merge it with Defense, or strengthen the foreign policy operations of the Pentagon. All of those measures might be considered, particularly the first. For the State Department to have been as dependent as it was in the offset case on military analyses produced in the Pentagon was hardly excusable. The bias toward narrow "military" security and "military" interests seems a pervasive one. Important political and foreign policy concerns of the United States often are given short shrift. And other kinds of considerations go unrepresented as well. Obvious examples are classes of public economic interests in international relations: witness the government's woeful lack of preparation for the 1973 oil embargo. The United States spent upwards of twenty billion dollars a year insuring itself against the risk of a Soviet nuclear attack, but virtually nothing to hedge against an oil embargo.[7]

Welcome as some quite general reshuffling of responsibilities would be—and measures I have mentioned here go beyond what any American government is likely to contemplate—I doubt that it would be a sufficient answer to the fundamental problem imbedded in the offset history. That is so for several reasons. One is doubt about whether it would turn out as anticipated. Major reshuffling might have little effect on the operations of the major departments of government. An expanded State or a politicized Pentagon would still be dominated by the attitudes and procedures of its career services—the foreign service or the military.

Even if the changes produced were real, the new departments could be expected quickly to organize their operations around some new definition of primary mission. Again, there would be no guarantee that the range of considerations to which each attended would be as broad as the reorganizers expected. Even a governmental creature quite different from the present departments of State, Defense or

Treasury would be a poor candidate for handling, alone, a set of issues as multifarious as offset/troop level. For the cluster of issues labeled "energy" it is hard even to imagine what the creature would look like.

Atop these difficulties rests another. As offset makes evident, the faces of issues change, often imperceptibly and sometimes rapidly. Yesterday's efficient division of governmental labors may be today's rigid anachronism. To regard offset as a matter of military sales and balance-of-payments accounting, and to handle it accordingly, was barely acceptable in 1963; to continue to do so in 1966 was to narrow vision dangerously, courting crisis. Departments, however consti- tuted, can be expected to treat issues deputed to them in ways which change only slightly over time. They will be slow to acknowledge that an issue no longer falls completely within their domains and reluc- tant, by their own lights, to surrender or share control of the issue.

For all these reasons, the need to coordinate the operations of the major units of government seems unavoidable. On that point, the offset case speaks clearly.

If the offset affair underscores the need for coordination, it also testifies to the difficulty of obtaining it. The more neatly a set of issues seems to fit within the jurisdiction of a single department, the harder it will be for another department to inject consideration of other views and other interests in the process leading to decision. Witness the frustrations of the State Department in 1966. We may, perhaps, count ourselves fortunate not to have an "energy-as-energy" machine to compare with our "food-as-food" machine, the Depart- ment of Agriculture. USDA controls a range of actions with direct bearing on national well-being and the conduct of American foreign policy: it influences supply, hence price, and oversees exports and imports. It operates those levers to the advantage of *its* traditional constituency, support for which long has been regarded as Agricul- ture's primary mission: the American farm industry. Fortuitously, producer interests in large exports partially coincide with general foreign policy interests, although high prices and large sales abroad diminish the government's ability to grant food aid. American con- sumers are the most obvious losers. Yet there is no reason to believe that if a single machine similarly monopolized decisions affecting prices and supplies of energy products, national interests would be even as well served as they are in the case of agriculture.

The hazard will be compounded if, as in offset, the issues run to the central concerns of several great units of government. The issues will fall into channels that go deeper than procedure. They will become enmeshed in perspectives which condition what aspects of the issues will be perceived and what lines of reasoning applied. Those perspectives will lend force and legitimacy both to arguments on merits and bureaucratic stakes in retaining (or securing) control of the issues. Wrenching government action from the clutch of one perspective, or framing policies between the clash of two, will be difficult.

What was needed in 1966 was a kind of *early* early-warning: not merely recognizing that existing decentralized operations were likely to cause trouble or forfeit opportunities, but noticing that existing arrangements were shaping the issues and lining up the government in ways which would make later rescue difficult or costly, or impossible. Perhaps to call for performance of that task is to ask too much of governments which by their (political) natures must give precedence to the immediate, a time-span more likely to be measured in hours or days than in weeks or months. Yet it is an imperative if ponderous governments, allied to one another by custom and need, are to fine-tune their actions in ways which levy exorbitant domestic costs on neither and do not impose them on each other.

The implications of the offset story for government organization, writ large, cut against the grain of common wisdom. The case suggests attempts to prevent fixed perspectives from becoming embodied in policy "machines" and to keep sets of issues away from those combinations. The lesson pertains as much to how issues are defined as how they are handled, or through what structures and procedures; it goes to art as much as to policy science. Perhaps departments should be conceded only parts of issues, or structures should be kept fluid so that agencies seldom have long-standing claim to managing entire groups of issues. This would have implied breaking the balance-of-payments accounting portion of offset away from military sales. Selling weapons to the Germans was reasonable given allied military objectives, and protecting the American balance of payments was not in itself exceptionable; joining the two and vesting responsibility for the entire cluster in a single machine (albeit a bi-departmental one) was the error.

The style of operations in the Johnson Administration, I surmise, tended to foster the formation of internal rigidities. For large numbers of issues, the permanent government of officials below the Cabinet was told to come to consensus behind some policy, then present it to the government's senior political officials. In practice that generally meant that the bureaucratic combination in control of an issue retained it, either by securing ratification of its control or by frustrating formulation of government-wide policies which might have threatened it. That the SIG/IRG exercise could not wrest control of offset from Defense and Treasury is a case in point, notwithstanding the difference in procedure produced by the routing of the issue through SIG/IRG. The history of the Okinawa issue until 1969 is another. In both cases the *status quo* was perpetuated. The harm was more obvious in the offset case because McNamara used his continuing grant of license to put pressure on Bonn.

The Nixon NSC system, which I discussed in previous pages as an approach to managing specific issues, was also a more general reaction to the informal style of operations of the Johnson Administration.[8] Issues were to be kept open and subjected to thorough interagency analysis, with the President to decide, not merely to ratify a bureaucratic consensus. The system was conscious centralization, with the White House assuming more direct control over each stage of the process leading to decision. Staffing arrangements in the White House were beefed up to run the system. As time passed, however, centralization became privatization under the banner of preserving Presidential flexibility. More and more issues came to be decided after processes involving the participation of but a few officials. In many cases, even elements of Washington officialdom with clear claim to relevant expertise were excluded.

Thus, within two years the formal NSC system of 1969 yielded place in fact, adapting its form to something different, a "private" arrangement. In the next year the shape of that arrangement would become clear enough to be considered as a third form of organization.

The great foreign policy initiatives of 1971—the opening toward China and the devaluation of the dollar ushering in the "new economic policy"—were the results of deliberations of which few men beyond the President and an advisor or two even had knowledge.[9] In the China instance, almost no one but the President and Henry Kissinger knew what was afoot; in the case of the economic departure, Kissinger was disinterested or excluded, and without him, no one who might have advocated general foreign policy concerns could gain entry to discussions. In the first instance, with foreign policy experts on Japan out of play, ignorance of or pique with Japan on the part of the men who took decision was allowed full rein. The China initiative came as a profound shock to America's chief Asian ally, to which the U.S. government had pledged full consultation in advance of a change of policy on China. State's Europeanists similarly were excluded, and the action came as a surprise to European governments, though the shock registered less intensely in their politics than in Japan's. In the instance of economics, the political impacts of the policy shift, most obvious with respect to Japan and western Europe, simply went unrecognized. There was no one to give them representation in the process of decision.

In both cases, the outcomes resembled the early handling of offset, though for different reasons and through different mechanisms: policies reflected narrow conceptions of United States interest. In offset, decentralization meant that parochial considerations guided action; in the Nixon cases, privatization meant that important interests were not perceived or lacked for sponsors.

The "shocks" are stark commentary on the hazard inherent in any attempt to pursue "open options" across the board. Mechanisms for keeping elements of Washington officialdom from coalescing around lines of argument or policy seem hard to structure, harder still to keep healthy for long periods. Of course the choice is hardly an absolute one, centralization or decentralization. It is a question of degree: how far to move away from fixed and fairly permanent delegations of authority to departments toward direct White House control of the process leading to decision and action. Presidents, whatever their personalities, are certain to be tempted to vest responsibility for more and more kinds of issues in White House mechanisms directly accountable to them. Doing so preserves freedom for maneuver. Yet the peril surrounding those mechanisms is clear. Even if they work as intended, centers of decision may become disconnected from the implementers, those in the bureaucracy whose job it is to convert governmental policy into action. And over time, as those at the top of government become more comfortable with the exercise of power, natural temptations to restrict deliberations may be abetted by the existence of a formal White House coordinating apparatus.

I have presumed that either *ad hoc* mechanisms for special issues or more general coordinating structures would center on the White House. That presumption is a bias borne of the offset cases in part. The focus on coordination and on issues of Presidential level insured that the White House role would be substantial. So, too, did the addition of economics. White House coordination on matters involving international economics is natural, given the deep involvement in those issues of the "domestic" economic departments—Treasury, Commerce and Agriculture—and the political constituencies they represent. But I believe the presumption holds more widely.

191

There are several reasons why the Secretary of State and his Department seem unlikely to be able to play the coordinating role, either in specific instances or more generally. One is the number of tasks the Secretary is called upon to perform. Expecting him at once to manage his department, oversee the missions, perform the ceremonial duties which accompany his position *and* act as the President's agent of coordination is asking too much of any single human being. Each task is a full-time job, at least.

Moreover, the tasks are not easily compatible with one another. Managing the Department requires building confidence downward—sustaining subordinates, issuing clear guidelines. By contrast, acting as the President's agent means preserving options and policing the departments; both are likely to require that the Secretary, on occasion, undercut his own Department. Secretary Dulles chose to attend his President rather than manage the Department. So, it appears, did Secretary Kissinger. Nor, on the evidence, did any President between Eisenhower and Ford in fact desire the State Department to play the preeminent role. That was true despite ritual affirmations by all concerned that the State Department ought to be the center of American foreign policy-making.

The offset cases underscore a central fact of postwar United States foreign policy-making: departments in addition to State also have a clear and legitimate right to participation. That fact was given structural form in the National Security Act of 1947. It underlies the currency of terms like "national security" in contrast to older words like "diplomacy." The State Department can be the first among equals, with skill and Presidential acquiescence. It can lead, by cajoling and persuading, with skill and perseverance. But in ordinary times it can hardly take decisions on major issues; only the President can. Nor can State often play the part of arbiter, ring holder and manager of the debate. To do so would be to act as both advocate and judge. And the experience of the 1966 offset affair bears remembering: trouble arose not because the Department of State did not coordinate but rather because it did not play a strong *departmental* hand within the coordinating structure.

If I am correct, procedures and staffing arrangements in the White House will be subject to a variety of pressures. That is obvious if the White House must maintain formal, centralized systems like the Nixon NSC. Yet the *ad hoc* White House arrangements of 1966 and 1967 were also subject to strains. The strains may have been somewhat different in character than were those of 1969; they were not too different in magnitude.

If decentralized operations by the various departments are taken for granted, the White House will be called upon to rescue issues from those operations in given instances, as in 1966. It may do so through specially fashioned *ad hoc* mechanisms, like the Rostow group, or through resort to special procedures, fixed but intended for use in specific instances. Strain will descend on the White House role as manager and arbiter, case by case. If, by contrast, an attempt is made to preserve options for the President, not in specific cases but for classes of issues, White House staffing arrangements must assure that options are not lost in privatized deliberations and that implementation does not slip. That implies strains like the foregoing, plus the addition of pressure on the White House role as maintainer of institutions regarded by the rest of the government as legitimate. The strains involved in the case-by-case and the more general strategies seem commensurate. So do the costs of failing to cope with them.

V. THE POLITICS OF ALLIANCE

The offset history suggests a final set of lessons. These pertain to the substance of United States relations with its major allies more than to the processes and structures of government used to handle that substance. But the conduct of policy-making and the content of policy are obviously intertwined. The lessons about the substance of relations arise, in large part, from an understanding of the limits on American policy-making (and that of its allies). In turn, the substantive suggestions carry clear implications for the organization of policy-making.

In offset, as in other recent instances in American relations with allies, the United States' reach exceeded its grasp. Offset arrangements and the link to force levels were an ostensibly cooperative endeavor, yet one which entailed obvious demands on the Federal Republic. Those demands bore on Germany's basic political processes—determining government expenditures and raising revenue. Their fulfillment was bound, sooner or later, to become a matter of contention within Bonn and between Bonn and Washington. At the same time, the history of demands made and complied with left Washingtonians to presume that their enterprise was reasonable. Moreover, the issues became entangled in, and in turn reinforced a fundamental division in the "inner" government. When German circumstances called the offset arrangements into question, the United States was little able to adjust its actions to account for German politics. A snarly summit conference ensued. That and subsequent events left a residue of suspicion, in the minds of Americans as well as Germans, that Washington had nudged Erhard over the brink.

The offset history, set beside Suez, Skybolt and other similar instances, suggests some of the dimensions of alliance relations from which may arise constraints on American action with respect to those allies. Several of these are general across the spectrum of dealings between the United States and a given ally.[10] Another set has to do with the nature of particular issues and their contexts. None of these dimensions necessarily applies only to relations between *allies*.

The first dimension is the closeness of the alliance. Relationships regarded as alliances may range from consortia, fixed and quite enduring, to nominal associations. As a general matter, the closer the alliance, the more the actions of one partner will bear on the other, hence the more constrained both will be. To the extent that both recognize the closeness of their alliance, and regard that proximity as desirable, they may *feel* constrained as well. On the other hand, some relations which might be regarded as close alliances by formal definition may not be recognized or desired, by one party or both. Relations between the U.S. and some nations of southeast Asia or Latin America may fall into that category. That suggests a second dimension of alliance.

The character of alliance relations is affected by the degree of dependence of one ally on its partner. This category, like the rest, is not of course independent of the others. The degree of dependency may well affect the closeness of the alliance, especially in perception. Yet a nation which is completely dependent on an ally, even a close one, may not be able to constrain the actions of its ally, at least while the weaker nation recognizes its dependency and sees no practical alternative to it. This formulation applies to relations between the U.S. and western industrialized nations; if the discussion were extended to American relations with poorer countries, different sorts, as well as degrees, of dependence should be considered. In the case of offset, American perceptions lagged behind reality, as I have suggested: the Federal Republic was perceived as totally dependent when it had ceased to be so (though it remained dependent). Germany's growing economic strength and political maturity were thought to increase Bonn's capabilities (for instance, to raise armies or assist those of its allies) but were not perceived in Washington to widen the Federal Republic's political options or freedom of action.

A related but separable dimension is more economic than political. It is the interconnection of allies' economies, the extent of their "interdependence" in the language of the 1970s. That may limit their ability to achieve political goals and complicate their political relations in myriad ways. It may constrain either's scope for the conscious pursuit of linkage strategies or, perhaps more important, it may compel linkages that neither sought and that cause problems for the domestic politics of both. In one sense, economic interdependence was at the root of the offset/troop level link. The American balance of payments depended, to some degree, on German procurement policies and Bundesbank actions: hence Washington's initial quest for levers to influence Bonn's actions in those regards, to use issues in which it perceived itself "strong" to shore up its position where it saw itself "weak."[11] Or looked at in another light, the form and extent of monetary interdependence between the United States and the Federal Republic constrained Washington's ability to pursue its military goals in Europe and its political interest in easy, close relations with Bonn.

The final two general factors are the familiarity of the allies to one another, and the wherewithal each possesses to understand the other. The two are obviously related to the closeness of the alliance but are not identical to it. Anglo-American relations differed from German-American along those dimensions, as Neustadt notes.[12] Both were close alliances, but Washingtonians had an easy familiarity with London's institutions and officials, not to mention its government buildings, streets and restaurants; and bilateral relations were, in public perception as well, those of family. By contrast, German institutions were foreign to most Americans, those in public life included, and Bonn's leaders remained strangers.

Familiarity and resources for understanding one another seem more directly related than closeness and familiarity, but again they are not identical. To use an example outside alliances, the U.S. government has at hand swarms of professional experts on the behavior of the Soviet government, although the two nations are hardly familiar to one another. More important, familiarity may not impel Washington to employ wisely what technical expertise exists, or to consult it at all. The lesson of Suez and Skybolt is precisely that it did not. In the instance of offset, sources of expertise on German delibera-

195

tions, themselves barely adequate, were again used poorly, this time due more to Washingtonians' perception of Germany's dependence than of its familiarity. If the American government lacks the professional resources necessary to comprehend an ally or is unlikely to use those it has at its disposal, it may find itself constrained in ways it does not understand and did not foresee. It would be foolhardy to frame any policies which depend on complicated responses from its ally.

Other constraints may inhere in particular issues or sets of issues. The form of the issue itself may imply clear constraints on the range of subsequent action, for one or the other government or, worse, for both. Additional limitations, subtler and less easily anticipated, may derive from particular features in the intersection of that form with the politics and governing processes of the two countries. The two categories of constraints are closely akin to one another. The second may be a specification of the first. But it may be not merely that, for, as in offset, issues may become enmeshed in internal complexities in a way which is not merely a result of the form of those issues.

The form of offset—German military procurement to balance American military balance-of-payments deficits—entailed sharp constraints on both sides of the Atlantic. Those were clear from the outset, whether or not officials in either country recognized them. Offset compliance, for the Germans, depended on a stream of decisions resulting from the central process of government— budgeting—hence depended on both economic capability and political will. Compliance also hinged on procurement choices, technical decisions bound up with domestic politics and European cooperation. For the U.S., once offset became an important instrument attached to a general matter of urgent concern—the balance of payments—the constraint was obvious. Adjustments in the instrument would run to the general concern, threatening consequences larger than some decrement in German procurement. What Washington sought for its balance-of-payments purposes had to be granted from a process at the center of German politics. That alone should have signaled danger to responsible officials in both countries.

Aspects of the political process surrounding offset elaborated the constraint on American action. The form of offset served the purposes of two major departments of the American government, Defense and Treasury. The coincidence became ingrained in procedures for handling the issue. Other purposes became attached to offset: those were served by linking offset to the question of force levels in Europe.

Concerns involved in that link were crucial ones to the four major departments of the American government, each buttressed by constituencies in Congress and outside government. The specific issues fell into a government divided along two broad perspectives which had become rigid over time. Questions of offset and force level were first shaped by one perspective, then caught between the two.

By 1966, offset was similarly bound up in the politics and processes of governance in the Federal Republic. The constraints on German action were commensurate with those on American. The specifics from whence derived those constraints are familiar from chapter III: Cabinet politics of budget-cutting in a time of fiscal stringency; Bundestag procedures for reducing expenditures, in particular automatic disbursements; party politics of succession to the chancellorship, approaching with or without offset; and the character of relations between the central government and the Bundesbank.

When Washington confronted Bonn over offset and force level in 1966, its range of action was extremely narrow. Germany was a close enough ally so no Washingtonian doubted that American actions affected it. But the unfamiliarity of Bonn and the limited expertise Washington commanded to understand it meant that the nature of those effects remained shadowy to U.S. officials. And perceptions of the Federal Republic's dependence suggested that Washington need not fine-tune its actions to account for probable German responses; Bonn would have to do as the U.S. wished. Moreover, the form of the issues and the internal politics surrounding them in Washington left little room in which to do the fine-tuning. What unfamiliarity made uncomfortable and what dependence suggested would be unnecessary, Washington's politics seemed to make impossible to consider.

That offset took the form it did initially is suggestive of the hazards to alliance relations when those relations no longer can be neatly divided into separate agendas labeled "politics" or "economics" or "military strategy." Allies, not least the United States, may be tempted to pursue objectives of one sort disguised as projects of another. For weaker allies, doing so may be reflective only of necessity. Prime Minister Macmillan no doubt thought he had little choice but to pursue his Tory *political* interest in prolonging Britain's independent nuclear deterrent through as technically dubious a military enterprise as the Skybolt missile. In other instances, the crossing of objectives may be abrupt, tactical decisions taken at the top of government. At the last minute, apparently, President Nixon struck a bargain with Japanese Prime Minister Sato linking Okinawa and

197

textiles: the U.S. would agree to Okinawa reversion on Japanese terms but expected, in return, that the dispute over Japanese textile exports to the U.S. would be settled on American terms, with Sato agreeing to limit exports.[13]

The crossings of objectives represented in Skybolt and Okinawa are interesting, and the costs they entail for alliance relations often are high, but they are not my primary subject here. Rather, I focus more on American policy than that of its allies, and on linkages across issues which are, or may come to be, more strategic than tactical. The connections I have in mind are those which resemble the link between offset and force level in the cases discussed in previous chapters. That link was employed to tactical advantage in offset negotiations with the Germans, in 1973 as well as 1966, and tactical considerations based on domestic politics may have motivated it initially; but it became an enduring element in United States action, a consistent part of American balance-of-payments policy. What began as a simple joining of congruent purposes, German and American, came to be a means of applying pressure on Bonn. In effect, the United States used a domain where it perceived itself to be relatively strong—military security—to exact advantage in an area where it felt relatively weak—international finance. Germans (and other Europeans) were presumed to care more about the presence of the troops than the United States. That being the case, they should be prepared to pay in one coin or another.

The approach embodied in the link was a paradox. Put somewhat too bluntly: either it was in the *United States'* interest to maintain an existing level of forces in Europe or it was not. If it were, then the United States should have been prepared to sustain the foreign exchange cost of doing so, leaving the necessary adjustments to economic arenas. (That statement applies with particular force to the period after 1971, when a fixed dollar exchange rate ceased to be sacred, but it was true with some qualification earlier as well.)[14] On the other hand, if a given level were not in the American interest, then matters of money should have played little part in the decision to thin the force.

The apparent paradox arose of course because the Washington consensus which had supported the maintenance of 300,000 American troops in Europe, at least through the Berlin crisis of 1961, eroded during the 1960s. What was a barely acceptable minimum level for the Joint Chiefs of Staff and a modest dollar cost to the State Department became a swollen garrison and an intolerable burden in the view of some Senators. The Johnson Administration, like its successor, sought to preserve a tenuous truce. If European assistance to the United States could be made to demonstrate that Europeans wanted the American troops to stay and if Germans at any rate could be pressed to do more, then perhaps Congress could be stayed from having the U.S. do less.

Yet if the genesis of offset was reasonable enough, the side effects of its continuation were unhappy ones. In 1966 those effects, especially on German politics, were obvious. Sustaining offset as then in effect implied continuing a particular pattern of German military procurement. Yet that pattern was bound to become unacceptable, even to the ostensible military experts of the Federal Republic. By 1966, the first round of German rearmament was more or less completed, and a continental arms industry, in Germany and in neighboring countries, competed with American suppliers for limited orders. By the same time, however, offset had become imbedded in particular politics and procedures in Washington. Those dictated that the Federal Republic should be exhorted to continue a joint venture for whose substance it no longer had any enthusiasm. That occurrence was, I think, predictable from the start.

The wider side effects of offset and the link to force levels on public attitudes in both countries were no less adverse. The rigidities which grew up around the issues within the two governments fed misunderstandings without. In neither country did the handling of the issues serve the cause of public education about matters of international economics or military security.

That the particular ways the issues were framed, in Bonn as in Washington, seemed politically necessary to the two nations' leaders is hardly an excuse. The American government's insistence that questions of force level not be divorced from offset encouraged the public impression that the United States was providing the Europeans a service by stationing troops on the continent, not pursuing its own interest. Continual exhortations to the Europeans to "share the burden" of budget and foreign exchange costs added to that impression (regardless of whether the "burden" actually was or is shared unfairly).

The role of offset in the domestic politics of the Federal Republic fostered attitudes which were just the obverse of those prevailing in the United States. For purposes of their politics, German leaders found it convenient, in 1966 and after, to cast the United States in the role of "heavy." Their purposes were served by portraying American offset demands as tough, to which the Federal Republic assented only in part and only after hard bargaining. From there, it was but a short step to the public perception that American demands were not only tough but unreasonable, that the United States was compelling Germany to buy unneeded weapons. That perception influenced German attitudes toward the troops. If Americans tended to think they were providing a service, Germans often felt they were purchasing one. That increased jitters about the permanence of the U.S. garrison and, with them, worries about how committed the United States actually was to the defense of Europe, through nuclear means if need be. Hiring mercenaries is clearly worse than engaging in a cooperative endeavor with an ally which stations troops on *your* soil in pursuit of *its* own self-interest.

The issues of troops in Europe and how they are paid for are still with us. Their current configuration hardly encourages optimism that sensible policies will be reached, on either side of the Atlantic, or that interallied outcomes will be happy ones. Domestic pressures in all the allies argue for smaller defense budgets, not larger (with inflation eroding the purchasing power of whatever budgets remain) and for conserving or earning foreign exchange, not spending or donating it. At the same time, two decades of assertions that any substantial reduction in American forces in Europe would have serious adverse consequences for European politics and security—arguments made both by Europeans to Americans and by the American Executive Branch to Congress—have left their mark. Prophecies repeated so many times may become self-fulfilling.

The situation allows little room in which to accommodate the needs of the allies' domestic politics, least of all those of the United States. Barring another Czechoslovakian invasion or other Soviet adventure (or perhaps even notwithstanding it), some American troops are likely to be withdrawn from Europe in the next half decade, not merely redeployed as in the support-forces-for-combat-troops exchanges of the mid-1970s. A decision to reduce the force level almost surely would be influenced by considerations of money—an American perception of its own incapability or of Europe's insufficient generosity—touching off recriminations all around. The offset cases stress the importance of process and form in dealings among allies; consultations may be as important as their subjects. But the allies seem to be frozen into a situation in which to discuss reductions in American forces is tantamount to making them. They seem precluded from engaging in the atmospherics that could diminish the political costs to all of them, and to their alliance, of withdrawals that may be inevitable despite the American retrenchment of 1975 and 1976. Instead they pin hopes on the prospect of mutual reductions negotiated with the Warsaw Pact nations. Yet the allied dilemma is as plain to the Russians as to Americans or Europeans. The Soviets would be foolhardy to agree to mutual withdrawals unless they are forced to them by domestic pressures of their own.

More generally, links across issues of different kinds, like that in offset, seem certain to occur with increasing frequency in alliance relations of the years ahead. The reasons are easy to find. One is the waning of the postwar preoccupation with military security. Security fears retain an edge in the Federal Republic that they have long since lost elsewhere in NATO. But even that is changing. Some tension was inherent as Bonn simultaneously pursued an *Ostpolitik* based on the lessening of strains with Germany's eastern neighbors, yet treated an armed attack from the East as a real possibility.

As security fears have waned, economic issues have risen higher on the agenda of North Atlantic relations. The hierarchy of issues— security first, then economics—which characterized the first two postwar decades of those relations no longer retains the force it once had. No longer is a bargaining threat which touches military ar- rangements regarded by the allies as too risky to be contemplated. Moreover, matters of economics, imbedded in domestic politics, are contentious ones in dealings among allies. That is surely true in the short run, when conflicts are more apparent than harmonies, how- ever much the U.S. and its major allies may share common economic interests over the long term.

Allies may be tempted to engage one another in projects involving a mixture of politics, economics and military strategy, endeavors whose constituent elements may not all be acceptable on their merits to the nations concerned. Temptation of that sort is inherent in alliance since by definition allies share an interest in sustaining their political relationship. They presumably judge the alliance to be in their long-term interest and will act to sustain it, even at some short-term cost. One or another ally can play upon its partner's interest in sustaining the alliance in order to secure a short-term gain, most often economic in character. Prime Minister Sato no doubt agreed to textile quotas finally because of his specific Okinawa objec- tive, but his earlier inclination to meet U.S. demands derived more from his general desire to maintain his close ties with Washington. The United States may be especially prone to such manipulations, since its perception of Europe's continuing dependence amounts to a belief that the alliance is a creature of necessity more for Europeans than for Americans. Of course, perceptions on either side of the Atlantic may not square with reality. For example, Americans during the 1966 offset affair exaggerated the extent of Bonn's dependence on the United States.

The more frequent crossing of economics and politics will abet the temptations, particularly for the United States. The U.S., or its allies, will be tempted to assemble packages of actions ranging across economic, political and military concerns. American allies may feel compelled to assent to a package, even though not all of the actions which comprise it are acceptable to them. The joining of the actions may represent American design, or it may emerge in the absence of conscious planning, from misperception or convenience. If neglecting the requirements of form and process in alliance relations is dangerous, so too is the converse. A community of interests may be taken for granted when none exists, and the United States may come to assume that Europeans will share its enthusiasm for a given action if only the proper form of interallied consultation can be found. What we do may come to seem less important than how we communicate our intentions to our allies. Of course, no matter how just their grievances, the Europeans have encouraged that American attitude by harping on deficiencies in "consultation" when often what they disliked were the American policies themselves. The flap over NPT consultation in 1966–67 is an example. American policy was bound to create troubles for German governments, no matter how intimate and full of goodwill were the consultations between the two governments with respect to that policy.

The end of "separate tracking" of economic and security issues may create especially serious dangers for the United States. In the American government, compromises across issues of different sorts must be reached in public to a much greater extent than is true in the capitals of major American allies in Europe. Differences among Executive departments and between Executive and Congress are played out in view of domestic groups with stakes in particular outcomes; no equivalent of the British Official Secrets Act keeps the American press at a safe distance from serious deliberations. Erhard could not manage a successful policy with regard to offset in the fall of 1966, but he could keep the issue away from his ministries when he chose to do so. On the American side, by contrast, while a new policy was in the making, McNamara still could run offset to suit his purposes. And

Senators could make their own separate threats to thin the U.S. force in Europe. In the major European governments, clusters of issues like offset and force level are likely to produce cabinet stalemate, leaving ministers fearful of losing the issues to ministerial compromise. In the United States, however, those clusters may produce multiple, conflicting "government" policies.

Framing cooperative actions in the years ahead will be a perilous endeavor. But I assume it will be a necessary one. The trappings and even many of the formal institutions of alliance may fall away. It is clearly conceivable that NATO might not persist in anything like its present form. But for the rest of this century the United States and the major countries of western Europe seem certain to regard themselves as allied to one another, if not necessarily as "allies" in the sense which the word acquired in the Second World War and has retained. *They* will continue to perceive *us* as instrumental to their purposes, economic and other, and we will regard them in a similar way. The relationship will remain something more than that of purely self-interested trading partners.[15] That will imply that the United States should take somewhat more account of its allies' politics in framing its own actions than is the case in American relations with other foreign countries. The assumption of continued alliance with western European countries is, however, neither immutable nor absolute. It should be continually examined to see what common interests exist and how far they extend.

Offset and other recent cases are testimony to the difficulty of framing cooperative efforts. They suggest several prescriptions, tentative and provisional, about what sort of joint ventures the United States should seek, what sort of demands it should make—and refrain from making—on allied governments.

Offset reinforces a lesson Neustadt drew from the Suez and Skybolt episodes. It is the injunction to limit demands, even those made within what has been regarded traditionally as a single domain of issues, to "outcomes which do not depend for their achievement on precise conjunctions of particular procedures, men and issues."[16] In offset, the United States claim on German politics went to essentials, to the complex and sensitive process of allocating government expenditures, hence depended for its fulfillment not only on a healthy German economy but also on senior German officials who were both willing and able to manage their machine in circumstances which were bound to be difficult in any case. Skybolt was similar, with the roles reversed, the United States having made a pledge which depended on the outcomes of processes of budgeting and technical development.

The offset cases counsel special caution in framing endeavors which combine politics, economics and military strategy by cloaking objectives of one sort in projects of another. Such enterprises may come, like offset, to bear heavily on the political center of an American ally in ways Washingtonians did not foresee and find themselves little able to remedy at critical junctures. The dangers seem likely to be especially acute if the partner in the joint enterprise is an ally on the order of the Federal Republic: close but strange to Washington, with the U.S. in possession of little expertise for comprehending the details of its governance; dependent on the United States but less so than in the past, with acquiescence to American wishes no longer an imperative of domestic politics, implying that subsequent action by the ally may be constrained in ways to which U.S. officials are unaccustomed. One American ally seems to fit this description as well as the Federal Republic, perhaps better—Japan. Yet the dangers do not seem much less even if the ally is more familiar than those two or if the U.S. commands more professional understanding of it.

Two examples bespeak the dangers. First the famous, now infamous, MLF (multilateral force)—a proposal for a NATO surface fleet, manned by sailors of different nationalities and armed with nuclear missiles under American control. For several years before Lyndon Johnson sank it, in December 1964, the fleet had been official U.S. policy and had been given a hard sell in Europe by committed State Department officials.[17] The MLF was a military venture for political purposes. It was, in the minds and hearts of its Washington supporters, the solution to a series of European political problems, not all of which, it turned out, existed. MLF was advertised in Washington, for instance, as an answer to NATO's "German problem"—the second-class status in the alliance to which the Federal Republic supposedly was relegated by being denied participation in nuclear defenses. But MLF threatened, in fact, to split Erhard's government at the seams. The "Gaullists" in his party wanted nothing of something so obviously made in America, and, to boot, so deeply scorned in Paris. In the process of layering purposes for MLF on top of one another, Washington did not see that the idea of the fleet was less an expression of interests the allies shared than a projection, by Washington, of *its* conceptions onto its allies. The U.S. finally made that realization, but not before its MLF advocacy had created political heat for the men in Bonn, London and Rome.

American calls for cooperation among the oil-importing nations after the 1973 Arab oil embargo bore a similarity to the MLF affair. The issues ran not only to foreign policy but to economics, international and domestic, enmeshed in domestic politics. Charting a course on that terrain, amid the constraints invoked and implied, was risky business. No matter how reasonable a policy of solidarity among major consuming nations appeared to Washington, the costs and benefits—economic and political—of that strategy were bound to be assessed differently in the capitals of European countries which depended almost completely on Arab oil. That fact, simple enough, Washington ignored at its peril. Yet for some time it did ignore it, instead laying Europe's reluctance to excessive timidity or advancing decadence.[18]

A return to the "separate tracking" of issues, which characterized the last two decades of Atlantic relations, seems unlikely. That practice kept military issues apart from matters of economics (the offset/troop-level link excepted), and trade and international money were treated in distinct arenas despite obvious connections between the two sets of issues. The "tracking" produced gains in all sets of relations which might have been possible in none of them had they been joined. Yet I doubt that the custom of the 1960s will be repeated in the late 1970s or the 1980s. The reasons have been mentioned before. Prominent among them are the diminished salience of security concern and the increased political visibility of economic interests, often divisive.

At a minimum, the offset cases suggest that the United States should be circumspect in assembling package deals in alliance relations. Insofar as possible the constituent elements of those packages should be acceptable *on their merits* to allied leaders and their relevant experts. Making determinations of acceptability will not be easy, for the officials who govern in allied capitals often have reason to disguise their purposes, and elements of Washington officialdom may have interests in accepting those disguises as real. If Washington decides a particular mixed venture is important or meritorious enough to pursue against doubts about some elements' attractiveness to allies, it should know wherein it treads. It should closely monitor the venture and be prepared to fine-tune its actions in order to prevent excessive burdens on the politics of its allies. The offset cases, however, offer small grounds for optimism that monitoring can be effective, less still that the United States will be able to change course quickly enough to prevent mishaps.

205

NOTES TO CHAPTER VI

[1] Richard E. Neustadt, *Alliance Politics* (New York: Columbia University Press, 1970), pp.118–19, 142–43.

[2] For a discussion of the problem of avoiding "overloads" on the politics of an ally, *see* Francis M. Bator, "The Politics of Alliance: The United States and Western Europe," in Kermit Gordon, ed., *Agenda for the Nation* (Washington: The Brookings Institution, 1968), p.352.

[3] The most detailed work on Okinawa reversion has been done by Priscilla Clapp. One version is a case she prepared for the federal Commission on the Organization of Government for the Conduct of Foreign Policy, "The Status of Okinawa, 1961—1969," in Appendix K to the Report of the Commission (Washington, 1975).

[4] The management problem was first formulated in this way, so far as I can tell, by Francis M. Bator in testimony before the Heineman Commission in 1967. For a more recent version, *see* his testimony in *U.S. Foreign Economic Policy: Implications for the Organization of the Executive Branch,* Hearings before the Senate Committee on Foreign Affairs and its Subcommittee on Foreign Economic Policy, 92 Cong., 2 sess.(1972), pp.109–11.

[5] For further description of the character and operation of informal working groups, *see* Bator's testimony in *ibid.,* pp.107–21.

[6] For a discussion of the 1969 NSC system, *see* John P. Leacacos, "Kissinger's Apparat," *Foreign Policy,* 5 (Winter 1971–72), pp.3–27. For a more critical view, *see* I. M. Destler's article, "Can One Man Do?" in *ibid.,* pp.28–40. My understanding of the system owes much to discussions with Morton Halperin.

[7] Graham Allison has pointed out to me that the maintenance of large oil stockpiles by the U.S. Navy serves as an antidote to the argument that no one could have predicted the embargo, hence no one could have prepared for it.

[8] The system also reflected mistrust of the State Department on the part of Nixon and Kissinger. But that goes beyond my purposes here.

[9] For a brief description of policy-making preceding the "shocks," *see* a study prepared by I. M. Destler for the federal Commission mentioned above, "The Nixon 'Shocks' to Japan," in Appendix K to the Report of the Commission (Washington, 1975). Another discussion is contained in Graham T. Allison, "American Foreign Policy and Japan," in Henry Rosovsky, ed., *Discord in the Pacific* (Washington D.C.: The American Assembly, 1972). For a discussion of the actions' effect on Europe, *see* Wilfrid Kohl, "The Nixon-Kissinger Foreign Policy System and U.S.-European Relations: Patterns of Policy-Making," *World Politics,* XXVIII, 1 (October 1975), pp.1–43.

[10] My discussion of this category draws on Neustadt, cited above, p.149.

[11] For a provocative general discussion of these phenomena, *see* Joseph S. Nye and Robert O. Keohane, "World Politics and the International Economic System" in C. Fred Bergsten, ed., *The Future of the International Economic Order: An Agenda for Research* (Lexington, Mass.: Lexington Books, 1973). They also develop a useful distinction between "sensitivity" and "vulnerability" interdependence. In their terms, the United States balance-of-payments position in 1966–67 was sensitive to German actions within the existing monetary structures. But the United States was not vulnerable to changes in

the structure, while the Federal Republic was, for only the United States had the power to compel a systemic alteration on its own. It did just that in 1971, abruptly, and then forced other countries to bear the burden of adjustment. America's power to upset the system suggests that German willingness to engage in offset and other forms of assistance to the U.S. balance of payments before 1971 had economic as well as political/security motivations; not only did Bonn want to ensure that large numbers of American GIs stayed in Germany, but it also wanted to preserve a monetary structure in which it could amass surpluses and in which most of the burden of adjustment in domestic economic policies fell on deficit nations.

[12]Neustadt, p.149.

[13]This deal is referred to in both the Destler study and the Clapp case, cited above.

[14]For similar analyses of the post-1971 period, *see* Edward R. Fried, "Foreign Economic Policy: The Search for a Strategy," in Henry Owen, ed., *The Next Phase in Foreign Policy* (Washington: The Brookings Institution, 1973), p.183; and Twelve North American, European and Japanese Economists, *Reshaping the International Economic Order* (Washington: The Brookings Institution, 1973), p.23.

[15]This would hold true, I believe, even under the quite radical assumption that the North Atlantic military relationship were completely dismantled, consonant with what Robert W. Tucker labels "a new isolationism." *See* his *A New Isolationism: Threat or Promise?* (New York: Universe Books, 1972), especially pp.77–86.

[16]Neustadt, p.149.

[17]The most concise version of the MLF history is Philip Geyelin's "MLF— Or, How He Does It," chapter seven of *Lyndon Johnson and the World* (New York: Praeger Publishers, 1966). *See* also John Steinbruner, *The Cybernetic Theory of Decision* (Princeton: Princeton University Press, 1974).

[18]For an insightful, concise discussion of French and German positions before and after the oil crisis of 1973, *see* Horst Mendershausen, *Coping with the Oil Crisis: French and German Experiences* (Baltimore: Johns Hopkins University Press, 1976).

LIST OF PERSONS INTERVIEWED

All of the people with whom I conducted more or less formal interviews consented to let me list their names. That list follows. It is composed of persons who were participants in the event described in this study, at some level, in Europe or the United States. I have not listed the academics and newspaper people with whom I discussed offset. The titles and dates given for each person are intended to suggest how much association with the events discussed in the study each had, what kind and when.

Americans

Raymond Albright — Office of National Security Affairs, Treasury, 1966–67.

George Ball — Under Secretary of State, 1966.

Francis M. Bator — Deputy Special Assistant to the President for National Security Affairs, 1966–67.

Robert W. Bean — Office of National Security Affairs, Treasury, 1966–67 until 1974.

C. Fred Bergsten — Bureau of Economic Affairs, State Department, 1966–67; National Security Council staff, 1969.

Robert Bowie — State Department Counselor, 1966–67.

James Cheatham — Bureau of Economic Affairs, State Department, 1973.

Geryld B. Christianson — Bureau of European Affairs, State Department, 1974.

Richard N. Cooper — Bureau of Economic Affairs, State Department, and then consultant to the McCloy task force, 1966–67.

Clyde Crosswhite — Office of National Security Affairs, Treasury, 1974, and earlier.

Frederick Deming — Under Secretary of the Treasury for Monetary Affairs, 1966–67.

Edward Fried — National Security Council staff, 1968.

Ellen Frost — Legislative Assistant to Senator Alan Cranston, 1974.

H. Kent Goodspeed—Economic Counselor, U.S. Mission to NATO, 1973–74.

Morton Halperin — Deputy Assistant Secretary of Defense, International Security Affairs, 1966–67; National Security Council staff, 1969.

Edward Hamilton — Deputy to Francis Bator, 1966–67.

Lucian Heichler — Bureau of European Affairs, State Department, 1974.

Donald G. Henderson — Staff, Senate Foreign Relations Committee, 1974, and earlier.

Martin Hillenbrand — Deputy Chief of Mission, U. S. Embassy in Bonn, 1966–67; Assistant Secretary of State for European Affairs, 1970–71; Ambassador to Germany, 1974.

John Knubel — National Security Council staff, 1973–74.

John Leddy — Assistant Secretary of State for European Affairs, 1966–67.

Eugene McAuliffe — Member, McCloy task force, 1966–67; Deputy Chief of Mission, U.S. Mission to NATO, 1974.

William Miller — Aide to Senator John Sherman Cooper, 1966–67 and later.

James C. Nelson — Bureau of European Affairs, State Department, 1973.

Walter Pincus — Consultant, Senate Foreign Relations Committee, 1970.

William Prendergast — Defense Advisor, U.S. Mission to NATO, 1973–74 and earlier.

Eugene Rostow — Under Secretary of State for Political Affairs, 1966–68.

Nathaniel Samuels — Deputy Under Secretary of State for Economic Affairs, 1969–71.

Roger Shields—Office for International Security Affairs, Defense Department, 1974.

George Springsteen — Aide to George Ball, 1966; Deputy Assistant Secretary of State for European Affairs, 1973.

Timothy Stanley — Defense Department participant in Trilateral working group, 1966–67.

Charles Stevenson — Legislative Assistant to Senator Harold Hughes, 1974.

Charles Sullivan — Director of Office for National Security Affairs, Treasury, 1966.

James Sutterlin — Bureau of European Affairs, State Department, 1971–73.

Richard Violette — Aide to Henry Kuss, Deputy Assistant Secretary of Defense for International Logistics Negotiations, 1966–67; Deputy Director, Defense Security Assistance Agency, 1974.

Leonard Weiss — Economic Minister, U.S. Embassy in Bonn, 1968–69;

Deputy Director, Bureau of Intelligence and Research, State Department, 1973.

Theodore Wilkinson — U.S. Mission to NATO, 1973.

Adam Yarmolinsky — Counsel, Defense Department, 1966–67.

Britons

Sir William Armstrong — Joint Permanent Secretary of the Treasury, 1966–67.

David Bendall — Political Counselor, British Embassy in Washington, 1966–67.

Sir Frank Figgures — Third Secretary of the Treasury, 1966–67.

Angela Gillon — Research Department, Foreign and Commonwealth Office, 1974.

George Leitch — Deputy Under Secretary of State for Policy and Planning, Ministry of Defense, 1966–67; Chief Executive of Procurement Executive, 1974

Derek Mitchell — Deputy Under Secretary of State, Ministry of Development and Economic Affairs, 1966–67; Second Permanent Secretary of the Treasury, 1974.

John Owens — Historical Department, H. M. Treasury, 1974 (retired Treasury official).

Sir Michael Pallister — Private Secretary to the Prime Minister, 1966–67.

Sir Michael Stewart — Minister, British Embassy in Washington, 1966–67.

David Tidy — Head of DS12, Ministry of Defence, 1973.

Germans

Otmar Emminger — Vice President, Bundesbank, 1973 and earlier.

Per Fischer — Chancellor's Office (in charge of foreign affairs, defense and development assistance), 1973.

Walther Grund — State Secretary, Finance Ministry, 1966–67.

Günther Harkort — Assistant Secretary for Foreign Economic Policy, Foreign Office, 1966–67; State Secretary, 1968–69.

Rüdiger Hartmann — Foreign Office, 1973.

Peter Hermes — Assistant Secretary for Foreign Economic Policy, Foreign Office, 1973–74.

Joachim Hiehle — Assistant Secretary, Budget Division, Finance Ministry, 1973–74.

Hermann Jung — Executive Secretary, Bundestag Foreign Affairs Committee, 1974 and earlier.

Peter Klemm — Budget Division, Finance Ministry, 1973.

Hans-Clausen Korff — Assistant Secretary, Budget Division, Finance Ministry, 1966–69.

Heinz Massberg — Financial Counselor, German Mission to NATO, 1973 and earlier.

Hans Neusel — Chancellor's Office, 1966–69; Personal Assistant to Karl Carstens, CDU Bundestag leader, 1973.

Horst Osterheld — Chancellor's Office (working on foreign policy and defense issues), 1966–67.

Helmut Rocke — Finance Ministry, 1973 and earlier.

Jürgen Scholl — Division for Foreign Economic Policy, Foreign Office, 1971–74.

Hans-Otto Seydel — Procurement Division, Defense Ministry, 1973.

Admiral Herbert Trebesch — Defense Ministry, 1966–67; Director, Office for Politico-Military Affairs, Inspector General's staff, 1973.

Karl Günter von Hase — Director, Press and Information Office, 1966–67; State Secretary, Defense Ministry, 1968; Ambassador to the United Kingdom, 1973.

Kai-Uwe von Hassel — Minister of Defense, 1966.

Ludger Westrick — Senior advisor to Erhard, 1966.

Hans-Georg Wieck — Director, Planning Staff, Defense Ministry, 1973.

Peter Würtz — Member, Bundestag (SPD specialist on defense budget), 1973.

BIBLIOGRAPHY

As mentioned in the preface, I drew lightly on the customary academic sources—books, journals and the like—for descriptions and documentation of the events described in this study. Those sources were most useful as general background, with respect to both the substance of the issues and the nature of the policy-making processes of the governments involved, and as bases for comparing the offset history with other recent episodes in the making of American foreign policy. The following list of sources does not include individual newspaper articles. I used a great many of these, most often as a rough check on the reliability of information about the cases which I received from interview and other private sources. I made most extensive use of the following newspapers and magazines:

United States: *New York Times*
                 Washington Post
Federal Republic: *Die Welt* (Hamburg)
                 Frankfurter Allgemeine Zeitung (Frankfurt)
                 Süddeutsche Zeitung (Munich)
United Kingdom: *London Times*
                 The Economist
France: *Le Monde* (Paris)
Switzerland: *Neue Zürcher Zeitung* (Zurich)

Allemann, Fritz René. "The Changing Scene in Germany." *The World Today,* XXII, 2 (February 1967), 49–62.

Allison, Graham T. "American Foreign Policy and Japan." *Discord in the Pacific*. Edited by Henry Rosovsky. Washington: The American Assembly, 1972.

————. *Essence of Decision: Explaining the Cuban Missile Crisis*. Boston: Little, Brown, 1971.

———— and Halperin, Morton H. "Bureaucratic Politics: A Paradigm and Some Policy Implications." *Theory and Practice in International Relations*. Edited by Raymond Tanter and Richard H. Ullman. Princeton: Princeton University Press, 1972.

Arkes, Hadley. *Bureaucracy, the Marshall Plan and the National Interest*. Princeton: Princeton University Press, 1973.

Art, Robert. "Bureaucratic Politics and American Foreign Policy: A Critique." *Policy Sciences*, 4 (1973), 467–490.

Bator, Francis M. "The Political Economics of International Money." *Foreign Affairs*, XLVII, 1 (October 1968), 51–67.

————. "The Politics of Alliance: The United States and Western Europe." *Agenda for the Nation*. Edited by Kermit Gordon. Washington: The Brookings Institution, 1968.

Bauer, Raymond A.; de Sola Pool, Ithiel; and Dexter, Lewis Anthony. *American Business and Public Policy: The Politics of Foreign Trade*. New York: Atherton Press, 1963.

Baumann, Gerhard. "Devisenausgleich und Sicherheit." *Wehrkunde*, XVII, 5 (May 1968), 245–250.

Bergsten, C. Fred. "The New Economics and U.S. Foreign Policy." *Foreign Affairs*, L, 2 (January 1972), 199–222.

Bertram, Christoph. *Mutual Force Reductions in Europe: The Political Aspects*. Adelphi Paper No. 84. London: International Institute for Strategic Studies, 1972.

————. "The Politics of MBFR." *The World Today*, XXIX, 1 (January 1973), 1–7.

Birrenbach, Kurt. "Die Zukunft unserer Sicherheit: Risken und Notwendigkeiten einer Konferenz." *Die Politische Meinung*, XV, 130 (1970), 29–40.

Boeck, Hans, and Kragenau, Henry. "Truppenstationierung, Devisenausgleich und Burden-Sharing." *Wirtschaftsdienst*, LI, 2 (February 1971), 91–94.

Calleo, David. *The Atlantic Fantasy: The U.S., NATO and Europe*. Baltimore: Johns Hopkins Press, 1970.

Carstens, Karl. *Politische Führung*. Stuttgart: Deutsche Verlags-Anstalt, 1971.

Clapp, Priscilla. "The Status of Okinawa, 1961–1969." Appendix K of the Report of the Commission on the Organization of Government for the Conduct of Foreign Policy. Washington: 1975.

Clark, Keith C., and Legere, Laurence J., eds. *The President and the Management of National Security*. New York: Frederick A. Praeger, 1969.

Cohen, Stephen D. *International Monetary Reform, 1964–69: The Political Dimension*. New York: Praeger Publishers, 1970.

Committee for Economic Development, Research and Policy Committee. *Congressional Decision Making for National Security*. New York: Committee for Economic Development, 1974.

213

Cooper, Richard. *The Economics of Interdependence: Economic Policy in the Atlantic Community.* New York: McGraw-Hill, 1968.

Dahrendorf, Ralf. *Society and Democracy in Germany.* Garden City, New York: Doubleday and Co., Inc., 1967.

Davis, David H. *How the Bureaucracy Makes Foreign Policy.* Lexington, Mass.: D.C. Heath and Co., 1972.

de Rivera, Joseph. *The Psychological Dimension of Foreign Policy.* Columbus, Ohio: Merrill, 1968.

Destler, I.M. "Can One Man Do?" *Foreign Policy,* 5 (Winter 1971–72), 28–40.

_____. "The Nixon 'Shocks' to Japan, 1971." Appendix K of the Report of the Commission on the Organization of Government for the Conduct of Foreign Policy. Washington: 1975.

_____. *Presidents, Bureaucrats and Foreign Policy.* Princeton: Princeton University Press, 1972.

Downs, Anthony. *Inside Bureaucracy.* Boston: Little, Brown and Co., 1967.

Duckwitz, Georg Ferdinand. "Truppenstationierung und Devisenausgleich." *Aussenpolitik,* IIXX, 8 (August 1967), 471–475.

Enthoven, Alain C. "Arms and Men: The Military Balance in Europe." *Interplay,* 2 (May 1969), 11–14.

_____ and Smith, K. Wayne. *How Much Is Enough? Shaping the Defense Program, 1961–1969.* New York: Harper and Row, 1971.

_____. "What Forces for NATO? And From Whom?" *Foreign Affairs,* XLVIII, 3 (October 1969), 80–96.

Ernstoff, Lois; Piekarz, Rolf; and Wetzler, Elliot. *United States Exports Induced by Department of Defense Expenditures in Europe.* Washington: Institute for Defense Analyses, 1965.

Fox, Annette Baker. "Domestic Pressures in North America to Withdraw Forces from Europe." *European Security and the Atlantic System.* Edited by William T. R. Fox and Warner R. Schilling. New York: Columbia University Press, 1973.

Fried, Edward R. "Foreign Economic Policy: The Search for a Strategy." *The Next Phase in Foreign Policy.* Edited by Henry Owen. Washington: The Brookings Institution, 1973.

_____, and others. *Setting National Priorities: The 1974 Budget.* Washington: The Brookings Institution, 1973.

Frye, Alton. *A Responsible Congress: The Politics of National Security.* New York: McGraw-Hill, 1975.

Garnet, John. "BAOR and NATO." *International Affairs,* XLVI, 4 (October 1970), 670–681.

Gelb, Leslie H. and Halperin, Morton H. "Why West Europe Needs 300,000 GI's." *Atlantic Community Quarterly,* IX, 1 (Spring 1971), 56–60.

George, Alexander L. "The Case for Multiple Advocacy in Making Foreign Policy." *American Political Science Review,* LXVI (1972), 741–785.

Germany, Federal Republic of. Bundestag. *Deutscher Bundestag* (proceedings). 5th Wahlperiode, 44–115 Sitzungen (1966–67).

Germany, Federal Republic of. Press and Information Office. *White Paper 1971–72: The Security of the Federal Republic of Germany and the Development of the Federal Armed Forces.* Bonn: Press and Information Office of the German Federal Government, 1971.

Germany, Federal Republic of. Statistisches Bundesamt. *Statistisches Jahrbuch für die Bundesrepublik Deutschland, 1970.* Frankfurt am Main: Statistisches Bundesamt, 1970.

Geyelin, Philip. *Lyndon Johnson and the World.* New York: Praeger Publishers, 1966.

Goldman, Guido. *The German Political System.* New York: Random House, 1974.

Grundler, Gerhard E. "Die Grosse Koalition—Eine Zwangshandlung." *Frankfurter Hefte,* I, 1 (1967), 3–6.

Halperin, Morton H. *Bureaucratic Politics and Foreign Policy.* Washington: The Brookings Institution, 1974.

————. "The President and the Military." *Foreign Affairs,* LI, 1 (January 1972), 310–324.

————. "Why Bureaucrats Play Games." *Foreign Policy,* 2 (Spring 1971), 70–90.

Hanreider, W. F. *The Stable Crisis: Two Generations of German Foreign Policy.* New York: Harper, 1970.

————. "West German Foreign Policy: Background to Current Issues." *Orbis,* XIII, 4 (Winter 1970), 1029–1049.

"How Do the West Germans Feel About NATO in 1969?" Analysis by Erich Peter Neumann of a poll conducted by the Institut für Demoskopie Allensback. *Atlantic Community Quarterly,* VII, 3 (Fall 1969), 440–447.

Hunter, Robert E. "Troops, Trade and Diplomacy." *Atlantic Community Quarterly,* IX, 3 (Fall 1971), 283–292.

International Institute for Strategic Studies. *The Military Balance, 1972–73.* London: International Institute for Strategic Studies, 1972.

"Interview mit Karl Blessing." *Der Spiegel,* May 3, 1971, 82.

Joffe, Josef. "Amerikanische Präsenze und europäische Stabilität: zur Problematik amerikanischer Truppenabzüge aus Europa," *Europa Archiv,* XXV, 6 (March 1970), 191–204.

Johnson, Lyndon B. *The Vantage Point: Perspectives on the Presidency 1963–69.* New York: Holt, Rinehart and Winston, 1971.

Kaiser, Karl. *German Foreign Policy in Transition: Bonn Between East and West.* London: Oxford University Press, 1968.

Keohane, Robert O., and Nye, Joseph S. "World Politics and the International Economic System." *The Future of the International Economic Order.* Edited by C. Fred Bergsten. Lexington, Mass.: D. C. Heath and Co., 1973.

Kohl, Wilfrid. "The Nixon-Kissinger Foreign Policy System and U.S.-European Relations: Patterns of Policy-Making." *World Politics,* XVIII, 1 (October 1975), 1–43.

Krasner, Stephen D. "Are Bureaucracies Important?" *Foreign Policy,* 7 (Summer 1972), 159–178.

Krause, Lawrence B. "A Passive Balance of Payments Strategy for the United States." *Brookings Papers on Economic Activity.* Washington: The Brookings Institution, 1970.

Lawrence, Richard D., and Record, Jeffrey. *U. S. Force Structure in NATO: An Alternative.* Washington: The Brookings Institution, 1974.

Leacacos, John P. "Kissinger's Apparat." *Foreign Policy,* 5 (Winter 1971–72), 3–27.

Loewenberg, Gerhard. *Parliament in the German Political System*. Ithaca: Cornell University Press, 1967.

Lowi, Theodore. "American Business, Public Policy, Case Studies and Political Theory." *World Politics,* XVI, 4 (July 1964), 677–715.

Mansfield, Mike. "And Another View." *Atlantic Community Quarterly,* VIII, 1 (Spring 1970), 13–17.

May, Ernest R. "The 'Bureaucratic Politics' Approach: U.S.-Argentine Relations, 1942–47." *Latin America and the United States: The Changing Political Realities.* Edited by Julio Cotler and Richard R. Fagen. Stanford: Stanford University Press, 1974.

Mayntz, Renate and Scharpf, Fritz W. *Policy-Making in the German Federal Bureaucracy.* Amsterdam: Elsevier, 1975.

Mendershausen, Horst. *Coping with the Oil Crisis: French and German Experiences.* Baltimore: Johns Hopkins University Press, 1976.

————. "Defense Policies and Developments in the Federal Republic of Germany." P-3792. Santa Monica: The Rand Corporation, 1968.

————. *Troop Stationing in Germany: Value and Cost.* RM-5881-PR. Santa Monica: The Rand Corporation, 1968.

————. "Truppenstationierung in Deutschland—dauerhaftes Provisorium." *Wehrkunde,* XVIII, 11 (November 1969), 560–563.

Meyers, Kenneth A. "Ostpolitik and American Security Interests in Europe." Monograph, The Center for Strategic and International Study, Georgetown University, 1972.

Milbrath, Lester. "Interest Groups and Foreign Policy." *Domestic Sources of Foreign Policy.* Edited by James Rosenau. New York: The Free Press, 1967.

Military Spending Commission, Members of Congress for Peace through Law. *The Economics of Defense: A Bipartisan Review.* New York: Praeger Publishers, 1971.

Morgan, Roger. "The German Federal Republic." *European Political Parties.* Edited by Stanley Henig and John Pinder. London: Allen and Unwin, 1969.

————. "Washington and Bonn: A Case Study in Alliance Politics." *International Affairs,* XLVII, 3 (July 1971), 489–502.

————. *The United States and West Germany, 1945–1973: A Case Study in Alliance Politics.* London: Oxford University Press, 1974.

Nerlich, Uwe. "Federal Republic of Germany." *Nuclear Proliferation: Phase II.* Edited by Robert M. Lawrence and Joel Larus. Lawrence, Kan.: University of Kansas Press, 1974.

Neustadt, Richard E. *Alliance Politics.* New York: Columbia University Press, 1970.

————. *Presidential Power: The Politics of Leadership.* New York: Wiley, 1961.

————. "White House and Whitehall." *The Public Interest,* 2 (Winter 1966), 55–69.

Newhouse, John and others. *U.S. Troops in Europe: Issues, Costs and Choices.* Washington: The Brookings Institution, 1971.

Paul, Roland. *American Military Commitments Abroad.* New Brunswick: Rutgers University Press, 1973.

Percy, Charles H., U.S. Rapporteur. "North Atlantic Assembly Draft Report on Burden-Sharing and the Economic Aspects of the Common Defense Effort." *Congressional Record,* daily edition (July 10, 1970), 23758.

Percy, Charles H. "Paying for NATO," *Washington Monthly,* July 1970, 32.

Pfaltzgraff, Robert L., Jr. "NATO and European Security: Prospects for the 1970's." *Orbis,* XV, 1 (Spring 1971), 154–177.

Plischke, Elmer. "West German Foreign and Defense Policy." *Orbis,* XII, 4 (Winter 1969), 1096–1136.

Richardson, Elliot L. "U.S. and Western European Security." *Atlantic Community Quarterly,* VIII, 1 (Spring 1970), 5–13.

Roberts, Geoffrey K. *West German Politics.* London: The Macmillan Press, Ltd., 1972.

Rostow, W. W. *The Diffusion of Power: An Essay in Recent American History.* New York: The Macmillan Company, 1972.

Schmidt, Helmut. "Germany in an Era of Negotiations." *Foreign Affairs.* IL, 3 (October 1970), 30–40.

Schmückle, Gerd. "Die NATO-Strategie und die Truppenverminderung." *Europa Archiv,* XXII, 15 (1967), 551–557.

Schultze, Charles L. "The Economic Content of National Security Policy." *Foreign Affairs,* LI, 3 (April 1973), 522–540.

———— and others. *Setting National Priorities: The 1972 Budget.* Washington: The Brookings Institution, 1971.

Shelper, Cora E., and Campbell, Leonard C. "United States Defense Expenditures Abroad." United States. Department of Commerce. *Survey of Current Business* (December 1969), 40–47.

Snitzer, Martin. *East and West Germany: A Comparative Economic Analysis.* New York: Praeger Publishers, 1972.

Sommer, Theo. "Detente and Security: The Options." *Atlantic Community Quarterly,* IX, 1 (Spring 1971), 34–39.

Sontheimer, Kurt. *The Government and Politics of West Germany.* London: Hutchinson University Library, 1972.

Speier, Hans. *Germany in American Foreign Policy.* P-332. Santa Monica: The Rand Corporation, 1966.

Stanley, Timothy W. "Mutual Force Reductions." *Survival,* XII, 5 (May 1970), 152–160.

————. "NATO and the Balance of Payments." Revision of a proposal made to the London Assembly of the Atlantic Treaty Association, 1971.

————. *NATO in Transition: The Future of the Atlantic Alliance.* New York: Praeger Publishers, 1965.

————. "The Political Economics of Defense: Burden-Sharing." *Atlantic Community Quarterly,* IX, 4 (Winter 1971–72), 442–451.

Steinbruner, John. *The Cybernetic Theory of Decision.* Princeton: Princeton University Press, 1974.

Strauss, Franz-Josef. "An Alliance of Continents." *International Affairs,* XLI, 2 (April 1965), 191–203.

Thiel, Elke. "Devisenausgleich und Lastenteilung im atlantischen Bündnis." *Europa Archiv,* XXVI, 10 (1971), 353–362.

————. "Hinweise zur Beurteilung der wirtschaftlichen Voraussetzungen für Offset-Vereinbarungen." Monograph, Munich, Stiftung Wissenschaft und Politik, 1967.

————. "Truppenstationierung und Devisenausgleich," *Europa Archiv,* XXIV, 7 (1969), 221–228.

————. "Truppenstationierung und Wirtschaft: Betrachtungen zum Devisenausgleich." *Wehrkunde,* XVII, 9 (September 1968), 470–473.

Tucker, Robert W. *A New Isolationism: Threat or Promise?* New York: Universe Books, 1972.

Twelve North American, European and Japanese Economists.*Reshaping the International Economic Order.* Washington: The Brookings Institution, 1973.

United Kingdom. House of Commons. *House of Commons Official Report.* London: Her Majesty's Stationery Office, 1966 and 1967.

United Kingdom. Ministry of Defence. *The Defence Review, Part 1 of Statement on the Defence Estimates 1966.* London: Her Majesty's Stationery Office, 1966.

United Kingdom. Foreign Office. *Agreement between the Government of the United Kingdom of Great Britain and Northern Ireland and the Government of the Federal Republic of Germany for Offsetting the Foreign Exchange Expenditures on British Forces in the Federal Republic of Germany,* Bonn, July 27, 1964. British Treaty Series No. 58. London: Her Majesty's Stationery Office, 1964.

United Kingdom. Foreign Office and Treasury.*Protocol for the Extension and Modification of the Agreement of 27 July 1964 Between the Government of the United Kingdom . . . [same as foregoing].* Bonn, July 20, 1965. British Treaty Series No. 63. London: Her Majesty's Stationery Office, 1965.

————.*Agreement Between the Government of the United Kingdom of Great Britain and Northern Ireland and the Government of the Federal Republic of Germany for Offsetting the Foreign Exchange Expenditure on British Forces in the Federal Republic of Germany,* Bonn, May 5, 1967. British Treaty Series No. 52. London: Her Majesty's Stationery Office, 1967.

United Kingdom. Foreign and Commonwealth Office. *[same title as foregoing],* Bonn, April 11, 1968. British Treaty Series No. 65. London: Her Majesty's Stationery Office, 1968.

————. *[same title],* Bonn, September 1, 1969. British Treaty Series No. 116. London: Her Majesty's Stationery Office, 1969.

————. *Exchange of Notes Between the Government of Great Britain and Northern Ireland and the Government of the Federal Republic of Germany for Offsetting the Foreign Exchange Expenditure on British Forces in the Federal Republic of Germany,* Bonn, March 18, 1971. British Treaty Series No. 41. Her Majesty's Stationery Office, 1971.

United States. Arms Control and Disarmament Agency. *Arms Control and Disarmament Agreements, 1959–72.* Washington: Government Printing Office, 1972.

————.*Documents on Disarmament, 1968.* Washington: Government Printing Office, 1969.

United States. Congress. House. Committee on Appropriations. *Military Construction Appropriations for 1970, Part 2: Department of the Air Force and Department of the Army. Hearings* before a subcommittee of the Committee on Appropriations. 91 Cong., 1 sess., 1969.

United States. Congress. House. Committee on Armed Services. *The Ameri-*

can Commitment to NATO. Hearings before the special subcommittee on NATO commitments of the Committee on Armed Services, 92 Cong., 1 sess., 1971–72.

————. *Military Posture. Hearings* before the Committee on Armed Services, 92 Cong., 2 sess., 1971.

United States. Congress. House. Committee on Foreign Affairs. *Conference on European Security. Hearings* before the subcommittee on Europe of the Committee on Foreign Affairs, 92 Cong., 2 sess., 1972.

————. *United States Forces in NATO. Hearings* before the Committee on Foreign Affairs and its subcommittee on Europe, 93 Cong., 1 sess., 1973.

————. *United States Foreign Economic Policy: Implications for the Organization of the Executive Branch. Hearings* before the Committee on Foreign Affairs and its subcommittee on Foreign Economic Policy, 92 Cong., 2 sess., 1972.

————. *United States Relations with Europe in the Decade of the 1970's. Hearings* before the subcommittee on Europe of the Committee on Foreign Affairs, 91 Cong., 2 sess., 1970.

United States. Congress. Joint Economic Committee. *Changing National Priorities. Hearings* before the subcommittee on Economy in Government of the Joint Economic Committee, 91 Cong., 2 sess., 1970, Pt. 1.

————. *1968 Economic Report of the President. Hearings* before the Joint Economic Committee, 90 Cong., 2 sess., 1968. Pt. 4, "The Dollar Deficit and German Offsetting."

————. *The United States Balance of Payments in 1968. Report* by the Brookings Institution to the Joint Economic Committee, 90 Cong., 2 sess., 1968.

United States. Congress. Senate. Committee on Armed Services. *Authorizations for FY 1973 Appropriations. Report* of the Senate Armed Services Committee, 92 Cong., 2 sess., 1972.

United States. Congress. Senate. Committee on Foreign Relations. *United States Forces in Europe. Hearings* before the subcommittee on Arms Control, International Law and Organization of the Committee on Foreign Relations, 93 Cong., 1 sess., 1973.

————. *United States Security Issues in Europe: Burden Sharing and Offset, MBFR and Nuclear Weapons. Staff Report* prepared for the subcommittee on United States Security Agreements and Commitments Abroad of the Committee on Foreign Relations, 93 Cong., 1 sess., 1973.

————. *United States Troops in Europe. Hearings* before the combined subcommittee of the Committees on Foreign Relations and Armed Services, 90 Cong., 1 sess., 1967.

United States. Congress. Senate. Committees on Foreign Relations and Armed Services. *Assignment of Ground Forces of the United States to Duty in the European Area. Hearings* before the Committees on Foreign Relations and Armed Services, 82 Cong., 1 sess., 1951.

United States. Department of State. "The Dollar Crisis and United States Forces." Briefing memorandum, May 13, 1971.

United States. President. *Economic Report of the President 1970.* Washington: Government Printing Office, 1970.

219

Volger, Gernot. "Devisenausgleich als militär und Zahlungs-bilanzpolitisches Instrument." Unpublished monograph, 1972.

Wallace, William. "Issue Linkage Among Atlantic Governments." *International Affairs*, LII, 2 (April 1976), 163–79.

Watt, D. C. "Manoeverings in Bonn." *The World Today*, XXII, 12 (December 1966), 509–511.

Williams, Philip. "Whatever Happened to the Mansfield Amendment?" *Survival*, XVIII, 4 (July/August 1976), 146–53.

Wilson, Harold. *The Labour Government, 1964–70*. London: Weidenfeld and Nicholson, and Michael Joseph, 1971.

Wyle, Frederick S. "European Security: Beating the Numbers Game." *Foreign Policy*, 10 (Spring 1973), 41–54.

––––––––. "The United States and West European Security—Interests, Forces and Finances." *Survival*, XIV, 1 (January-February 1972), 8–15.

INDEX

Acheson, Dean—110, 113, 117
additionality criterion—13-14, 17, 29
  n.7, 42, 104, 140
Adenauer, Konrad—32, 39, 57-59,
  61-64, 71, 73, 87, 90, 93 n.5, 98,
  168-69
Agriculture, Department of, U.S.—138,
  188, 191
Ailleret, Michel—64
Allison, Graham—xiii, xiv n.2
Anderson, Robert—32-33, 51 n.1, 105
Armed Services Committee, House of
  Representatives, U.S.—106-7
"Atlanticists," German—63-64, 78, 82,
  87, 95 n.8, 110, 151, 174-75

Bahr, Egon—88
Ball, George—113, 115, 117, 119-21,
  143, 159-61
barracks renovation program—17-18,
  45, 49, 54 n.30, 82-85, 104
Barzel, Rainer—64, 70, 78, 144
Bator, Francis—xiii, 106, 113, 117-21,
  123, 126-28, 130-33, 141, 143-45, 156,
  160, 163
Bergsten, C. Fred—xiii

Blessing, Karl—16, 69, 76, 85-86, 131
Bowie, Robert—123, 125-27
Brandt, Willy—37, 44, 48, 50, 78, 80-81,
  87-88, 90, 92, 178
Brentano, Heinrich von—58
Brezhnev, Leonid—45
British Army of the Rhine (BAOR)—33,
  35-36, 38-39, 92, 123, 129, 131-32,
  141-42, 147, 151-52
Brosio, Manlio—44, 79
Brown, George—123, 132, 143
Budget Bureau. U.S.—105
"budget-cutting" measures (*Sparmassnahmen*)—82
"building bridges" speech of October,
  1966, President Johnson's—90, 96
  n.51
Bundesbank—15-17, 37, 39-40, 45, 60,
  69, 76, 80, 82-83, 85-86, 91, 105, 112,
  122, 130, 131, 145, 151, 156, 171, 195,
  197
Bundesrat—58
Bundestag—35, 37, 41, 57-60, 62-64,
  69, 76-80, 122, 140, 144, 161, 167-68,
  175, 197
Bundeswehr—13, 25, 33-34, 84, 89, 139
Bundy, McGeorge—113

222

Burns, Arthur—105
"Buy American" procurement policies, U.S.—9, 49

Callaghan, James—35, 124, 141-42
Camp David agreement—177
Carstens, Karl—37, 79-80, 123, 152
Central Intelligence Agency (CIA)—124
Chancellor's Office—68, 70-71, 87-88
Christian Democratic Union (CDU)—37, 58-59, 61-64, 67, 70, 74-78, 90, 100, 144
Christian Social Union (CSU)—58-59, 62-64, 75-78, 90
Church, Frank—134 n.9
"clubs"—see sub-Cabinet working groups
Commerce, Department of, U.S.—138, 191
Commission on the Organization of Government for the Conduct of Foreign Policy—xiii
Council of Economic Advisors—105, 112
Cranston, Alan—47
CRESTED CAP, U.S. military exercise—53 n.20

Dahlgrün, Hans-Georg—67, 72, 91-92
Defense, Department of, U.S. (see also Pentagon)—10, 19, 20, 27, 44, 49, 101-2, 104, 114-15, 119, 127, 138-40, 159-60, 172-74, 177, 186-87, 190, 196
International Logistics Negotiations, Office of—103
International Security Affairs (ISA), Office of—103, 114, 118, 121, 124-25
Systems Analysis, Office of—20, 116, 126
Defense Ministry, German—66-67, 69-70, 72-73, 79, 81, 83-86, 142-43
Budget Department—66
Procurement Department—66, 83
Planning Office—84
Deming, Frederick—52 n.4, 103, 121, 123, 126-27, 130-31, 183
Deming group—127, 135 n.22, 183
Democratic Policy Committee, Senate, U.S.—126
Destler, I.M.—xiii
detente—90
deterrence—xi, 1, 24-25, 84
Deutsche Gesellschaft für Auswärtige Politik—xiv

devaluation, American—10, 13, 16, 44, 48, 85, 103, 130, 190, 198
devaluation, British—39, 142
Dillon, Douglas—32
direct support of U.S. forces in Germany—7, 13, 17, 32-35, 40-42, 45, 47, 82-83, 87, 104
"dollar drainers"—2, 9-10, 174
"dual-basing" of U.S. forces—7, 19, 100-1, 128
Duckwitz, Georg Ferdinand—80, 87, 131, 152, 165 n.10
Dulles, John Foster—63, 168, 192

Economics Ministry, German—83, 86-87, 148
Economic Stabilization Program, German—41, 48, 61-62, 70, 76, 119, 142-43, 160
Eisenhower, Dwight—32, 177, 192
Erhard, Ludwig—1, 2, 26, 31-32, 34-37, 56-66, 68-77, 79, 81, 85, 88-89, 92, 97-98, 100, 105, 114, 116-118, 120-22, 137, 140-46, 150-52, 156, 158-60, 162-64, 167, 169-73, 175-76, 178, 194, 202
downfall—x, 36-37, 56, 60-65, 71, 74-80, 88, 91, 98, 117, 121, 144, 146, 158, 162-63, 169-71, 175-76, 178, 194
July 5 letter—35-36, 158-60
visit to Washington—1, 2, 26, 31-32, 35-37, 56, 60 ff., 69-70, 73-74, 79, 98-99, 111, 117, 120, 130, 145-46, 154, 156, 158, 160, 163
European Defense Improvement Program (EDIP)—44-45, 54 n. 27
European Economic Community (EEC)—108
"Europeanists," U.S.—113, 117

Federal Reserve, U.S.—16, 105, 111
Finance Ministry, German—66-68, 70, 72, 79, 81-84, 86, 112, 142, 145, 150
Ford, Gerald—50, 192
Foreign Affairs Committee, House of Representatives, U.S.—106-7
Foreign Office, German—66, 68, 71-73, 78-82, 84, 86-88, 138-39, 178
Fowler, Henry—35-36, 103, 105, 112, 115-16, 119, 121-23, 127, 130, 132, 145, 157, 161, 176
Free Democratic Party (FPD)—37, 44, 58-59, 62-64, 67, 76-78, 81, 83, 88
Fulbright, J. William—30 n.3, 134 n.9

Gaulle, Charles de—57, 63-65, 73-74
"Gaullists," German—63-64, 75, 79, 82,
  90-91, 100, 114, 141, 146, 150, 152,
  204
General Agreement on Trade and
  Tariffs (GATT)—14
Gerstenmaier, Eugen—63, 70, 78
Gilpatrick, Roswell L.—33
Godesberg Program, SPD—59
gold, U.S.—108, 111
  risk of run on—118, 171
"gold budget" (U.S. balance-of-
  payments savings program)—10, 34,
  40
"gold bugs," American—108, 110, 112,
  157, 174
gold pledge, German—10, 13, 15-17, 34,
  38-39, 85-86, 105, 128, 131, 151, 154,
  156
Goodpaster, Andrew—29 n.12, 50 n.14
"graduated presence," German military
  doctrine of (Abgesturzpräsenz)—95
  n.7
Grand Coalition—37, 56, 59-60, 68, 70,
  75-78, 80-82, 88-90, 100, 152-53
Gromyko, Andrei—90
Guttenberg, Karl Theodor, Baron von
  und zu—63

Halperin, Morton—xiii, xiv n.2, 206 n.6
Hase, Karl von—67, 70, 92, 140, 142
Hassel, Kai-Uwe von—35, 63, 65,
  67-79, 71-72, 74, 100, 105, 115, 117-
  18, 122, 138, 140, 159
Hickenlooper, Bourke—134 n.9
Hillenbrand, Martin—35 n.15, 133 n.1,
  160
Hughes, Harold—108
Humphrey, Hubert—47, 109

INR—see State, Department of, U.S.
International Institute for Strategic
  Studies—xiv
ISA—See Defense, Department of, U.S.

Jackson, Henry—47-51, 108, 134 n.9
Jackson-Nunn Amendment—47-50
Javits, Jacob—126
Johnson, Lyndon—1-3, 26, 28, 32,
  35-37, 39-40, 45, 62, 64-65, 68-69, 73,
  89-92, 98, 105-7, 116, 121, 126, 133,
  140, 143-45, 149-53, 155, 157-60,
  163-64, 169, 171, 175, 180-83, 189-90,
  199, 204
Joint Chiefs of Staff—20, 27, 44, 101,
  124-25, 128, 149, 153, 174, 181, 198

Joint Staff—155

Katzenbach, Nicholas—30 n.14 and 23,
  52 n.4
Kennedy, David—41, 105, 177-78
Kennedy, John—10, 33, 177
Kennedy Round Trade Negotiation—
  112, 118, 138
Kiesinger, Kurt-Georg—37, 39, 75,
  78-80, 89, 92, 133, 146, 150-52
Kissinger, Henry—24, 42, 46, 50, 106,
  157, 182-83, 190, 192, 206 n.8
Knappstein, Heinrich—73, 144
Krone, Heinrich—87
Kuss, Henry—103, 124, 139

Laird, Melvin—45, 81, 102, 178
Leddy, John—110, 117, 126, 132
Lemnitzer, Lyman—64
Lowenthal, Abraham—xiii
Lübke, Heinrich—72, 93 n.5

Macmillan, Harold—169, 177, 197
Management and Budget, Office of,
  U.S. (OMB)—68
Mansfield, Mike—30 n.24, 39-40,
  44-45, 47, 50, 89, 101, 107-10, 126,
  129, 157-58
Marshall, George—5
Marshall Plan—ix, 43
Martin, William—16, 131
May, Ernest—xiii, xv n.2
Mayo, Robert—105
McCloy, John—37-38, 74, 101, 110, 113,
  117, 120, 123-29, 131-33, 133 n.1,
  143-44, 149, 152, 155-57
McGhee, George—89-90, 119-20
McNamara, Robert—xi, xiv n.1, 8, 10,
  19-20, 25, 34-36, 38, 67-68, 70, 72, 74,
  89, 99, 102-3, 105, 110, 112-13, 115-
  23, 126-30, 133, 138-41, 143, 145,
  153-64, 169, 172, 174-79, 186, 190,
  202
McNaughton, John—103, 121, 123-24,
  126-27, 133, 181
Mendes, Erich—77
Miller, Jack—134 n.9.
Moorer, Thomas—29 n.11
Multilateral Force (MLF)—63-64, 74,
  95 n.8, 113, 204-5
multi-role combat aircraft (MRCA),
  European—84, 95 n.40
Muskie, Edmund—109

Mutual (and Balanced) Force Reductions (MBFR or MFR)—25-26, 45, 54 n.29, 149

National Democratic Party (NPD)—63
National Security Act of 1947—192
National Security Council (NSC)—42, 44
staff—106
National Security, Assistant to the President for—182
National Security Council system, Johnson—116, 154, 159, 180, 182, 190
Inter-departmental Review Groups (IRGs)—116, 182
Senior Inter-departmental Group (SIG)—116, 159, 164, 182
National Security Council System, Nixon/Ford—46, 154, 156-57, 180-83, 190, 192
Interdepartmental Groups (IGs)—157, 182
National Security Decision Memoranda (NSDMs)—42, 46, 182
National Security Study Memoranda (NSSMs)—41-42, 44, 46, 156, 182
Review Group—182
Under Secretaries Committee—157, 182-83
Neustadt, Richard—xi, xiii, xiv n.2, 166-67, 170, 177, 195, 203
"New Atlantic Charter" speech, Henry Kissinger's—24, 46, 55 n.33
Nixon, Richard—24, 42, 44-45, 48, 87, 106, 110, 157-58, 182-83, 190-92, 206 n.8
Non-Proliferation Treaty (NPT)—39, 90, 111, 113-14, 128, 133, 138, 140-41, 152, 202
North Atlantic Treaty Organization (NATO)—1, 2, 5, 19-23, 25-26, 32-34, 40, 44, 47, 49, 63, 76, 79, 84, 90, 94, 100, 103, 106-7, 111, 125, 138, 141, 147-49, 153, 155, 158, 160, 179, 201, 203-4
French withdrawal from—34, 112
Military Payments Union proposal, American—100, 115-18, 139, 159, 164, 175
NSSM/NSDM system—see National Security Council system, Nixon/Ford
Nunn, Sam—29 n.13, 47-51
Nunn Amendment, 1974—21
Nye, Joseph—xiii

offset, forms of—
arms procurement—13-14, 33-35, 39, 40-43, 47, 49, 65-67, 76, 79, 83-84, 89, 91, 100, 104, 108-9, 114-15, 122, 125, 128-30, 139, 154, 186, 189, 195-96, 199-200 in Britain—34, 92, 147, 152
civilian purchases (or procurement)—2, 13-14, 34, 40, 42, 49, 62, 69, 87, 104, 119, 122, 139-40 of space hardware—139 in Britain—92, 115, 141
payments—17, 32, 42, 44-45, 47, 83, 104
purchases of Treasury securities (also bond purchases, loans)—14-16, 38-43, 45-46, 49, 85-86, 100, 104-5, 119, 121-22, 128, 130-31, 151, 156 Eximbank—43 in Britain—91, 151 non-convertibility of—69 U.S. attitudes toward—105
oil embargo, 1973—ix, 24, 44, 48, 187, 205
Okinawa—177-78, 186, 190, 197-98, 201
Ostpolitik—23, 26, 77, 81, 88, 90, 201

Pastore, John—109
Pearson, James—134 n.9
Pell, Claiborne—109
Pentagon—21, 71, 101, 117-18, 124-25, 187
"Phantom" jets, German purchases of—41, 84, 43, 45
"plate-glass" doctrine—19
Polaris submarine—176-77
"privatized" U.S. policy-making—190-91, 193

recession, German, 1966—2, 61-62
REFORGER, U.S. exercise—8-9, 53 n.20
revaluation of Mark—86
Richardson, Elliot—30 n.14, 23, 42, 157, 183
Rostow, Eugene—99, 124, 126-27, 131-32, 150, 155-57, 180, 183-84, 193
Rostow, Walt—52 n.10, 113, 121, 123, 132, 144
Rostow group—126-28, 131-32, 135 n.22, 150, 155-57, 160, 180, 183-84, 193
Rumsfeld, Donald—30 n.16-18, 22
run on the pound—34-35, 141-42
Rush, Kenneth—7, 30 n.16, 18
Rusk, Dean—19, 70, 74, 90, 110, 113,

116-19, 123, 127-29, 132, 140-41, 153, 159-60, 176-77

Samuels, Nathaniel—157
Sato, Eisaku—197-98, 201
Schiller, Karl—61, 83
Schlesinger, James—21, 29 n.10, 30 n.13
Schmidt, Helmut—45, 48-51, 55 n.41, 81, 84, 88, 1u4
Schröder, Gerhard—41, 58, 63-64, 66, 72-74, 78, 80, 82, 84, 87-90, 92, 100, 144-45, 151-52, 167, 169
Security Council (Bundessicher-heitsrat)—83, 86-87
Shultz, George—49, 82
SIG/IRG system—see National Security Council System, Johnson
Skybolt—167-68, 170, 172-73, 176-77, 194-95, 197-98, 203-4
Social Democratic Party (SPD)—37, 43, 58-65, 68, 74-78, 80-81, 83, 88, 100
Sparkman, John—134 n.9
Special Drawing Rights (SDR)—39, 42, 52 n.5, 112, 118
"Spiegel affair"—77
"Starfighter" jets, German problems with—65
State, Department of, U.S.—20, 27, 38, 44-46, 64, 71, 75, 86, 89, 99-101, 112-113, 115, 117-19, 123-24, 127, 138, 155, 157, 159-61, 167-70, 173-76, 178-79, 182-83, 186-88, 191-92, 198, 204
  Economic Affairs (E), Bureau of—100, 115
  European Affairs (EUR), Bureau of—99-100, 116, 124, 126
  Intelligence and Research (INR), Bureau of—161
  Regional Politics and Military Affairs, (RPM), Bureau of—100
Stennis, John—134 n.9

Stoltenberg, Gerhard—69
Strauss, Franz-Josef—33, 43, 58, 62–64, 75, 77–79, 82, 89, 91–92, 131, 146, 151–52
sub-cabinet working groups—123, 126–28, 131–32, 135 n.22, 150, 155–57, 160, 163, 180–81, 183–85, 206 n.5
Suez crisis—167, 170, 194–95, 203
summit meeting, Erhard-Johnson (see also Erhard, visit to Washington)—1, 72, 145, 175, 194
Symington, Stuart—108, 134 n.9

Taylor, Maxwell—165 n.15
Thomson, George—37, 152, 165 n.12
Treasury, Department of, U.S.—27, 41–42, 45–46, 49, 82–83, 86, 89, 100–101, 103–105, 115, 119, 124, 138–40, 156, 159–60, 172–74, 177, 186, 188, 190–91, 196
  National Security Affairs, Office for—103, 114
Trilateral Negotiations—x, 2–3, 9, 12, 15, 19–20, 23, 32, 36–40, 56–57, 66, 69, 73, 75–76, 79–80, 85–86, 88, 91–92, 98–99, 103, 107, 119–20, 122–24, 126, 129, 132–33, 137, 143–44, 146–49, 151–56, 158, 162–63, 169, 171, 176, 179
Twentieth Century Fund—xiii

Vance, Cyrus—116
Vietnam War—1–2, 5, 8, 17, 34–35, 50, 101–2, 108–11, 113, 117, 138, 140, 158–59, 163, 174, 179, 183

Warsaw Pact—19, 21, 23, 26, 125, 147–49, 153, 201
Wehner, Herbert—78
Westrick, Ludger—71–73, 76, 144
Wilson, Harold—34, 37, 120, 123–24, 131, 141, 146–47, 151, 164 n.3, 169
Wyle, Frederick—124